Underground Railroad in Pennsylvania

WILLIAM J. SWITALA

STACKPOLE
BOOKS

Published by
STACKPOLE BOOKS
5067 Ritter Road
Mechanicsburg, PA 17055
www.stackpolebooks.com

Printed in the United States of America

10 9 8 7 6 5 4 3 2 1

FIRST EDITION

Cover design by Caroline Stover

Cover illustration: The Underground Railroad *by Charles T. Webber, 1893.*
Cincinnati Art Museum, Subscription Fund Purchase.

Back cover illustration: The Resurrection of Henry "Box" Brown, *c.1853.*
The Friends Historical Library of Swarthmore College.

Maps by Kevin J. Switala

Library of Congress Cataloging-in-Publication Data

Switala, William J.
    The underground railroad in Pennsylvania / William J. Switala. — 1st ed.
        p.   cm.
    Includes bibliographical references and index.
    ISBN 0-8117-1629-5 (PB)
        1. Underground railroad—Pennsylvania.   2. Fugitive slaves—Pennsylvania—
History—19th century.   3. Afro-Americans—Pennsylvania—History—19th century.
4. Pennsylvania—Race relations.   5. Historic sites—Pennsylvania.   6. Pennsylvania—
History—1775–1865.   I. Title.

E445.P3 S95   2001
973.7′115—dc21

                                                                00-061201

CONTENTS

PREFACE

The Underground Railroad was a system developed before the Civil War to guide slaves to freedom. This mysterious and highly secretive network is the subject of renewed interest and considerable study today, especially at the local level, where historical societies are researching sites connected with the railroad.

This book is devoted to examining the operation of the Underground Railroad in Pennsylvania. The state had three major escape routes, roughly divided into geographic regions: the Western, Central, and Eastern Routes.

Although many books deal with the Underground Railroad, only four contain extended descriptions of the operations in Pennsylvania. The earliest is William Still's 1872 work, *The Underground Railroad: A Record of Facts, Authentic Narratives, Letters, & c.* The author, an agent in the cause, gives an in-depth look at the general operations of the railroad but limits his scope to Philadelphia and a few counties around it. The second work, *History of the Underground Railroad in Chester and the Neighboring Counties of Pennsylvania,* by Dr. Robert C. Smedley, published in 1883, provides rich insights into many personalities and sites of the railroad but limits this treatment to York, Lancaster, Chester, Delaware, and Philadelphia Counties. Wilbur Siebert's *The Underground Railroad from Slavery to Freedom,* written in 1898, is still the most fundamental study of the overall movement as it existed in America. Siebert gives some details of the system's organization in Pennsylvania. He also includes a map showing the major routes of the railroad in the United States; however, many of the lines of the routes in Pennsylvania are incomplete, and some are missing entirely. *The Underground Railroad in Pennsylvania,* written by Charles Blockson in 1981, examines the workings of the railroad in Pennsylvania county by county. It includes many valuable references to sites and individuals, but it is short on narrative and lacks maps.

The purpose of this book is to fill in the gaps found in the other studies and to expand on and provide visual representation for the escape routes. The special features of this work include the organization of the many escape paths into specific routes, a set of detailed maps tracing the major routes as they traversed the state, a discussion of the role Indian trails and early roads played in the operation of the Underground Railroad, a number of new sites not found in previous works, and an examination of the efforts put forth by several religious organizations in helping fugitives reach freedom. Each major route is described in a separate chapter, which includes a detailed map. The study also lists the names of those individuals who were recorded as having helped in the operation of the railroad. They are mentioned in a variety of sources and are included in this work to provide recognition for their efforts and because many of the descendants of these individuals still live in Pennsylvania.

I used a wide variety of resources in researching this work: eyewitness accounts in letters, diaries, speeches, and newspaper articles; early histories of counties and churches, written shortly after the Civil War, that mentioned the Underground Railroad and its operation; and modern-day scholarship on the subject, including source material found on the Internet. I conducted most of this research in the Gumberg Library at Duquesne University and the Hillman Library at the University of Pittsburgh, and did additional research in the libraries of the Senator John Heinz Regional History Center in Pittsburgh, Dickinson College, Shippensburg University, Washington and Jefferson College, and the Pennsylvania State University. Finally, I retraced a number of the routes and examined many sites still in existence today. I give special thanks to three of my sons, who helped in the researching of this work: Kevin J. Switala, a geographic information systems analyst, for creating the maps in this study; and William J. Switala, Jr., and Michael J. Switala, both history teachers, for their help in researching sites and taking pictures of them.

I hope this work will act as a guide and bring some degree of unity to the multitude of descriptions of how the Underground Railroad functioned in Pennsylvania, and that it will enhance the reader's understanding of this monumental endeavor to secure individual freedom in American history and the role that local communities played in it.

The Escape of
Henry "Box" Brown

The old adage "desperate times call for desperate measures" sums up many of the escape attempts made by slaves during the era of the Underground Railroad. Daring, inventiveness, endurance, and heroism were all qualities the runaway needed to have in the attempt to gain freedom. The annals of the Underground Railroad abound with tales illustrating these qualities. One such story is the saga of Henry Brown.

Brown was a slave living in the city of Richmond in the late 1840s. His tale was told in the writings of William Still, the great black abolitionist and member of the Underground Railroad network in Philadelphia. Still was directly involved in Brown's escape and gives all the details of the event. He refers to Brown as "a man of invention as well as a hero."[1] According to Still, Brown could no longer endure being a slave, and in 1848, he decided to seek freedom by fleeing to Pennsylvania. Brown knew that attempting to leave Richmond would be a hazardous undertaking. Slave catchers patrolled the border with Pennsylvania, and this made land and water travel very risky, and if caught, he would face the wrath of his master. Brown came up with an ingenious and radical plan: He would enclose himself in a wooden crate and have himself shipped to abolitionists in Philadelphia. Still described the crate Brown had made for himself:

> The size of the box and how it was to be made to fit him most comfortably was of his own ordering. Two feet eight inches deep, two feet wide, and three feet long were the exact dimensions of the box, lined with baize.
>
> His resources with regard to food and water consisted of the following: One bladder of water and a few small biscuits. His mechanical implement to meet the death-struggle for fresh air, all told was one large gimlet (a small tool for drilling holes). . . . He entered his box, which was safely nailed up and hooped with five hickory hoops, and was then addressed by his next

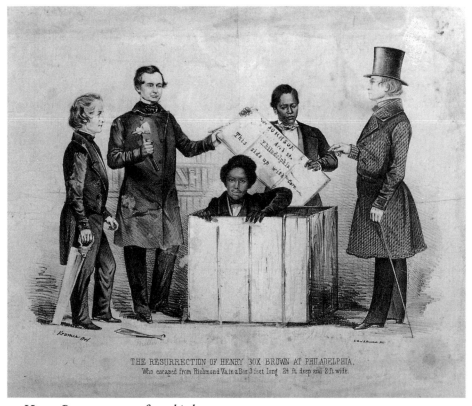

THE RESURRECTION OF HENRY BOX BROWN AT PHILADELPHIA.
Who escaped from Richmond Va. in a Box 3 feet long 2½ ft. deep and 2 ft. wide.

Henry Brown emerges from his box. THE FRIENDS HISTORICAL LIBRARY OF SWARTH-
MORE COLLEGE

friend, James A. Smith, a shoe dealer, to Wm. H. Johnson, Arch street,
Philadelphia.[2]

Smith took the crate to the Adams' Express office and shipped it to
Philadelphia. What followed next had to be a ride of agony aboard freight
wagons and a railway boxcar. The complete journey lasted about twenty-six
hours, with Brown traveling on his head part of the way because the team-
sters handling the crate ignored the label "This End Up," which had been
placed on the side of the crate.

The crate containing Brown arrived in Philadelphia, and through the pay-
ing of a bribe, the members of the Anti-Slavery Society in the city had it delivered to their offices at 107 North Fifth Street. Present when the crate arrived
were society members J. M. McKim, C. D. Cleveland, Lewis Thompson, and
William Still. Still recorded what happened when the crate was opened:

The witnesses will never forget that moment. Saw and hatchet quickly had the five hickory hoops cut and the lid off, and the marvelous resurrection of Brown ensued. Rising up in his box, he reached out his hand, saying, "How do you do, Gentlemen?" The little assemblage hardly knew what to think or do at the moment.[3]

From that day on, Brown was known as Henry "Box" Brown because of his clever method of escape. Brown stayed with James and Lucretia Mott and then with William Still in Philadelphia. While living in Still's home, he related all the details of his tale to Still, who incorporated them into the memoirs of his experiences with the Underground Railroad. Eventually, Brown left Philadelphia and went to Boston.

Back in Richmond, Smith tried to send two other fugitive slaves to Philadelphia in a similar manner. Unfortunately, the publicity about Brown's successful escape had alerted the authorities, and the two were caught. Smith was arrested, convicted of aiding runaway slaves, and sentenced to eight years in the penitentiary.[4]

Not all the people living in the North were as sympathetic to the anti-slave movement and the activities of the Underground Railroad as were James Smith or the group who aided runaways in Philadelphia. There were those who thought nothing ill of the institution of slavery. Some informed of the whereabouts of escapees and even participated in the recapture of runaways. These individuals were frequently motivated by the large financial rewards offered for their capture and return.

Even among the white abolitionist groups, there were those who absolutely opposed the operation of the Underground Railroad. They believed in the gradual abolition of slavery as an institution through legal means and thought that aiding slaves in escaping from their masters was immoral and illegal.[5] In the religious arena, not all of the churches in the North, nor all the members of a given congregation, felt the same way about the institution of slavery and aiding runaways.

According to Charles Blockson, many of Pennsylvania's white citizens were sympathetic to the South and the institution of slavery, but an even greater number were apathetic toward the plight of slaves and those attempting to flee. Many incidents of fugitives being aided by Underground Railroad agents took place in front of whites who simply did not care enough to assist them or to notify the authorities or help capture the runaways.[6]

A myth that has developed over the years is that white people, and especially Quakers, were solely responsible for the success of the Underground Railroad in Pennsylvania. There is ample evidence in the original source material, especially in the writings of William Still and Robert Smedley, that blacks played an important role in the success of the railroad. Blockson's research goes even further and shows that in many cases, fugitives were able to reach safe havens due solely to the efforts of fellow blacks. Finally, while many of the fugitives depended on others to help them along the way, a good number of slaves relied completely on their own wits and were not aided by anyone.[7]

The passage of the fugitive slave laws, the hostility of many whites in the North, and even the disagreements among the abolitionists and church leaders all led to the necessity of secrecy surrounding the workings of the Underground Railroad. This secrecy is a major reason why researching the railroad is so difficult. The number of primary sources is limited, and the almost mythological nature of the railroad colors the secondary source material. However, careful sifting of the sources, physical inspection of the existing sites, knowledge of the terrain and geographic features along a suspected route, and a heavy dose of logical speculation can provide a fairly accurate picture of the Underground Railroad in a given area. Those are the factors on which the assumptions in this book are made.

The Setting

The history of blacks in this country dates back to the earliest days of the Colonial period. They made their appearance in 1619 when twenty captured Africans were sold to the English colonists at Jamestown.[1] This trade in human beings from Africa continued throughout the seventeenth and eighteenth centuries, and that factor, coupled with natural reproductive rates, resulted in the population of blacks increasing to 757,208 by 1790. Of this number, 697,681 were slaves and 59,527 were free. The population of white Americans, at the same time, was 3,172,006. Just prior to the onset of the Civil War in 1860, these numbers had increased to 26,923,000 whites and 3,953,760 enslaved blacks, or almost 13 percent of the total population of the country. Of these, 3,838,765 were enslaved in the South. Most of the 488,370 free blacks lived in the North.[2] Pennsylvania exhibited an opposite trend during approximately the same time period. In the census of 1790, 3,737 blacks were listed as enslaved in the state and 6,500 were listed as free. By 1860, the number of slaves appears as zero in the state census and the number of free blacks as 57,000.[3]

Many in the North became convinced of the evils of slavery and actively worked to put an end to the institution. The earliest evidence of this effort comes from Germantown, Pennsylvania. On February 18, 1688, a group of men with strong religious convictions—Garret Hendrick, Daniel D. Pastorius, and the brothers Derick and Abram op de Graeff—published a document entitled *The Resolutions of the Germantown Mennonites*. In this manifesto, they roundly condemned slavery and made a religious argument for the freedom of all people from bondage.[4] The sentiments expressed would go on to establish the basic reasons for the abolition of slavery in America. They included the following:

1. Since the Moslem Turks sell people into slavery, is it not worse for Christians to do it?
2. Just because these people are black in skin color, that is no reason to enslave them.

3. The mentioning of the Biblical dictum ". . . that we should do to all men as we will be done to ourselves . . ." followed by the question ". . . would we enslave whites?"
4. In Europe people are oppressed for the sake of their beliefs, here it is because of their color.
5. The Bible says that we should not commit adultery, and yet, when wives are forcefully separated from their husbands in slavery and given to others, is this not encouraging adultery?
6. It is unlawful to steal, and yet, these people were stolen from their native country.[5]

The Quakers were also pioneers in the early movement to abolish slavery in America. In 1693, the Quaker George Keith printed a pamphlet that argued against slavery. The pamphlet was circulated throughout the colonies.[6] This antislavery sentiment among the Quakers continued to develop, and in 1754, at the yearly meeting of the Friends, the group publicly condemned slavery as an institution and many of them freed what slaves they had.[7]

As the colonies neared the eve of their independence from Great Britain, others, in addition to the Quakers and Mennonites, were morally distressed by the fact of slavery. Individuals began to meet to discuss the evils of the practice and make plans to bring about its demise, or at least to help slaves gain their freedom. Once again, Pennsylvania was the site of an early effort to organize opposition in a formal way to slavery. The first abolitionist society in America, called the Society for the Relief of Free Negroes Unlawfully Held in Bondage, began in Philadelphia in the year 1775. Over the years, people came to refer to it as the Pennsylvania Abolition Society.[8]

Opposition to slavery in this country involved two major initiatives in the years during the American Revolution and shortly thereafter. The first of these dealt with the changing of laws. Legislation was enacted in various forms to curtail the practice, at least in the North. Several of the newly formed states either made antislavery laws part of their new constitutions or enacted separate legislation that banned slavery immediately or arranged for its gradual elimination. Vermont in 1777, Massachusetts in 1781, New York in 1799, Connecticut and Rhode Island in 1799, and New Jersey in 1804 changed their constitutions or formulated new laws that banned the institution.[9]

In Pennsylvania, the state legislature passed a law on February 29, 1780, designed to abolish slavery over a period of time. Called the Gradual Abolition of Slavery Act, the law contained a number of provisions to bring about an ultimate end to the practice of enslaving others in the state. The first of these provisions held that no child born in Pennsylvania would be a slave.

The exception to this was that children born to black or mulatto slave mothers would be emancipated automatically when they reached the age of twenty-eight. Another provision stated that all slaves currently living in the state had to be registered with local governments by their masters before November 1, 1780. Failing to do so would result in the automatic freeing of their slaves.[10]

Not all those who opposed slavery were successful in getting their own states to ban the practice as did the states in the North. In 1785, the Methodist Church in Virginia petitioned the state legislature to abolish slavery on the grounds that it violated the basic teachings of Christianity and the tenets of the Virginia Declaration of Rights. They failed in their effort, however, because the lawmakers were completely opposed to this suggestion.[11]

On the national scene, efforts were made to slow the growth of slavery. The Northwest Ordinance, which was passed on July 13, 1787, stated in article 6, "There shall be neither slavery nor involuntary servitude in the said territory." This effectively eliminated the practice of slavery in what was about to become the states of Ohio, Indiana, Illinois, Michigan, and Wisconsin.[12] The most important legislative action taken during this early period was the passage of the Act to Prohibit the Importation of Slaves by Congress. The most important provision of the law was "that from and after the first day of January One thousand eight hundred and eight, it shall not be lawful to import or bring into the United States or the territories thereof from any foreign kingdom, place, or country, any negro, mulatto, or person of colour, as a slave, or to be held to service or labour." This law was the first attempt on a national scale to curb the rising tide of slavery.[13]

The second initiative against slavery in the pre–Civil War era was the creation of the abolitionist societies. These groups contained citizens who lived mostly in the North. Their role was to speak out against slavery. They published newspapers, wrote pamphlets, and spoke out at every occasion in an attempt to raise the consciousness of the American people about the horrors of the practice of slavery. Some of the most famous writers, speakers, and reformers of the day belonged to these groups. They also raised funds to care for those individuals who managed to flee from their enslavement in the South, and they supported those who provided aid and assistance for those still enslaved in their attempt to flee.

The first of these societies was formed in Pennsylvania in 1775. Some years later, in 1830, James and Lucretia Mott, the renowned Quaker reformers, established a new group in Philadelphia, which they called the Pennsylvania Anti-Slavery Society. The goal of the group was the elimination of slavery and the assistance of those trying to flee from enslavement.[14] The year 1831 gave witness to the founding of two other prominent abolitionist groups. Arthur and Lewis Tappan organized the New York Committee for a National Anti-Slavery Society, and in New England, William Lloyd Garrison, the outspoken critic of slavery, started the New England Anti-Slavery Society. Garrison also began to publish the most famous abolitionist paper of the day, *The Liberator.*[15] In 1833, at the urgings of the Motts and Robert Purvis, these two major abolitionist societies were amalgamated into one major group, which was called the American Anti-Slavery Society. Pennsylvania played a major role in this union, because the new society got its start in Philadelphia.[16] On December 4, 1833, the organization published its Constitution and Declaration of Sentiments, making it clear that the society was an avowed enemy of slavery and would do everything in its power to oppose it. Article II states that "the object of the Society is the entire abolition of Slavery in the United States." The document went on to elaborate that the society would attempt to do this through persuasion of state and national legislatures to put an end to the domestic slave trade, stressing that these goals would be achieved through peaceful methods. At the heart of this document, reminiscent of the Mennonite Resolutions of 1688, is the sentiment that slavery is opposed to natural justice and Christianity.[17]

Not all of the organizations formed to address the question of slavery advocated freedom for blacks in America. There was a group of individuals, made up of both white and black Americans, who advocated the deportation of all slaves to Africa, and especially to the newly formed country of Liberia, for resettlement. They felt that the granting of full rights to former slaves in this country would never work, and the only solution was to send them back to the place of their origin. To this end, the American Colonization Society began operating in 1817.[18]

Most of the black elite in the North were opposed to the suggestion of the American Colonization Society, although they were not absolutely against the concept of emigration, seriously considering the merits of places like Haiti, Trinidad, and Canada.[19] Many blacks felt that the continuing success of former slaves in Canada was of special importance in that they served as proof of the "fitness of freedom" for members of their race. To this end, during the 1830s, they founded several settlements near the Canadian towns of Windsor, Chatham, and St. Catharines. While these settlers did face some racial discrimination, they still found more security and far greater political and economic opportunities there than they could in the United States.[20] Haiti was also considered an acceptable home for émigrés, and black abolitionist James Forten of Philadelphia, who strongly opposed the plan to deport former slaves to Africa, viewed Haiti as a "symbol of black nationalism."[21] Forten also helped organize the Convention of Free Negroes in 1830.

The convention developed a position against the deportation scheme and advocated the abolition of slavery and the granting of first-class citizenship to all former slaves. Forten is also said to have had a great influence on the development of William Lloyd Garrison as an abolitionist.[22] At the end of the 1830s, free blacks in the North were also interested in emigrating to Trinidad.[23] By 1841, however, only a small number were emigrating to Haiti and Trinidad, and Canada had become the main destination point.[24] Canada had already existing black settlements in which fugitive slaves could receive aid and comfort.

Free blacks in the North were also ardent in their opposition to slavery and played a major role in aiding those escaping from bondage in the South. The earliest example of this effort to help their fellow blacks came in 1787, when two ministers in Philadelphia, Rev. Absalom Jones and Rev. Richard Allen, formed the Independent Free African Society of Philadelphia.[25] The society was designed to aid those who had recently gained their freedom, having either purchased it or escaped. Reverend Allen later founded the African Methodist Episcopal Church, which went on to play a critical role in the operation of the Underground Railroad.[26]

In addition to forming societies and holding conventions, several black Americans began to publish newspapers and magazines that were abolitionist in nature and were widely read throughout the country. The first of these was the newspaper *Freedom's Journal,* which appeared in 1827 and was the creation of John B. Russwurm and Samuel Cornish. Russwurm was the first black to receive a college degree in the United States, having graduated from Bowdoin College in 1826. They followed this with another newspaper in 1828, entitled *The Rights of All.* The object of these two papers was to advocate the elimination of slavery and equal rights for all blacks in the United States. Many of the leading abolitionists of the day wrote articles for these two newspapers.[27] *The Mystery,* which first appeared in 1843, was one of the most widely read abolitionist papers. It was by Martin Delany, the most famous of the black newspaper publishers and both an abolitionist and an advocate of the plan of the American Colonization Society.[28] The quarterly journal *The Mirror of Liberty* also appeared during this same time period. It was the creation of David Ruggles, an escaped slave, and advocated the rights of blacks and the abolition of slavery.[29]

The effect of all of these activities—the antislavery legislation, the abolitionist societies, and the publications—was the creation of an atmosphere in which many people could see the evils of slavery and develop a desire to do something about it, even at the risk of their own well-being. It was in this atmosphere that the Underground Railroad would find support and the opportunity to grow over a large portion of the United States—particularly in Pennsylvania.

Operation of the Railroad

Detailing the operation of the Underground Railroad poses special problems for the historian. Larry Gara, in his critical work *The Liberty Line: The Legend of the Underground Railroad,* states that this organization functioned in great secrecy and did not have a unified structure or a clear chain of command. Gara also points out that as the years have passed, the Underground Railroad has taken on mythological qualities and thus is difficult to pin down with accuracy.[1] Nevertheless, there is enough material in primary sources written by eyewitnesses such as Frederick Douglass, William Still, Dr. R. C. Smedley, Rev. Calvin Fairbanks, Samuel Ringgold Ward, Levi Coffin, William and Ellen Craft, and Howard Wallace, as well as governmental reports, letters, diary entries, and newspaper articles from that time period, to paint a reasonable picture of this organization and its major functions.

EARLY REFERENCES TO THE UNDERGROUND RAILROAD

The earliest references to slaves running away and receiving aid in their attempt to escape come from George Washington. In a letter to Robert Morris dated April 12, 1786, Washington mentioned a Mr. Dalby, of Alexandria, Virginia, going to Philadelphia to take part in a lawsuit involving an escaped slave of his, whom Quakers had aided in his effort to gain freedom. Washington went on to say that if the Quakers' practice of helping runaways did not stop, anyone visiting Philadelphia with a slave ran the risk of losing the slave.[2] Later that year, in a letter to William Drayton dated November 20, Washington mentioned having apprehended a runaway on his property who belonged to Drayton. He said that he sent him back to Drayton under the custody of an overseer, but when they got to Baltimore, the slave, a man named Jack, escaped. Washington told Drayton that he presumed that Jack headed for Philadelphia, where "there are numbers who had rather facilitate an escape than apprehend a runaway."[3] In a series of letters from that same year, Washington appeared to be torn between the existing practice of slavery as an economic necessity and his ardent desire to see it abolished. He concluded the letter involving the lawsuit in Philadelphia by stating that he sincerely hoped for the abolition of slavery in this country, but that it should be done through the legislative process and over a gradual period of time.[4] On May 10, he wrote to the Marquis de Lafayette, praising him for purchasing an estate in the colony of Cayenne with the idea of emancipating the slaves living on it. He told Lafayette, "Would to God a like spirit would diffuse itself generally into the minds of the people of this country; but I despair of seeing it."[5] Finally, in a letter dated September 9, sent to a friend named John Francis Mercer, Washington stated that he would never purchase another slave and reiterated his wish to see slavery abolished.[6]

There were several other early references to slaves fleeing their masters and being aided in their attempt. Wilbur Siebert, in his monumental work on the Underground Railroad, states that in 1787, a Philadelphian by the name of Isaac Harper was aiding escaped slaves flee to freedom.[7] Also in 1787, Samuel Wright laid out a town in Lancaster County, Pennsylvania, which was to become a major hub of activity on the Underground Railroad. He named his town Columbia and set aside the northeastern corner of it for manumitted slaves. Because of its proximity to the border of Maryland, Columbia was the site of many escapes to freedom.[8] Western Pennsylvania became part of the effort on February 17, 1789, when the "Washington [County] Society for the Relief of Free Negroes" was established. The officers of this pioneering organization for the combating of slavery were Thomas Scott, president; Daniel Reddick, vice president; Alexander Addison, secretary; and Absalom Baird, treasurer.[9]

By 1804, the practice of assisting fugitive slaves was so prominent in Columbia that many feel the Underground Railroad actually had its birth in that town.[10] Between 1815 and 1817, Ohio and western Pennsylvania were very active in the Underground Railroad network. One of the pioneer organizers of the railroad there was Owen Brown, the father of John Brown, who later became famous for leading rebellions in Kansas and at Harpers Ferry, Virginia.[11] By 1830, the Underground Railroad was operating in both the North and the South.

NAMING OF THE UNDERGROUND RAILROAD

The actual historical event that resulted in the use of the name Underground Railroad may never be known with complete certainty. There are three versions of this event in three different sources. The first of these accounts is by

Siebert, who relates that in 1831, a fugitive slave by the name of Tice Davids was fleeing from Kentucky with his former master in hot pursuit. Upon coming to the Ohio River near Ripley, Ohio, Davids had to dive into the river and swim to the other shore. The pursuing Kentuckian crossed the river in a boat, keeping the slave in sight. Once on the opposite shore, however, he could not find Davids. Returning to Ripley, still searching for the fugitive and not finding him, the slave owner is reported to have stated that the slave "must have gone off on an underground road."[12] Eventually the phrase "underground road" became the Underground Railroad.

A second version is found in the writings of R. C. Smedley. In his history of the Underground Railroad, Smedley dwells on the importance of Columbia, Pennsylvania, as a major depot on the escape route from Maryland. He tells of the frustration that slave hunters had when pursuing runaways across the border into Pennsylvania and tracking them to Columbia, where they were unable to locate the fugitives despite all their efforts. They then supposedly said, "There must be an underground railroad somewhere."[13]

Rev. Calvin Fairbanks relates yet a third version. He tells the story of the famous Underground Railroad personality Levi Coffin and his wife, who once hid three fugitive girls in Indiana between the feather bedding and mattress on their bed. When the Coffins allowed the slave hunters to search their house for the runaways, they could not find them. At this point, Fairbanks records the hunters as having said, "That old Quaker must have an underground railroad, for once a slave gets here, he is never seen again."[14]

THE NUMBER OF FUGITIVES WHO ESCAPED

The exact number of slaves who reached freedom on the Underground Railroad will never be known. Because of the perils involved in aiding escapees, the people involved in the railroad did not keep accurate records. However, there are several sources that offer approximations as to the numbers who reached safety in Canada or the Northern states.

Siebert quotes two Southern politicians who gave estimates as to the number of slaves fleeing captivity. North Carolina senator Clingman said that 30,000 fugitives had escaped from bondage in the South. Louisiana governor John A. Quitman, estimated that a much higher number had fled, up to 100,000 between 1810 and 1850.[15] The report given to the Freedmen's Inquiry Commission in Washington, D.C., in 1864 estimated that between 30,000 and 40,000 slaves had reached Canada during 1800 to 1864. The report also said that in 1852, the Anti-Slavery Society of Toronto determined the black population of Canada to be 30,000.[16] However, Gara cites that the

Canadian census of 1860 listed only 11,000 blacks as living there.[17] Supporting the estimates of the Freedmen's Commission Report, Samuel Ringgold Ward, a fugitive himself, says in his autobiography that in 1855 there were between 35,000 and 40,000 "coloured people" in Canada. Of these, he states that about 3,000 were free-born and the rest were fugitives.[18]

The numbers offered by the two Southern politicians must be taken in the context in which they were stated. In both instances, the men were lamenting the loss of the fugitives as property amounting to millions of dollars. Both were calling for treaties with Canada to recoup lost revenue, and both were painting a picture of dire economic hardship if the Underground Railroad continued to help slaves escape.[19] Under these circumstances, it would be natural for them to exaggerate the numbers to create an image of greater need in the form of a treaty or other legislation. While the numbers given by the Freedmen's Commission Report and by Ward are within reason, both are based on census data collected before 1860 in Canada. Unfortunately, these data were not particularly accurate when it came to calculating the population of blacks, and somewhat less than 30,000 fugitives probably found refuge in Canada by way of the Underground Railroad.

DESTINATIONS OF FUGITIVES

Men and women fleeing bondage in the South sought several areas in which they might find freedom. At first, the goal was to reach one of the Northern states where slavery was no longer practiced. However, as the imminent threat of being recaptured by slave hunters from the South was always present, especially after the passage of the Fugitive Slave Law of 1850, many sought safety and freedom in foreign lands. The chief of these was Canada, but Florida and Mexico were other destinations.

Prior to the acquisition by the United States of the Florida Territory from Spain in 1821, this Spanish-held land was a destination for many runaway Georgia slaves, who sought freedom among the Seminole Indians or in the Spanish towns and surrounding lands. The number was sufficiently large enough to cause the Georgia General Assembly to write of the problem to George Washington on December 22, 1789. In his reply, Washington recognized the substantial financial loss experienced by Georgia plantation owners as a result of slaves escaping to Spanish lands. He concluded with a statement indicating that if this escape route were not blocked soon, then Florida as a goal for runaways could reach national proportions.[20]

Another area to which fugitives fled from captivity in the Deep South was the Mexican-held lands of the American Southwest and Mexico proper.

Detail of The Underground Railroad, *painted in 1893 by Charles T. Webber (1825–1911).* CINCINNATI ART MUSEUM, SUBSCRIPTION FUND PURCHASE

The Freedmen's Inquiry Commission Report of 1864 stated that Mexico became a goal for runaways as early as the War of 1812.[21] The numbers fleeing to these lands had grown so large that Congress, at the urging of Southern legislators, proposed a treaty with the Mexican government in 1827 for the return of runaway slaves. To its credit, the Mexican Senate rejected the offer.[22] To make matters worse for slave holders in Louisiana, Alabama, and Mississippi, the Mexican Constitution of 1829 granted freedom and equality to blacks. Louisiana was especially affected by this act because it bordered the Mexican lands of what was to become the state of Texas.[23]

Canada was by far the leading foreign country to which fugitives from slavery headed. It was far more accessible to a greater number of runaways than either Florida, which ceased to become a major escape possibility after 1821, or the Mexican-held lands, which necessitated travel through slave-owning states in order to reach them. A well-organized escape mechanism in the form of the Underground Railroad made the journey to Canada much easier. In addition, large settlements of free black émigrés already living there provided aid and comfort to the fugitives.

As early as May 5, 1772, steps were taken in Canada to make it an ultimate haven for those seeking freedom. On this date, Lord Chief Justice Mansfield of Great Britain stated that any slave reaching British soil was automatically set free.[24] In order to deal with the problem of slaves who were already the property of Canadian masters, the provincial governor of Canada, on July 9, 1793, issued an act stating that all children born of female slaves were to be set free upon reaching the age of twenty-five.[25] Siebert states that although some runaways were reaching safety in Canada in the late 1700s and early 1800s, it was not until after the War of 1812 that any sizable numbers of fugitives reached this northern land. Stories of Canada and its safe haven for runaways were told by veterans returning from the war, and it did not take long for news of this "promised land" to reach the slaves toiling on the plantations. Siebert reports that by 1815, a steady traffic of fugitives was crossing Ohio and Pennsylvania headed for Canada.[26] On January 24, 1821, the General Assembly of Kentucky passed a resolution petitioning Congress to protest the official reception of fugitives in Canada. The petition asked that Congress negotiate a treaty whereby the acceptance of fugitives would cease and all runaway slaves would be returned to their former masters. When overtures were made to the British government in 1827 on this matter, Britain refused to negotiate such a treaty.[27] A few years later, in 1833, Parliament put an end to further discussion on the matter by formally abolishing slavery in all British colonies.[28] This action made Canada even more attractive as a goal for runaways.

ORGANIZATION OF THE RAILROAD

The organization of the Underground Railroad was similar to that of a real railroad. Terminology was used that reflected railroad structures and lines of communication. Safe havens, or houses where fugitives could find refuge, were known as depots or station houses. Levi Coffin, the "president" of the Underground Railroad, states that these depots were located at distances ranging from ten to twenty miles apart, the distance that a fugitive could travel through the course of a single night.[29] When a traveler arrived at a depot or station house, the usual procedure was to signal his or her arrival by a tap on the door or a window after sundown. The runaway would then be admitted into a darkened room. The windows were covered, the lights turned up, and food and shelter provided. The fugitive would then be hidden and conveyed the next night, if possible, to another station. This was usually done by hiding the individual in a wagon and traveling at night over secondary roads.[30] While the runaway stayed at a depot, he or she was hidden in a number of ways. Some simply hid in woods or thickets near the depot.[31] William Still mentions the hiding of a fugitive named Hezekial Hill under the floor boards in one of the rooms of a depot to avoid detection.[32] Others were hidden in barns, in secret rooms built into houses or barns, and even in rooms constructed inside corn shocks or hay piles in the fields.[33]

Assisting those escaping from the plantations and farms in the South was a special group of extremely brave individuals known as conductors. These were the men and women who actually traveled in the South encouraging, making arrangements, and guiding fugitives on their journeys to freedom. The most famous of these were two black women who had been slaves at one time themselves, Harriet Tubman and Sojourner Truth, and a white minister named Calvin Fairbanks. Fairbanks recorded his adventures as a conductor in a book entitled *During Slavery Times*. Tubman and Truth appear in almost every work written on the Underground Railroad in the nineteenth century.

Others involved in the operation of the railroad were agents and superintendents. Agents were individuals whose homes were used as depots and who often coordinated escape routes in the immediate vicinity of their homes. The writings of Wilbur Siebert and R. C. Smedley contain long lists of the names of agents who operated in Pennsylvania and the other Northern states during the years of the Underground Railroad. Superintendents coordinated the operation of the railroad in an entire state. They were the ones who maintained lines of communication among the depots and station houses, maintained escape routes, and gathered financial support to aid fugitives in passing though their state.[34] The superintendent of the line in Indiana, J. T. Hanover, even gave specific code names to the routes fugitives were to take, giving them the names of trees, such as linden, oak, maple, or hickory.[35]

METHODS OF ESCAPE

Runaways and conductors used many methods to flee the South, traveling overland on foot, in specially designed wagons, on railways, on steamers, in canoes or skiffs, and on coastal schooners. Some even were shipped in containers. Others made use of disguises and forged documents. Following is a sampling of methods employed in documented escape attempts.

OVERLAND TRAVEL ON FOOT

The most common manner in which slaves escaped was to travel overland on foot, northward to freedom. The location of "northward" was taught to them by word of mouth and by conductors who ventured southward to help enslaved individuals escape. North meant Canada, and Canada meant freedom. Since the fugitives, in most cases, did not have access to maps and a compass, they had to rely on natural features to guide them northward. The major natural feature was Polaris, the North Star, which can be found in the night sky by tracing a line from the two stars that make up the end of the Big Dipper (Ursa Major). By traveling in the direction indicated by the line formed by these two stars, the fugitive had a good approximation of north. When slaves were taught to follow this natural indicator, it was usually referred to as the "Drinking Gourd."[36]

With this guide before them, the fugitives would travel, mostly at night, along whatever routes were available to them. During the day, they would hide in underbrush, thickets, dense woods, or outbuildings on farms. If they were lucky, they would find refuge in the hands of an Underground Railroad station master on his or her property. Most fugitives followed existing roads or railroad beds that they knew headed north. As they traveled these routes, they had to maintain constant vigilance against a chance encounter with slave hunters prowling the area or even residents of the area who might not be sympathetic to their attempts to gain freedom. When encountering streams or rivers, they would cross by wading, swimming, riding in a stolen boat or skiff or on a hastily constructed raft, or clinging to a floating log.[37] Whatever the route, many of them walked great distances to freedom.

TRAVEL IN WAGONS

Travel in some type of wheeled conveyance was another method used for escape purposes. This type of travel almost always took place when the fugitive was in the hands of the Underground Railroad network, though occasionally a runaway would steal a horse or wagon from his former master and make an initial escape in this manner. Levi Coffin always kept a wagon ready to transport runaways in the middle of the night over less traveled secondary roads to the next depot.[38] Rev. Calvin Fairbanks, who had traveled to the South and led hundreds of runaways to freedom, wrote that he regularly employed wheeled travel to help in his escape attempts. Buggies, wagons, and carriages were all used. Often the fugitives were hidden in false bottoms in the vehicles or under loads of hay, straw, old furniture, boxes, and bags.[39] In a few cases, fugitives disguised themselves as white people and simply drove a carriage or buggy or rode in a stagecoach to safety, openly through hostile territory.[40]

TRAVEL ON RAILWAYS

Runaways took advantage of the railways to escape in two general ways, either hiding on a train in some fashion or riding on the train in some disguise or using some kind of subterfuge. William Still recounts the story of John Thompson, who at age nineteen decided to escape bondage from his master in Alabama. Thompson traveled the incredible distance from Huntsville, Alabama, in the Deep South to freedom in the North largely by train. He had made careful note, while working for his master, of the trains that followed northern routes out of Huntsville. Leaving his master's property one night, he went to the railyards in Huntsville, where he climbed onto the top of a passenger car and clung to the roof of the car as it left the station in darkness. In this manner, by riding on the top of passenger cars at night and hiding wherever he could during the day, he ultimately reached Canada.[41]

In one amazing escape story, discussed in more detail later, William and Ellen Craft rode several trains openly among white Southerners while Ellen was disguised as a white male and William pretended to be her slave.[42]

TRAVEL BY WATER: STEAMERS, CANOES, SKIFFS, AND SCHOONERS

Travel by water was another option runaways had for reaching freedom. Rev. Calvin Fairbanks used steamboats several times as a means of getting fugitives to safety. In June 1842, he helped a young woman flee from a plantation in Montgomery County, Kentucky, by traveling with her to Frankfort on a train, and then putting her on a steamboat bound for Cincinnati, where she was met by Levi Coffin. In another case, he rescued a runaway named Helen

Payne from slave catchers in Cincinnati by putting her on a steamboat headed to Pittsburgh. The steamboat captains either cooperated through goodwill or were bribed.[43] There are also accounts of escapees disguising themselves as white Southerners and simply booking passage on a steamboat and traveling to safety.[44]

Less elaborate vessels were used at times. Frederick Douglass told how he and several companions planned to escape by paddling canoes up the Chesapeake Bay, pretending to be fishermen. They then were going to abandon the canoes and travel the rest of the way through Maryland on foot, following the North Star.[45] A number of people escaped along the coast by using a variety of oceangoing vessels. Many fled from Portsmouth, Virginia, to Philadelphia in open skiffs.[46] Some traveled in more substantial ships, such as schooners. William Still recounts the tale of one such attempt, in which a sympathetic captain whom he refers to as "Captain F," in order to protect his identity, cleverly hid twenty-one fugitives aboard his schooner while he was docked in Norfolk, Virginia. Despite a careful search by proslavery port officials, the fugitives were not found and the vessel sailed to safety in Philadelphia.[47] Still also relates stories of using coastal steamers as a means of escape, but under conditions that were rather harsh for the fugitives. One such tale involved the escape attempt by James Mercer, William Gilliam, and John Clayton, who secretly boarded the steamer *Pennsylvania* before it sailed and hid themselves in the coal bin of the ship's boiler room. They stayed hidden there enduring heat, lack of air, dust, thirst, and no food, while the ship left Richmond, Virginia, and traveled to Philadelphia on February 26, 1854. By the time they reached Philadelphia, they were almost dead, but they managed to leave the ship and reach safety in the hands of the Underground Railroad in the city. Eventually they made it to freedom in Canada.[48]

TRAVEL BY CONTAINER

One of the more imaginative methods of escaping from slavery was the use of a container. In this method, the runaway hid in a box, crate, chest, or barrel, and the container was then shipped to some Northern destination. Once again, William Still is a source for a number of these unusual methods of escape. The most famous of these is the story of Henry "Box" Brown, which has already been discussed.

Still tells two other escape stories that involved containers. In 1857, a twenty-one-year-old woman who was a slave in a wealthy household in the city of Baltimore had herself sealed in a wooden crate, which was taken by a male accomplice to the express office and shipped to a Mrs. Myers in

Philadelphia. The journey from Baltimore took a day and a half, and for a large part of the time, she was upside down in the box, much like Brown had been. Adding to her woes was the fact that her escape took place during the winter, and the cold was severe in the crate. She had taken along a small pair of scissors, with which she pried a small breathing hole in the side of the box. When she finally reached the Myers home, she was almost dead. Eventually, she managed to get to Canada. Another young woman, named Lear Green, gained her freedom by being shipped in a chest aboard a steamer from Baltimore to Philadelphia.[49]

DISGUISES AND FALSE DOCUMENTS

Many fugitives managed to escape by using a variety of disguises or forged documents. Disguises included cross dressing, wearing wigs, false beards, or some form of makeup; or dressing like a white gentleman or lady, an option open only to very light-skinned blacks. R. C. Smedley recounts the story of a large, masculine-looking woman named Rachel Harris, who eluded slave catchers by dressing as a man.[50] Levi Coffin tells a similar story dealing with an incident where he was trying to aid two young girls fleeing from their master. They had reached Coffin's home, but the master and some slave catchers were in hot pursuit. Before Coffin could get them out of the house, the slave catchers appeared outside. To effect their escape, Mrs. Coffin had the girls dress like boys. They then went outside and walked past their former master, who did not recognize them in their disguises.[51]

There are many stories of runaways who dressed as white Southerners to escape. Levi Coffin tells the story of a man named Jackson who was the slave of Vice President William R. D. King, during the presidency of Franklin Pierce, and who lived on the King plantation in Alabama. He had married a freed woman who was a Creole from Louisiana and who had a light olive complexion. Jackson conceived a daring escape plan. He dressed his wife like an elegant Southern lady and had her book passage on a steamboat bound for New Orleans. He then put on a woman's outfit and accompanied his wife as her personal servant. Upon reaching New Orleans, they took a boat to Cincinnati, telling everyone that their ultimate destination was Baltimore. Once they reached Cincinnati, they sought the aid of Levi Coffin and made it safely to Detroit via the Underground Railroad network. From Detroit, they crossed over into Windsor, Canada, and gained their freedom.[52]

Coffin also writes of an Underground Railroad conductor in Virginia named John Fairfield, who aided slaves in escaping to Pennsylvania. Fairfield's favorite technique was to disguise the fugitives as Southern gentry, using wigs and makeup. Then he would buy them railroad tickets in Harpers Ferry, Virginia (now West Virginia), on a train that made a regular run to Pittsburgh. From there they would go to Cleveland and then to Detroit and freedom.[53]

Fairbanks tells of helping a woman, Emily Ward, to safety from her bondage in Kentucky using two different disguises. Ward was very light skinned, and when Fairbanks got her out of Kentucky, he dressed her as a young boy. Once in Cincinnati, he sought the help of Levi Coffin and the Ohio Underground Railroad system to get Ward to Canada. Before they could arrange her departure from Cincinnati, however, her master from Kentucky appeared in pursuit. They clothed Ward in a silk dress, and she affected the mannerisms of a Southern belle. They left the house and walked right past her former master, who did not recognize her and tipped his hat to her. They boarded a carriage and left the city. Ultimately, Emily Ward reached freedom in Canada.[54]

Fairbanks also helped rescue a slave named William Minnis from Little Rock, Arkansas. Minnis was a light-skinned mulatto, and Fairbanks dressed him in the garb of a white Southerner and used a false beard, mustache, and some hair dye to disguise him as another man in Little Rock whom he resembled. Fairbanks also trained him to speak like a white Southerner. Then they simply bought tickets on a steamboat to Cincinnati. From there, Minnis eventually reached Toronto.[55]

The most famous disguise story is that of the daring and imaginative escape of William and Ellen Craft. The Crafts wrote a detailed account of their adventure after they had reached England, and their story appears in most nineteenth-century accounts of the Underground Railroad. The couple lived in Macon, Georgia, and decided to flee northward. They were 1,000 miles from the Pennsylvania border and safety, so William devised a strategy that involved a combination of several disguises and ruses. Ellen had a light complexion, and William had her dress as a white man. William would play the role of a manservant and travel with "him". To hide her lack of a beard and smooth face, he had Ellen wear a white handkerchief over her chin and head, pretending to be suffering from a toothache. In this way, she could muffle the female tone of her voice. He also had her wear green-tinted glasses. To complete the disguise, William cut Ellen's long hair in the style of a man's. To avoid having her write anything or sign her name, skills she lacked, he put her right hand in a sling. When all was ready, he had Ellen go to the railroad station and buy two tickets for herself and her "slave." They then went to Savannah, where they boarded a steamer bound for Charleston, South Carolina. From Charleston, they took another steamer to Wilmington, North Carolina, a train to Richmond, a steamer to Washington, D.C., a train to

Baltimore, and another train to Philadelphia. The Crafts settled in Boston, but because of the passage of the Fugitive Slave Law of 1850, they ultimately went to England.[56]

Falsified documents were also used by runaways or conductors to gain freedom. The most common technique was to forge a slave owner's signature on a travel pass, allowing the runaway to reach a Southern city close to a Northern state, thus providing a better opportunity to escape. Frederick Douglass, in his autobiography, discusses such a plan. In his aborted attempt to flee, for the first time, from his bondage, Douglass wrote fake notes for himself and his co-conspirators stating that they each had their master's permission to travel to Baltimore on an errand. Unfortunately, because of an informant, the plan was thwarted, and Douglass was forced to eat the slips before his master could find out what he had done.[57]

HAZARDS IN ESCAPING

Escaping was no easy matter. It was hazardous for the fugitive, for anyone aiding him or her, and even for those in pursuit. The punishments for the runaway, if caught and returned to a master, could be excessive and even result in death, and the penalties exacted on those aiding the runaway could be both physically and financially disastrous.

A review of advertisements in Southern papers for the capture of runaways gives some idea of the brutality shown toward them by their former masters:

> Committed to jail as a runaway, a negro woman named Martha, 17 or 18 years of age, has numerous scars of the whip on her back. (*Nashville Banner,* December 10, 1838)
>
> Ten dollars reward for my woman Siby, very much scarred about the neck and ears by whipping. (*Mobile Commercial Advertizer,* 1838).
>
> Ranaway, a negro fellow named Dick—has many scars on his back from being whipped. ([Vicksburg, Mississippi] *Sentinal,* August 22, 1838)
>
> One hundred dollars reward for my negro Glasgow, and Kate, his wife. Glasgow is 24 years old—has marks of the whip on his back. Kate is 26—has a scar on cheek, and several marks of the whip. ([Macon, Georgia] *Messenger,* May 25, 1837)[58]

These newspaper advertisements indicate that whipping was a common experience in a slave's life. If this was the norm in the daily life of a slave, how much worse could it be if the slave fled and was then returned to the master?

A review of eyewitness accounts shows the barbarity of the institution of slavery in this country. Among the more severe punishments inflicted were the following: Hot tar was poured on a runaway's head; another was whipped severely and then had his Achilles tendons severed to prevent further attempt at flight; in another instance, the runaway was dragged through brambles by his master, who was on horseback; one fugitive was strapped to a table and slowly hacked to pieces by his master with an ax; and still another was shot dead upon his return.[59] William Still recounts the punishment of a runaway named Henry Grimes, who, upon his capture and return, received 100 lashes and then had both of his insteps split to the bone to cripple him and prevent him from escaping again.[60]

Even if the fugitive avoided recapture, the hazards faced while on the journey were great. Not all white people were sympathetic to the runaway's plight. Frederick Douglass speaks of some who made a practice of encouraging slaves to escape and then capturing them and returning them to their masters for the reward money being offered.[61] The following exerpt from a January 9, 1839, letter written by the great abolitionist of western Pennsylvania, Dr. F. Julius LeMoyne, gives a glimpse into the physical hardships runaways sometimes faced:

> Lest you should not have seen the statement to which I am going to allude, I subjoin a brief outline of the facts of a transaction which occurred in Western Virginia, adjacent to this county, a number of years ago. . . . A slave boy ran away in cold weather, and during his concealment had his legs frozen; he returned, or was retaken. After some time the flesh decayed and sloughed—of course was offensive—he was carried out to a field and left there without bed, or shelter, deserted to die. His only companions were the house dogs which he called to him. After several days and nights spent in suffering and exposure, he was visited by Drs. McKitchen and Mitchell in the field, of their own accord, having heard by report of his lamentable condition; they remonstrated with the master; brought the boy to the house, amputated both legs, and he finally recovered.[62]

Dr. R. C. Smedley relates the story of another fugitive who had fled in midwinter and was poorly clad. His fingers froze so badly that the flesh fell off their tips, and his bones were sticking out over an inch. He had to have several fingers amputated, but he did manage to gain his freedom.[63]

Station masters, conductors, and anyone giving a fugitive aid also faced serious hazards. The Fugitive Slave Act of 1793 had made it a crime to assist fugitive slaves. It established a fine of $500 for anyone aiding a runaway.[64] Of more serious consequence, however, was the enactment of the Fugitive Slave Law of 1850. This federal law, enacted on September 18, 1850, increased the penalties for aiding fugitives and made it possible for slave catchers to return runaways to the South, even if they had been living in freedom in the North for some time. Under this new law a person would be fined $1,000 for each fugitive aided and possibly face a jail sentence of six months.[65] The law had such a chilling effect that fugitives who had settled in the Northern states left in droves for Canada and even, like William and Ellen Craft, for England.[66]

Two celebrated abolitionists suffered greatly for aiding fugitives—Rev. Calvin Fairbanks and Rev. Charles T. Torrey. Fairbanks was an ordained Methodist minister who spent years helping slaves escape from all over the South through the Indiana and Ohio route of the Underground Railroad. He was captured several times. In some cases, he was flogged, but in two cases, he was imprisoned. He spent a total of seventeen years and four months in prison. While in Kentucky prisons, he was harshly treated by guards and fellow inmates because of his Underground Railroad activities. By his own tally, Fairbanks recorded that between March 1, 1854, and March 1, 1862, he received a total of 35,105 whip lashes because of his work aiding fugitives.[67] Torrey was an ordained Congregationalist minister who lived with his wife and children in Albany, New York. He was an ardent abolitionist who spoke against the institution of slavery. In the late spring of 1844, he traveled to Maryland, where he attempted to escort a family of slaves named the Webbs to freedom in New York. He was caught in the act and formally arrested on June 24, 1844. His trial in Baltimore was covered by all of the leading newspapers of the day. Despite a spirited defense, which called into question the whole immoral principle underlying the institution of slavery, he was convicted and sentenced on December 3, 1844, to serve six years for each of the three slaves he was escorting. Despite pleas from many prominent individuals and petitions to the governor of Maryland and the president, and even though his health began to fail under the conditions of prison life, no pardon came. On May 9, 1846, Charles Torrey died in his cell.[68]

Apprehending runaways could also be hazardous for the slave catchers. Fugitives did not surrender easily and in many cases fought back with great determination. Sometimes those who were present when a slave catcher attempted to seize a runaway helped the fugitive get away and even inflicted physical damage on the pursuers. The most famous case involving a group of people thwarting an attempt to recapture fugitives was what became known as the Christiana Affair. On September 11, 1851, Edward Gorsuch came to the town of Christiana, Pennsylvania, to reclaim some fugitive slaves under the provisions of the Fugitive Slave Law of 1850. He had learned of their presence there through an informant. Accompanying him on the trip were Federal Marshal Henry H. Kline and a band of men. When they came to the house where the fugitives were meeting, one of them, William Parker, vowed that he would never be taken alive. He persuaded his two brothers-in-law, Alexander Pinkney and Abraham Johnson, to resist with force, if necessary. Meanwhile, an alarm was sounded, and in a few minutes, a large band of Parker's neighbors appeared on the scene. In the battle that followed, Edward Gorsuch was shot dead and several of the others with him were wounded. The marshal quickly left, as did a number of those with him. Parker, Pinkney, and Johnson fled to safety and were never apprehended.[69]

ESCAPE ROUTES

NATIONAL ROUTES

There were three major geographic routes by which fugitives could travel via the Underground Railroad in the United States to reach Canada: eastern, central, and western. The eastern route was the oldest of the three and dates back to the late 1700s. Coming overland from the state of Maryland or by water along the coast from Baltimore or one of several ports in Virginia or the Carolinas, the runaways would reach one of a number of towns or cities in eastern Pennsylvania. The main entry areas were Lancaster, Columbia, and Philadelphia. From these sites, fugitives then moved on to New Jersey, New York City, and then through the New England states or upper New York to Canada.[70]

The central route funneled fugitives from states all over the South through Kentucky, Virginia, and western Maryland to Indiana, Ohio, and Pennsylvania. Each of these Northern states had networks that were designed to convey runaways to Detroit; Cleveland and Sandusky, Ohio; and Erie, Pennsylvania. From these points, the fugitives could cross over into Canada.[71]

The western route ran along the Mississippi River Valley through the territories of Kansas and Missouri to Iowa and Illinois. Chicago was a main focal point on this route. From there, runaways were escorted through Michigan to safety in Canada, usually through the city of Detroit.[72]

PENNSYLVANIA ROUTES

There were three principle Underground Railroad routes running through Pennsylvania. The Eastern Route involved York, Lancaster, Chester, Delaware, and Philadelphia Counties, and the fugitives using this pathway were guided through the counties of northeastern Pennsylvania to New York and then into Canada.[73] The Central Route began in Adams and Fulton Counties and proceeded through Cumberland and Dauphin Counties and on northward. Fugitives would enter Pennsylvania from Maryland and pass through the towns of Mercersburg and Gettysburg. They would then travel to Harrisburg or Reading, and from there go on to either New Jersey or New York and then to Canada. The Western Route was mainly for runaways who had passed through Virginia, Maryland, or Ohio. Fugitives reached the main Underground Railroad towns of Bedford, Uniontown, and Washington. From these points, they were led northward by one of three major routes, passing through Clearfield, Indiana, or Pittsburgh. Ultimately the routes led to Canada.

NEW YORK

To New York
To Jamestown
Sugar Grove
To Salamanca
Warren
To Erie
Meadville
Barnes
River
Franklin
Allegheny
Sandy Lake
Clarington
Mercer
Shippenville
Clarion
Brookville
Summerville
Grampian Hills
Clearfield
Bellefonte
Philipsburg
Marion Center
Burnside
Cherry Tree
Indiana
Little Juniata River
Altoona
PENNSYLVANIA
Ebensburg
Hollidaysburg
Pittsburgh
East Freedom
Johnstown
Claysburg
Monongahela River
Geistown
Ligonier
Pleasantville
Saint Clairsville
Youghiogheny River
Fishertown
Bedford
To Uniontown
Schellsburg
Everett
Somerset
Manns Choice
Charlesville
Rainsburg
Patience
Chaneysville

Cumberland

VIRGINIA   MARYLAND

PENNSYLVANIA UNDERGROUND
RAILROAD STATIONS

**Bedford–Clearfield
Route**

Western Pennsylvania
1790–1860

SCALE IN MILES
0   5   10   15

Bedford–Clearfield Route

The most easterly of the major Underground Railroad routes in western Pennsylvania began at the Maryland-Pennsylvania border, ran northward to Bedford, and by several different subroutes, reached the town of Clearfield. From there, the route went in a northwesterly direction, ultimately linking with other routes heading to New York or Erie.

The town of Bedford was the entry point for fugitive slaves following this route. Located only twenty-six miles from Cumberland, Maryland, and at the head of several pathways leading northward, Bedford was well situated for such an important role on a major escape route. The fact that Bedford played this role is documented in the writings of Siebert (1898), Blackburn and Welfley (1906), Burns (1925), and Blockson (1981).[1]

CUMBERLAND TO BEDFORD

A study of the topography of the land between Cumberland and Bedford reveals several natural thoroughfares over which runaways could travel. One option was to leave Maryland at the small hamlet of Old Town, just nine miles to the east of Cumberland, and journey along the eastern slopes of Tussey Mountain to Everett, Pennsylvania, just six miles east of Bedford. A well-worn Indian trail, the eastern branch of the famous Warriors Path, traversed this area and made travel easier. This path led from Old Town to Everett, passing along the slopes of Tussey Mountain and through the town of Chaneysville.[2] The modern PA Route 326 follows this same trail today.[3] Blackburn and Welfley mention this easterly trail to Bedford and also state that some of the runaways used an alternative route at this point. This route lay on the eastern slopes of Evitts Mountain, located between the Cumberland Valley and the Indian Path on Tussey Mountain.[4] Blockson corroborates the use of this trail along modern Route 326, and he cites Chaneysville and Rainsburg as having had Underground Railroad stations. He says that the Lester Imes family operated a station in Chaneysville.[5]

Eventually, when those using this trail reached the towns of Everett and Mount Dallas, they would cross the Bedford-Chambersburg Pike and be just eight miles to the east of Bedford. Today this pike is U.S. Route 30. Blockson traces the escape route from this location to a station located at the Stuckey Farm on the eastern side of Snake Spring Valley next to the Narrows, a natural gap in Evitts Mountain through which all the roads leading to Bedford had to pass.[6] From the Stuckey Farm, it was a short trip to Bedford.

The most important route between Cumberland and Bedford followed the terrain of the Cumberland Valley. Bordered on the west by the ridge line of Wills Mountain and on the east by the slopes of Evitts Mountain, this trail provided ample cover in the form of groves of trees, dense underbrush, and hidden glens, in which runaways could hide to avoid pursuers. In addition, the central arm of the Warriors Path ran northward along the valley.[7] Ultimately, U.S. Route 220 followed the same course. Although the towns of Centerville, Patience, and Burning Bush lay along this route, there were no organized Underground Railroad stations in them. A fugitive would not reach a place of refuge until the outskirts of Bedford.[8] What small aid runaways could find along this trail was to be had at the hands of a few isolated black families living in the valley.[9]

The writings of Siebert, Blackburn, and Welfley list only these two routes as leading from Cumberland to Bedford. A case can be made for a third route, however. Blockson, in his research, found evidence that free blacks and whites who lived in the small town of Schellsburg, eight miles to the west of Bedford, provided shelter for runaways.[10] He suspects that the Knaugel House was a station in that town.[11] A possible trail that would bring one to Schellsburg was a third branch of the Warriors Path, which ran from Cumberland, along the western slopes of Wills Mountain, to Manns Choice, a small town just a few miles west of Bedford and southeast of Schellsburg. The trail then continued northward to Frankstown near Hollidaysburg.[12] Blockson speculates that the fugitives went from Schellsburg along the old Forbes Road to Ligonier, where they would have linked up with the Uniontown–Indiana Route. A more likely possibility is that from Schellsburg, they would have traveled the six miles up the Quaker Valley to the highly organized Underground Railroad stations in and around Fishertown.

Bedford was a logical site as the jumping-off point for this branch of the Underground Railroad in western Pennsylvania. Founded in 1750, by Robert MacRay as a trading post on the Raystown Branch of the Juniata River, Bedford quickly became a focal point for people traveling north from Maryland and west from Lancaster.[13] Between 1757 and 1758, Lt. Col. John Armstrong built a fort on the site to act as a staging area for Gen. John Forbes and his assault on the French at Fort Duquesne. Armstrong named it Fort Bedford after the fourth duke of Bedford, a nobleman in England.[14] By this time, a road reached Bedford from Shippensburg to the east, making the Fort even more accessible to travelers.[15] It was from this site that Forbes launched the cutting of a road through the wilderness to Ligonier.[16]

Bedford grew rapidly in the 1760s. By 1761, twenty-seven log homes were built near the fort, and in 1771, it became the seat of the newly formed Bedford County.[17] George Washington used Bedford as a staging area in 1794 when he moved against the Whiskey rebels in western Pennsylvania. By 1800, the old Forbes Road underwent improvement and became known as the Pennsylvania Road. Other roads, such as a turnpike from Chambersburg to Bedford and from Bedford to Stoystown, a new road to Somerset, and a stage line linking Bedford to Cumberland, all helped establish Bedford as a travel center.[18]

The roads accelerated the growth of the community surrounding Bedford. As early as 1783, a traveler by the name of Johann Schoepf wrote a description of Bedford as being a "little town" having a courthouse, a mill, and a Lutheran and a Presbyterian church, and being surrounded by many farms.[19] Around 1800, John Melich discovered mineral springs near the town. John Anderson built a hotel near the springs in 1804, and by 1808, the springs were appearing in advertisements around the state as a source of "medicinal waters."[20] By the time the Underground Railroad became active there, Bedford had a sizable population.

There were a number of Underground Railroad stations in the Bedford area. Blackburn and Welfley list three black agents who lived there: Rev. John Fiddler, Elias Rouse, and Joseph Crawley.[21] Siebert adds a fourth person named Wyett Perry to this list of agents.[22] Recently, the name of James Graham has emerged as a fifth agent. Graham lived on a farm outside of Bedford with his wife and their sixteen children. He frequently conveyed runaways to safety by hiding them in his hay wagon.[23] Blockson identifies a dwelling in the town of Bedford, built in 1797 and called the Grove, where fugitives hid until they were moved westward or northward on their journey to freedom.[24]

BEDFORD WESTWARD

Once the runaways reached the vicinity of Bedford, there were several possible escape routes they could follow. Two of these involved traveling almost due west from the town.

SCHELLSBURG

One path to safety that fugitives could take was the western branch of the old Warriors Path, which ran from Maryland to Schellsburg. From there they could have gone along the Forbes Road to Ligonier, as Blockson suggested. Once in Ligonier, runaways most likely would have entered the Union-town–Indiana branch of the railroad and fled northward to safety. But what is more plausible is that they simply went six miles northward to Fishertown and entered the Bedford–Clearfield Route. In either case, the runaways' quest for freedom would have continued.

SOMERSET

Another trail led from Bedford to Somerset. Glades Road, linking Bedford with Somerset, was completed in 1772, following the Indian trail of the same name.[25] The road, which became modern PA Route 31, eventually went through the towns of Mount Pleasant, West Newton, Monongahela, and Washington, all of which had organized Underground Railroad stations.[26] Siebert includes William Willey and a Mr. Smith in his list of active agents in the Somerset area.[27]

BEDFORD TO CLEARFIELD

The most popular escape route from Bedford passed through Fishertown, a small Quaker community about ten miles to the northwest of Bedford on Chestnut Ridge. To reach it, fugitives would take the road that followed the old Conemaugh Indian Path through the Pigeon Hills. Today, PA Route 56 follows the same track.[28] The role of the Quakers in the operation of the Underground Railroad in eastern Pennsylvania is well documented. That they lived and aided escapees from slavery in western Pennsylvania is not as well known, but it was only natural that the Quakers living in Fishertown should be part of the escape network. Blackburn and Welfley list a number of individuals and their families who played a role in assisting and transporting escapees in the Fishertown area. Their names include Amos, Samuel, William, and Josiah Penrose; Eli Miller; Samuel Way; Samuel K. Miller; William Kirk; John Albaugh; and Nathan Hammond.[29]

Not all the runaways, however, chose to continue their journey to freedom through Schellsburg, Somerset, or Fishertown. Some stayed in the Bedford area and joined the existing black community that flourished there. There is evidence that a number of fugitives decided to stay within the black community located in Juniata Township, to the west of Bedford and bordering Somerset County at the base of Allegheny Ridge.[30]

The next stage in the Bedford–Clearfield Route led from Fishertown northward. With all of the Underground Railroad routes, there were few single, direct pathways between two points. The need for secrecy and for avoiding slave catchers and their sympathizers required conductors and runaways to zigzag, backtrack, and use alternate routes. This was the case with the next leg from Fishertown to Clearfield, which followed two different paths.

FISHERTOWN–JOHNSTOWN–CLEARFIELD ROUTE

One major escape route led from Fishertown to Geistown in Cambria County. Conductors would convey their charges along the Conemaugh trace from Fishertown to the town of Pleasantville. One can retrace the same path today by following Route 56. At Pleasantville, several agents, including Benjamin Walker, Samuel and George Hess, and George Harbaugh, took over the task of moving the fugitives.[31] While these men are formally listed as agents, other people also aided the travelers. John Albaugh does not appear on any list of agents, but it is apparent that he played an important role in the Underground Railroad nonetheless. Blackburn and Welfley mention him in recounting a story told by Mark Miller of Pleasantville, son of Eli Miller.

At the time referred to in this sketch, Eli Miller lived upon what is now known as the Claycomb farm, on Dunning's Creek, in East St. Clair township, on the road leading from Fishertown to Osterburg. On a Sunday evening in about the year 1840, Thomas Miller, then a lad about twelve years old, was watering horses at the creek, when he discovered four colored men sitting on the foot-log which crossed the creek near the watering place. They made inquiry as to their whereabouts, when Thomas told them to remain where they were until he had sent his father down to see them. Mr. Miller then went down, and after a short interview took them in charge, gave them something to eat, and furnished them appropriate shelter for the night. The next morning, fearing that their captors might come upon them before he could arrange for their removal to a more advanced station, he secluded them in a dense wood or thicket back of "Mount Miserable Hill," an abrupt elevation above the present county bridge. This was a rather secure fortress, as their position was accessible from the main road only on foot, and the elevation such as to afford them a good view of surroundings. Here they were kept for three or four days and nights, when by the assistance of John Albaugh, they were transferred under cover to Benjamin Walker's, who took them afoot across the mountain, Benjamin riding a white horse along the road, and the darkeys taking to the woods for safety, being guided in their course by keeping an eye on the white horse. On landing at William Sleek's they were soon forwarded to Johnstown, and probably got into the friendly hands of Mr. Cover, Mr. Helsop or Avery Allen. We should have noted in passing, that, in fifteen minutes after leaving Miller's, the pursuers of these poor fellows passed by the place from which they had so recently started, and two boys, Thomas Miller and Hiram Way, being in a shed by the roadside, heard them discussing the subject of capturing these slaves.[32]

Walker and the other agents conveyed their charges from Pleasantville over the mountains to Geistown in Cambria County. Once there, they turned the runaways over to William Sleek, the local agent in that area.[33] Sleek is mentioned as an agent in almost every source dealing with the Underground Railroad in Cambria County. Mark Miller's story gives evidence to the important role that Sleek played in the escape network.[34] Another story of fugitives passing through the area and being aided by Walker and Sleek was told by Thomas G. Walker, the son of Benjamin Walker, to Blackburn and Welfley.

In 1848 or '49 four negroes from the state of Alabama arrived along the underground railroad at the point in the mountain below Bedford Springs. It was a rare occurrence that fugitives from such a great distance succeeded in making their way to the north. Soon after they started from their master they found themselves pursued by bloodhounds, a mother dog and three pups. One of the negroes knew the old dog very well, and, calling her to him, stuffed the bell which she had on her neck with moss, so as to prevent its ringing, and the pups, being unable to follow their mother, became scattered and returned home: besides this, the negroes, on crossing a stream, followed down the same some distance before coming out on the other side, so as to defeat further pursuit of hounds. From their mountain retreat they pressed on toward Pleasantville, evading the main road and guided by the north star. On arriving at Benjamin Walker's they were conducted by him to the top of the mountain, and were there directed to William Sleek's, as many others had previously been. Their would be captors were in close pursuit, as they were met by Mr. Walker on his return down the mountain. As their capture was not heard of afterward, it is presumed that they finally escaped into Canada.[35]

Geistown is a suburb of Johnstown today, and in the early nineteenth century, it was only a short distance from that much larger town. William Sleek took fugitives from his home to Johnstown, where they received shelter from several individuals, including a Mr. Cover and Avery Allen.[36] Henry Wilson Storey, in his work on the history of Cambria County, identifies several other agents in Johnstown, including James Helsop, who was aided by his wife, as well as John Cushon, Henry Willis, William Barnett, and John Myers.[37] From Johnstown, the fugitives moved northward via one of two possible routes.

Johnstown–Wilmore–Ebensburg–Burnside Route

The more well known of the two routes proceeded from Johnstown in a northeasterly direction. Most sources have the escapees traveling all the way to Ebensburg, following the trace that eventually became I-219.[38] Blockson mentions a stop along the route at the hamlet of Wilmore, a small black community located about eight miles south of Ebensburg and near Portage. Godfrey Wilmore, a former slave from Maryland, is reported to have founded the community.[39]

Once they reached Ebensburg, the runaways found refuge with A. A. Barber, the resident agent in the town.[40] He sent them on their way north through a series of valleys, until they reached the small town of Cherry Tree, situated in Indiana County where Cambria, Clearfield, and Indiana Counties meet.[41] Dr. George Gamble was the agent in Cherry Tree.[42] The village was also located on the great Frankstown Path, the Indian trail that ran from Harrisburg to Kittanning and over which a great many people traveled.[43]

The escape route left Cherry Tree and continued along the track of modern U.S. Route 219 to Burnside in Clearfield County, where George Atchison was the agent.[44] The West Branch of the Susquehanna River, which begins near Cherry Tree, flows through Burnside, and the fugitives followed it to Grampian Hills, a town in central Clearfield County.[45] From here they continued along the river the ten miles to the town of Clearfield, the major Underground Railroad station in this part of western Pennsylvania.[46]

Johnstown–Conemaugh–Marion Center–Cush Cushion Route

The other route from Johnstown went northwest to the town of Conemaugh in Indiana County. Rev. David Blair, pastor of the Presbyterian church there, was the key agent in the vicinity.[47] Blair saw to it that the runaways made their way to the town of Indiana, where they entered another great Underground Railroad escape route, the Uniontown–Indiana Route. From Indiana, they went northward through Marion Center, but after reaching the town of Cush Cushion, they turned away from the Uniontown–Indiana Route and reentered the Bedford–Clearfield Route at the town of Burnside in Clearfield County.[48]

FISHERTOWN–HOLLIDAYSBURG–CLEARFIELD ROUTE

The second route from Fishertown to Clearfield followed the western slopes of the Dunning Mountain Ridge, running along the Warriors Path, as does modern U.S. Route 220. An entry in the diary of James Blackburn dated May 14, 1837, mentions runaways leaving Fishertown and going northeast to the town of St. Clairsville and says that another Quaker settlement there provided aid and transportation for runaways fleeing northward to Clearfield.[49] From there the fugitives made their way eleven miles northward to the hamlet of Claysburg, proceeded five miles to East Freedom, and continued northward another six miles to Hollidaysburg and Altoona in Blair County.[50] Siebert says William Nesbet was the major agent in Blair County.[51] From Altoona, there were two escape routes leading to Clearfield.

Altoona–Centre County–Clearfield Route

Blackburn and Welfley describe a route heading from Altoona through the mountains of Centre County to Clearfield, but they give no details as to the actual pathway it took.[52] A map of the area shows a clear possible track runaways may have followed. Leaving Altoona, they may have gone along the Bald Eagle Indian trail, which traverses the same line as modern U.S. Route 220, as far as the village of Bald Eagle, twenty miles northeast of Altoona. At this point, they likely took the road that led to Philipsburg, about fifteen miles to the northeast. Philipsburg was directly linked to Clearfield by the western branch of the Bald Eagle path and a road that became U.S. Route 322 in later years.[53] The names of the individuals who may have helped the fugitives along this route were not documented.

Altoona–Ebensburg–Clearfield Route

Storey gives another route leading from Altoona to Clearfield, saying that fugitives went from Altoona "over the mountain" to Ebensburg and from there to Canada.[54] Once in Ebensburg, runaways would have followed the well-established Ebensburg–Cherry Tree–Burnside–Clearfield route described above.

CLEARFIELD NORTHWARD

Like Bedford, Clearfield is included in all the sources that describe the Underground Railroad in western Pennsylvania. One measure of its importance is the number of agents operating in the area. Siebert's list of agents includes George and William Atchison, Isaac Cochran, James Gallaker, William Westover, and Jason Kirk and his sons.[55] Siebert also states that an "important branch" of the

Underground Railroad ran northwest from Clearfield to Shippenville, and then on to the town of Franklin. From Franklin, Siebert has the escape route going to Erie.[56] McKnight adds the town of Brookville to this route.[57] Brookville lies on the route between Clearfield and Shippenville. In addition, it is twenty miles closer to Clearfield than is Shippenville, making it a logical stopping place for escapees fleeing northward. A well-traveled Indian trail, the Venango-Chinklacamoose Path, ran from Clearfield through Brookville, passed just north of Shippenville, and reached Franklin. Later, a road, the precursor of U.S. Route 322, ran from Clearfield through Brookville and Shippenville to Franklin.[58] This meant that runaways had two excellent ways to go from Clearfield to Franklin.

Brookville was a station of some prominence on this escape route. McKnight lists a number of agents operating in and around the town, including Judge Elijah Heath and his wife, Mr. and Mrs. Arad Pearsall, Mr. and Mrs. James Steadman, and Rev. and Mrs. Christopher Fogel.[59] Judge Heath had a house at 64 Pickering Street in Brookville, in which he had a special room built in the basement for the purpose of hiding escaped slaves. Pearsall was a jailer at the Jefferson County Jail. On one occasion, he helped two captured runaways, Charles Brown and William Parker, escape from the jail and head toward Canada. Fogel, along with his first and second wives, operated safe havens in both Summerville (Troy at that time) and Brookville. In addition to using his home, he also hid fugitives at the tannery that he operated on Jefferson Street in Brookville.[60]

Two passages from a local newspaper, cited by McKnight, give some idea of the volume of runaways passing through the town of Brookville. The first states that "twenty-five fugitive slaves passed through Brookville Monday morning on their way to Canada." The second, dated October 14, 1850, says that, "forty armed fugitive slaves passed through Brookville to Canada."[61] Another indicator of Brookville's importance was the fact that the route from Clearfield was not the only one passing through the town. McKnight also mentions that fugitives came here from Punxsutawney, a station on the Uniontown–Indiana Route,[62] and he quotes a Mrs. Lowry, the daughter of Isaac P. Carmalt, a local Quaker station master, as saying that fugitives also came to Brookville from Bellefonte in Centre County.[63] Two different routes exited the town of Brookville.

BROOKVILLE–FRANKLIN ROUTE

The most widely used route leaving Brookville was the one that passed through Shippenville, either along the Venango-Chinklacamoose Path or the road that went all the way to Franklin.

BROOKVILLE–WARREN ROUTE

McKnight describes a second route that left Brookville and proceeded northward through Forest County. The first stop along this way was the village of Clarington, about fourteen miles north of Brookville, according to McKnight. The station master here was William Coon, who, along with his wife, gave aid and comfort to the weary runaways.[64] To get from Brookville to Clarington, and then to Warren, the fugitives could have traversed the Catawba Indian Path, which ran from Brookville past Clarington.[65] Warren was only twelve miles from the New York border.[66] Blockson records that the town of Barnes, which lies between Clarington and Warren, had an Underground Railroad station in the Presbyterian church.[67] Fugitives could have taken an alternate route from Barnes to Warren by going along an old hunting trail known as the Pigeon Path.[68] Once they reached Warren, the runaways had three alternatives.

Warren–Salamanca Route

One possible path was northeast from Warren on the Cornplanter-Venango Indian Trail. This trail proceeded north from the town for about three miles along Conewango Creek and then turned eastward at Hatch Run. It followed Hatch Run to Quaker Ridge, veered north for a few miles, and then proceeded eastward along Hodge Run until it met the Allegheny River.[69] From this point, fugitives would have gone along the banks of the river to Salamanca, New York.

Warren–Jamestown Route

A second possibility was to travel due north along the shores of Conewango Creek. A road paralleled the creek, and both crossed the Pennsylvania–New York border about twelve miles north of Warren. The creek eventually came into contact with the feeder stream for Lake Chautauqua and the town of Jamestown at the head of the lake.

Warren–Sugar Grove Route

A third route led northwest from Warren, along a road that later became PA Route 69, to the village of Sugar Grove. In recent years, much research has shown the importance of this town, which is on the Pennsylvania–New York border, in the Underground Railroad system.

Those choosing to follow the more common route from Brookville to Franklin entered Venango County and a well-organized Underground Railroad system there. According to Siebert, Venango County had many agents, including B. Ralph Clapp, a Mr. Conley, John W. Howe, John Hughes,

James Kingsley, James Lawson, Job Lawson, Alex McDowell, William Raymond, James Rodgers, S. H. Small, and Richard Travis.[70] Siebert's map of the Underground Railroad in Pennsylvania has two routes leaving Franklin.

Franklin–Meadville Route

One route leads from Franklin through Cooperstown to Meadville in Crawford County.[71] This is the path mentioned most often in the sources on the Underground Railroad. Both the Venango Indian Trail and a road (today U.S. Route 322) connected the two towns.[72] Once they reached Meadville, fugitives entered the complicated network of escape routes that ran throughout Crawford and Erie Counties.

Franklin–Mercer County–Ohio Route

The second route depicted on Siebert's map runs from Franklin through Mercer County to the Ohio border.[73] On the way to the Ohio border, runaways could have stopped and found aid in a little community in Mercer County. Siebert describes a small colony of escaped slaves living near the shores of Sandy Lake in Mercer County. The colony was only fifteen miles from Franklin and would have been about a day's travel from that town.[74]

The Bedford–Clearfield Route is a typical example of an Underground Railroad escape way. No direct road was taken between the major towns, but rather, a whole host of secondary roads and subroutes, each with its own advantages and unique features, allowed the fugitives to move ever northward toward freedom.

NEW YORK

OHIO

PENNSYLVANIA UNDERGROUND RAILROAD STATIONS

Uniontown–Indiana Route

Western Pennsylvania
1790–1860

SCALE IN MILES
0   5   10   15

To
Meadville

To
New York

To Ohio

Franklin

Rockland   Shippenville

Clarion

Brookville

Clearfield

Callensburg
Summerville
Rimersburg

Punxsutawney

Dayton

Burnside

Marion
Center

Cush Cushion

Indiana

Clarksburg

Homer City
Graceton
Black Lick
Blairsville

Pittsburgh
New Alexandria

Jeannette

Latrobe
Greensburg

PENNSYLVANIA

Mt. Pleasant

River

Allegheny

Ohio

River

River

Monongahela

Youghiogheny River

Uniontown

To Pittsburgh

Turkey Foot

From
Virginia

Greensboro
Bobtown   New Geneva
Mt. Morris   Somerfield   Addison

Morgantown

Cumberland

VIRGINIA

MARYLAND

Uniontown–Indiana Route

The second and third major routes of the Underground Railroad running through western Pennsylvania had their origins in and around the community of Uniontown. Situated at the western base of Chestnut Ridge, only twelve miles from what was then Virginia, and on the National Road, which came from Cumberland, Uniontown was a natural focal point for fugitives fleeing slavery in the South. Founded in 1767 by Thomas Douthet and Henry Beeson, and originally called Beesontown, the community of Uniontown grew rapidly. The fertile land between the western slopes of Chestnut Ridge and the Youghiogheny and Monongahela Rivers attracted new settlers eager for farmland. Beeson saw the potential for growth in the area and opened a blacksmith shop and a mill for grinding the grains grown on the new farms. In addition to being an enterprising businessperson, he was also a Quaker. Beeson recruited others of his faith to come west, and in a short time, a Quaker settlement grew around Uniontown.

Uniontown became the seat for the newly formed county of Fayette in 1784. By 1790, its population had swelled to 11,402.[1] Uriah Brown, an early traveler in western Pennsylvania, gave a description of the town in an 1816 entry in his personal journal:

> 23rd of the month [June] & 11th [first] of the week. . . . I am now in Union Town Formerly Beeson Town on the West Side of the Aleghany Mountain, the Back Bone of America. . . . This great western Road (the National Road) is Carried and Laid out a great part of the way on the same Identical ground & totally carried through on the General direction of Braddocks road. . . . I saw one handsome and Larg Brick House, with extensive back buildings of Brick on the Aleghany Mountains, also one Large Stone house that Looks as well as the Comonallity of the best Stone House, and many Very good & 2 Story log Buildings: and many Comfortable little farms & some Large farms. . . .

Union or Beeson Town is a Post & Country Town; where at it, dont look so promising as from laurel Hill, some good building of Brick in the same, too many wooden houses for the Credit of the place, its situation is handsome & the surrounding neighborhood is a handsome hill Country in a good State of Cultivation; Red-Stone Creek runs through this Town which affords a Merchant Mill in the vicinity of the Town. I have put up at Thomas Brownfield sign of the Swan as soon as I came to Town which was yesterday 5 or six o'Clock.[2]

Siebert makes special mention of the prominence of Uniontown to the Underground Railroad. "The most important of these [routes through western Pennsylvania] seem to have been the roads resulting from the convergence of at least three well-defined lines of escape at Uniontown in southwestern Pennsylvania from the neighboring counties of Virginia and Maryland."[3] He says that based on a map drawn by Amos M. Jolliffe of Uniontown, two routes ran northward from the town, both ending in Pittsburgh.[4] A further examination of Siebert's research, and that of other writers on this subject, shows that another route exited Uniontown and proceeded northward, not through Pittsburgh, but via the town of Indiana.

TO UNIONTOWN

There were several ways by which a runaway could reach Uniontown from the South. Siebert cites that there were three such paths. While he does not elaborate on the three, his map of Underground Railroad routes shows lines emanating from Cumberland, Morgantown, and an area to the west of Morgantown on the Virginia-Pennsylvania border.[5] Brewster, in "The Rise of the Antislavery Movement in Southwestern Pennsylvania," describes only two routes. The first agrees with Siebert's route, beginning in Cumberland, Maryland, and traveling along the National Road to Uniontown. The second crosses the Mason-Dixon Line and proceeds through Greene County to Uniontown.[6] Examination of these and other sources, the topography of the region, and the traces left by ancient Indian trails and early roads seems to indicate that there were three, possibly four, routes to Uniontown.

CUMBERLAND–UNIONTOWN ROUTE

One route led from Cumberland to Uniontown. Cumberland was the jumping-off point for many runaways fleeing the South. It is a well-established fact that Cumberland was linked to Uniontown from early times. In 1752,

Christopher Gist and Col. Thomas Cresap, acting for the Ohio Company, followed a trail that the Indian chief Nemacolin had blazed, known as Nemacolin's Path, from Cumberland to the area around present-day Uniontown.[7] Three years later, General Braddock, in his advance on Fort Duquesne, cut a road following the same Indian trail, passing just to the east of Uniontown and proceeding along Chestnut Ridge. At a point just west of Chalk Hill known as Half-King's Rock, Nemacolin's Path divides into two, with one branch going through a gap in the ridge and leading down the slope to what became Uniontown, and the other following the ridge line northward. It was this northward branch that Braddock chose to follow.[8] This shows that even before Douthet and Beeson founded the town, there was a link between Cumberland and Uniontown.

The connection between the two towns received further strengthening on March 29, 1806, when Congress approved plans for building the National Road, linking Cumberland to the western frontier. The road was to follow Braddock's Road over the summit at Laurel Hill to Brownsville, Pennsylvania. From there it was to go along the ancient Indian trail known as Mingo Path, until it reached the city of Washington. Upon leaving Washington, it was to proceed to Wheeling and the frontier. Many would call it the National Pike because it was to operate in the fashion of a turnpike, with tolls charged. By 1817, the road passed through Uniontown and the next year it reached the Ohio River.[9]

Blacks were familiar with travel on the National Road. Thomas B. Searight, in his recollections of life along the road, related how, as a young man, he saw blacks traveling over the road in two different ways:

> . . . for be it remembered that negro slaves were frequently seen on National Road. The writer has seen them driven over the road arranged in couples and fastened to a long, thick rope or cable, like horses. This may seem incredible to a majority of persons now living along the road, but it is true, and was a very common sight in the early history of the road and evoked no expression of surprise, or words of censure. Such was the temper of the times. There were negro wagoners on the road. . . . Wagoners, white and black, stopped over night at the same taverns, but never sat down together at the same table. A separate table was invariably provided for the colored wagoners, a custom in thorough accord with the public sentiment of the time, and seemingly agreeable to the colored wagoners themselves.[10]

This is an important observation in light of the fact that one of the most common methods employed to transport runaways was to conceal them in a wagon, hidden either in a secret compartment or under the load they were hauling. Fugitives now had a good path to follow, compatriots to aid them, and a means of getting from Cumberland to Uniontown and beyond.

The escape route along the National Road took the runaways through several towns that had Underground Railroad stations and agents. Upon crossing the Maryland-Pennsylvania border, the escapees would have gone just three miles before coming to the town of Addison. Although there is no documentation, local legend has it that several families in the town offered aid and comfort to runaways.

There seems to be some disagreement in the sources as to the next leg of the journey. Siebert's map has the route proceeding to Turkey Foot (modern-day Confluence) and then to Sommerfield [sic] following the National Road.[11] Brewster has the route going directly to Somerfield with no mention of Turkey Foot.[12] The problem with Siebert's map is that Turkey Foot was not on the National Road. A map of the area shows that Addison, Somerfield, and Turkey Foot form an equilateral triangle. Addison and Somerfield are at the base of the triangle and are only three miles apart. Turkey Foot is at the apex and is six miles from either Addison or Somerfield. A map of the region done by Reading Howell in 1792 has a series of roads connecting Turkey Foot to the National Road, but in a rather long, roundabout manner.[13] The traveler would have to leave the road after Addison, go back to the northeast, and then turn to the northwest before reaching Turkey Foot. Although it is possible that this was done to throw pursuing slave catchers off the track, this would have required runaways to travel an additional ten to twelve miles to reach Somerfield, when it was only three miles from Addison.

There is another possible explanation for the appearance of Turkey Foot on Siebert's map, however. The settlement of Turkey Foot was at the confluence of three waterways and several Indian trails. One of these trails, the Turkeyfoot Path, ran from Cumberland through Big Savage, Allegheny, and Negro Mountains, along a trace parallel to Nemacolin's Path, to the site of the Turkey Foot settlement. In 1751, a road was cut by the Ohio Company along this trail, linking Cumberland with the area where Turkey Foot developed. The road was even called the Turkey Foot Road, and it was later extended over Laurel Hill to Fort Pitt.[14] Here, then, was an alternate route for fleeing Cumberland and seeking freedom to the northwest. Siebert's map indicates a station located in Turkey Foot, so fugitives could have found support there. From this spot, they could have followed the road to Pittsburgh or rejoined the National Road at a number of places between Somerfield and Uniontown.

After leaving Addison, the next logical stop on this escape route would be Somerfield. One cannot visit the town today, however, because it is underwater. In 1948, the U.S. Army Corps of Engineers erected a dam on the Youghiogheny River, which created a large lake and inundated Somerfield.[15] From here, runaways then covered the twenty-one miles between Somerfield and Uniontown by traveling on the National Road.[16]

GREENE COUNTY–UNIONTOWN ROUTE

Greene County was the site of a network of escape routes that led from the South to the North. Brewster places many stations of the Underground Railroad in the county.[17] While Cumberland was the major departure point for runaways leaving Maryland for Pennsylvania, Morgantown and Wheeling acted in a similar role for those heading north from Virginia. Blockson, echoing the research of Greene County historian Andrew J. Waychoff, describes the Underground Railroad path coming from Virginia into Pennsylvania as doing so at a spot approximately one-half mile south of the town of Mount Morris in Greene County. This town had the advantage of being connected to Morgantown by a road. Waychoff says that at or near Mount Morris, the escape route split into two tracks. One ran northward through Bob Maple's Mill (now Bobtown) and continued on to Beesontown (Uniontown), while the other track led to Washington County and joined the escape route that ran through Pittsburgh. Blockson also cites an incident recorded by Waychoff illustrating the fugitive slave traffic along this route:

> During the year 1857, from twelve to fifteen slaves came in a body early one Sunday morning to Mt. Morris. They consisted of men and women and children who had escaped from near Clarksburg, and were armed with clubs and hoes. The most formidable being a corncutter. Not far from town they were overtaken by the slave hunters and a fight occurred during which two of the fugitive slaves were slightly hurt and a small girl captured. The slave hunters soon returned to Mt. Morris and to Virginia.[18]

Siebert's map cites Greensboro as the first station in Greene County.[19] This town was strategically placed on a bend in the Monongahela River and is in an almost direct northeasterly line running from Mount Morris, through Bobtown, to Greensboro. However, Siebert does not show how runaways got to Greensboro from Virginia. It is only logical to assume that they traveled the Mount Morris trail through Bob Maple's Mill to get there. How they got from Greensboro to Uniontown may be explained by referring to Howell's map of 1792, which describes a road covering the fourteen miles between these two towns.[20] Thus, a fugitive seeking freedom had a clear route from Mount Morris to Uniontown.

VIRGINIA–UNIONTOWN ROUTE

Siebert's map shows a third route emanating from the area around Morgantown and heading straight to Uniontown. But again, he gives no details about the route.[21] The map shows the route running to the east and parallel to the Monongahela River, with no towns listed along the way. This is atypical of Siebert and may reflect the fact that he had only sketchy details about this pathway.

An examination of old maps showing roads and Indian trails gives some substance to this route, however. The Catawba Indian Path ran from the area just east of Morgantown and the Monongahela River, northward across the Cheat River, through the settlements of Gans and Outcrop, directly to Uniontown.[22] Howell's map of early southwestern Pennsylvania indicates that a road followed a similar trace along the western edge of Chestnut Ridge from the area around Morgantown to Uniontown, while passing through the towns of Georges and Griffins in Pennsylvania.[23] Freedom seekers now had a ready course to follow and inhabited localities through which to pass.

ANOTHER POSSIBLE VIRGINIA–UNIONTOWN ROUTE

Did a fourth route exist starting in Virginia and ending in Uniontown? The possibility of such a route may be postulated from the topography and early trails in Greene County. The Warriors Branch Indian Path went from Moundsville on the Ohio River and across the whole of Greene County. It proceeded on a track parallel to the Virginia border and only four to five miles from that border all the way to the Monongahela River. It then crossed the river at New Geneva, just south of Greensboro, and worked its way to Uniontown. Later, the small communities of Morford, Nettle Hill, Bluff, Camp, and Luke sprang up along the path.[24] Once they got to New Geneva, near Greensboro, fugitives could have connected with the more established Greene County–Uniontown Route.

UNIONTOWN

Uniontown offered a place of sanctuary for many runaways due to its size and large population of black people. Siebert lists ten Underground Railroad agents in Fayette County, most of whom operated in and around Union-town.[25] Eight of this group were blacks: Joe Black, John and Joseph Jackson, Potan McClure, Jacob B. Miller, Thomas Walker, Joe Wares, and Cato Web-ster.[26] The other two, Joe Benson and Mathew Chalfant, were white. Siebert did not include the name of Howard Wallace, a black man who wrote a pamphlet on his recollections of the Underground Railroad in Uniontown.[27] In his work, Wallace gives the names of two other black agents in town: John Payne and a man named Curry.[28] Blockson adds the name of Alexander Green.[29] In all, twelve of the fourteen Underground Railroad agents in the area were black.

There were several Underground Railroad stations in Uniontown. Hadden, in his *History of Uniontown,* cites Baker Alley, a small street near the east end of East Main Street, as a station.[30] Swetnam, in *Pittsylvania Country,* calls this same alley the headquarters for the Underground Railroad in Uniontown.[31] Hadden states that a stable in the alley provided teams of horses and wagons in which fugitives made their escape during the night. He also speaks of agents hiding runaways under floorboards in their homes when slave catchers appeared to look for escapees. In one case, when slave catchers visited the home of an agent who was hiding runaways under his floorboards, the agent and his friends began to sing and dance in order to muffle any sound from the fugitives hiding under the floor.[32]

Among the slave catchers, Hadden mentions a man from Virginia named Stump, certainly the notorious Robert Stump, whom many writers on the subject cite as a slave catcher. He apparently made regular forays to Uniontown looking for escapees.[33] Baxter Ridge and Turkey Nest, two other parts of Uniontown, were inhabited by black residents who also offered aid and shelter to runaways.[34]

FROM UNIONTOWN TO INDIANA COUNTY

Siebert speaks of two routes leaving Uniontown and proceeding northward. He cites a map of Amos M. Jolliffe of Uniontown as showing both ending in Pittsburgh. Siebert also describes another route running east of the Allegheny River, through Greensburg, to Indiana County, and then on to Clearfield.[35] Hadden has an escape path going from Uniontown to Indiana.[36] Brewster describes four routes emanating from Uniontown, one of which proceeds through Indiana County.[37] Swetnam agrees with Siebert that two routes left Uniontown, but in Swetnam's description, only one of these went to Pittsburgh; the other went through Greensburg to Indiana.[38] It can be concluded that two major escape paths left Uniontown, with one heading to Indiana and the other to Pittsburgh.

Between Uniontown and Indiana, Siebert's map has a major station located in Greensburg. However, he shows no paths leading to the town.[39] Swetnam also has Greensburg as a station, and he connects it to Uniontown. Mount Pleasant, a town about two-thirds of the way from Uniontown to Greensburg, also appears to have had a station.[40] The fugitives likely traversed this rather long distance via Indian trails and early roads. The Catawba Path ran north from Uniontown to a point just west of Mount Pleasant. From there it went on to Ligonier and then to Indiana.[41] In addition to this possible pathway, Braddock's Road traced a route from the Uniontown area to Mount Pleasant.[42] And Howell's map shows a road beginning at Uniontown and extending to Hanna's Town, just passing Greensburg to the east.[43]

While Siebert does not include anyone from Westmoreland County on his list of Underground Railroad agents, there is sufficient evidence that agents and stations both existed there. Westmoreland County lies between Fayette and Indiana Counties, and fugitives could not have gotten from Uniontown to Indiana without having passed through Westmoreland County. Siebert includes a great many names of agents from these other two counties on his list, and his map shows Greensburg and New Alexandria as having stations on the Underground Railroad.[44] In addition, research shows that stations existed in the towns of Mount Pleasant, Latrobe, Jeanette, and New Kensington, all of which are in Westmoreland County.[45] Finally, Westmoreland had an active Anti-Slavery Society, which was founded on March 4, 1836.[46] Some of the members of this organization would most certainly have provided a cadre of sympathetic supporters for the effort by freedom seekers to reach their goal.

While the escape route from Uniontown passed through Mount Pleasant to Greensburg, the town of Jeanette, which had a station, lies only three miles west of Greensburg, and it is reasonable to assume that it was part of the Greensburg network. From Greensburg, the escape path appears to have divided, one route going through New Alexandria and the other through Latrobe.

NEW ALEXANDRIA–INDIANA ROUTE

There is a track on Siebert's map that clearly connects Greensburg with New Alexandria,[47] a little community only eight and a half miles to the northeast of Greensburg. Modern U.S. Route 119 connects the two today. Howell's map shows that an older road accomplished the same thing back in the early

1800s.[48] From New Alexandria, the route may have followed two possibilities, one through Clarksburg and the other through Blairsville.

New Alexandria–Clarksburg–Indiana Route

Siebert has the line of escape going from New Alexandria to Clarksburg. From there it moves on to Indiana.[49] Clarksburg was almost equidistant from both New Alexandria and Indiana. A problem with this route lies in the fact that there were no Indian trails or roads shown on early maps connecting all three sites. However, Siebert most likely had legitimate sources at his disposal supporting his contention that a route did indeed join the three.

New Alexandria–Blairsville–Indiana Route

Another possibility would link New Alexandria with Blairsville, a town only eight miles to the east just over the border in Indiana County. The Forbes Road joined the two communities, thus providing a ready path over which runaways could have traveled. In addition, there is excellent documentation indicating that Blairsville played an active role in the Underground Railroad movement.[50] For example, Stephenson cites the names of two prominent agents in the town, John Graff and Jesse Thomas.[51] Hadden names a third agent there, Lewis Johnson, who used his home as a station.[52] Based on the evidence that a readily available pathway existed between the two locales, and that there were people devoted to the cause of helping runaways move northward, it is safe to assume that the New Alexandria–Blairsville Route was another option the fugitives could have exercised on their journey.

LATROBE–INDIANA ROUTE

Latrobe, like New Alexandria, is only eight and a half miles due east of Greensburg. Howell has a road on his map going from Ligonier to Greensburg.[53] By the time of the activity of the Underground Railroad in the area, the town of Latrobe had sprung up right near the road. From Latrobe, it is only a short journey of ten miles to Blairsville. The predecessor of modern Route 217 ran through the valleys and farms that lay between the two towns. A single night's journey would have allowed the fugitives to traverse these ten miles.

INDIANA COUNTY

Indiana County had a well-established Underground Railroad network. An abolitionist group called the Anti-Slavery Society formed in the town of Indiana on July 31, 1837. On January 28, 1838, citizens in the Center Township, a community just south of the town of Indiana, formed their own Anti-Slavery Society.[54] Siebert lists a large number of Underground Railroad agents for Indiana County, including James and John Baker; Joseph Campbell; a Mr. Dixon; George Gamble; James Hamilton; a Mr. Henry; John and Robert Huston; Dr. Robert Mitchell; C. R., George, Samuel, S. K., and Zenas Rank; George Spaulding; Jane G. Swisshelm; Jesse Thomas; S. P. White; William White and his sons; and a person named Work and his brothers.[55] A number of other agents do not appear on this list but are cited below. Churches were especially active in the effort to move fugitives on to the North. Stephenson states that the congregation of the Universalist Church overwhelmingly opposed slavery and supported the efforts of the Underground Railroad, but the Presbyterian congregations in the county were divided on the issue.[56]

Fugitives who had chosen the Blairsville Route left that town and traveled in almost a straight line along the road that became U.S. Route 119, through a series of small communities, to the town of Indiana. First they passed through Blacklick and Graceton, where James Simpson was the agent. Then they proceeded to Homer City, where Joseph Campbell offered them shelter. Next, it was on to Yellow Creek and the assistance of Andrew Dixon, likely the Dixon on Siebert's list. Finally, the travelers reached Indiana. They may have stayed on the farm of Dr. Robert Mitchell, which was located nine miles east of town and had a small cabin for the purpose of providing shelter for fugitives. Mitchell suffered great financial loss for helping a runaway escape on the Underground Railroad. In 1845, a fugitive slave named Anthony Hollingsworth was captured by his master near the town of Indiana. His owner took him to a hotel in Indiana, and while there, a mob of abolitionists assembled to set Hollingsworth free. Mitchell went to court and, through a legal maneuver, quickly obtained the release of Hollingsworth, who returned with Mitchell to his farm outside of Indiana, where he stayed for a time, later fleeing to Canada. Two years after the incident, the man who had owned Hollingsworth sued Mitchell in the U.S. Circuit Court in Pittsburgh. Judge Robert C. Grier heard the case and determined that Mitchell had violated the Fugitive Slave Law of 1793. The case continued until 1853, and ultimately, Mitchell was forced to pay Hollingsworth's former owner the sum of $500 plus legal costs. He had to sell part of his land holdings to pay the amount, but even that did not deter his efforts to continue serving as an agent on the Underground Railroad. The network in the area was so extensive that even the constable of Indiana Borough, Joseph R. Smith, Esq., was involved, "one of the most valuable Underground Railroad members," according to Stephenson.[57]

The town of Indiana had its own group of agents and hiding places for runaways. Dr. Mitchell, in addition to his farm outside of town, also maintained a residence on the north side of Philadelphia Street.[58] James Moorhead, the editor of the abolitionist newspaper in Indiana, *The Clarion of Freedom,* was also an agent.[59] From a building at the corner of South 6th Street and School Street, where he published his newspaper, Moorhead directed others in aiding runaways on their journey.[60] Stephenson also reports that a major station existed in the cemetery near the house of Judge Silas Clark and that remnants of it were still surviving near the armory when he wrote his work in 1978.[61] Men were not the only citizens of Indiana who were active as agents in the Underground Railroad. The names of five women also appear on the roll of those helping runaways: Mrs. Daniel Stanard, Mrs. James Sutton, Mrs. John Sutton, Mrs. Thomas White, and Mrs. David Blair.[62]

INDIANA NORTHWARD

The pathway to freedom from Indiana imitated a pattern typical for major centers of the Underground Railroad, with three possible escape routes exiting Indiana County.

INDIANA–BURNSIDE ROUTE
Siebert's map indicates that a track existed between Indiana and the town of Burnside.[63] On this route, travelers first passed through the town of Marion Center, where they found comfort at the hands of William Work (likely the Work on Siebert's list of agents), the local agent there.[64] To reach this place, the fugitives followed the old Catawba Path or, later, a road that ultimately ran from Indiana to Punxsutawney, passing through Marion Center. This road eventually became U.S. Route 119.[65] The next stopping place was a community called Cush Cushion, where George Gamble and George Atchison guided the travelers across the border to Burnside in Clearfield County.[66] At Burnside, the runaways entered the Bedford–Clearfield escape route and went on to Clearfield and points northward.

INDIANA–PUNXSUTAWNEY ROUTE
Blockson cited Greene County historian Andrew J. Waychoff as saying that there was an escape route that led from Uniontown, through Indiana, to Punxsutawney.[67] On Siebert's map, a route extends to the north from Marion

Center, but it ends abruptly with no clear terminal point.[68] Extending this line brings it to Punxsutawney. To get from Indiana to Punxsutawney, a runaway could simply have traveled along a road that ran between the two places and passed through Marion Center, which itself was a station of the railroad.

Punxsutawney, founded in 1816, was a well-established town by the time of the operation of the Underground Railroad.[69] Two Underground Railroad routes apparently entered that community: the Uniontown–Indiana Route and a route that ran through central Pennsylvania, beginning in Baltimore and extending northward through York, Harrisburg, Bellefonte, and Grampian Hills, Pennsylvania, before reaching Punxsutawney.[70] There was only one route out of town, via a road (later PA Route 36) that went to the town of Brookville.[71] Once the runaways reached Brookville, they entered the northern leg of the Bedford–Clearfield Route.

INDIANA–FRANKLIN ROUTE

Siebert described a third trail leaving Marion Center. This one went to the northwest and ended at the town of Smicksburg, some seven miles away.[72] In his discussion of the activities of the Underground Railroad in Clarion County, Blockson details a route running through a series of small communities there.[73] These communities line up in northwesterly pattern between Marion Center and Franklin. This line also happens to coincide with the trace of the Frankstown–Venango Indian Path.[74] This would seem to indicate that runaways had a readily available track to follow in their journey from Marion Center to Franklin, and this pathway was dotted with Underground Railroad stations.

The sojourn along this particular route was an involved one. The first stage in the trip consisted of a journey of seven miles to Smicksburg. From this town, it was a short four miles to the next station at Dayton in Armstrong County. In Dayton, Rev. John Hindman, a Seceder Presbyterian minister, helped the fugitives and sent them on to William Blair. Blair lived in Porter Township just across the border in Clarion County. He took care of the next phase of the journey by sending the runaways to Rev. John McAuley, another Seceder clergyman, in the town of Rimersburg. James Fulton, another agent who lived just north of the town, shared in the duties of aiding fugitives along with Reverand McAuley. It fell to Fulton to convey escapees, hidden in his wagons, ten miles farther to Benjamin Gardner. Gardner lived three miles north of the town of Callensburg, where he was the local agent. At this point, the Uniontown–Indiana Route was running a few miles to the south and parallel to the Bedford–Clearfield Route through Clarion County.

Gardner saw to it that his charges made it safely across the county line into Venango County, where Elihu Chadwick, the station master in Rockland, took over and ushered the fugitives over the final ten miles of this branch of the route to Franklin.[75] It was in the town of Franklin that the Uniontown–Indiana and the Bedford–Clearfield Routes merged and headed north together. Like the Bedford–Clearfield Route, the Uniontown–Indiana Route was composed of many alternative pathways.

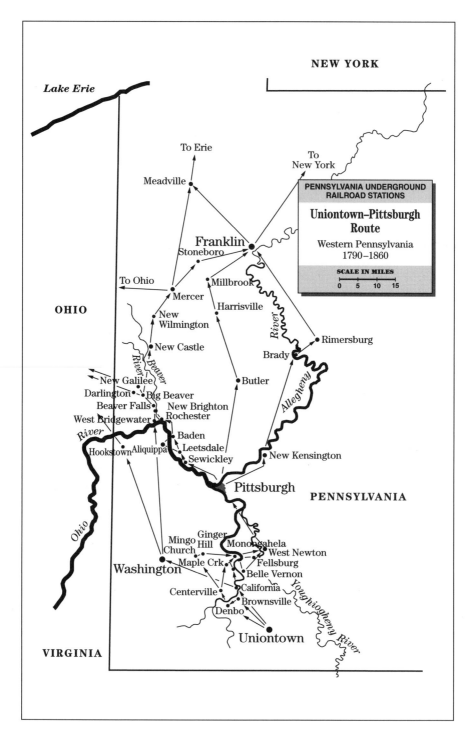

NEW YORK

Lake Erie

To Erie

Meadville

To
New York

**PENNSYLVANIA UNDERGROUND
RAILROAD STATIONS**

**Uniontown–Pittsburgh
Route**

Western Pennsylvania
1790–1860

SCALE IN MILES

0   5   10   15

Stoneboro

Franklin

Millbrook

To Ohio

Mercer

Harrisville

OHIO

New
Wilmington

River

New Castle

Rimersburg

Brady

River

Beaver

New Galilee

Butler

Darlington

Big Beaver

Beaver Falls

New Brighton

West Bridgewater

Rochester

Allegheny

River

Baden

Hookstown

Aliquippa

Leetsdale

Sewickley

New Kensington

Pittsburgh

PENNSYLVANIA

Ginger
Hill

Mingo
Church

Monongahela

West Newton

Maple Crk

Fellsburg

Washington

Belle Vernon

Ohio

Centerville

California

Youghiogheny River

Brownsville

Denbo

VIRGINIA

Uniontown

Uniontown–Pittsburgh Route

A second major route that the Underground Railroad took from Uniontown followed the course of the Monongahela River all the way to Pittsburgh. In typical railroad fashion, this route was filled with subroutes, backtracks, and alternatives. Because Pittsburgh was such a large city, it appears that a large number of runaways chose to follow this particular route.

UNIONTOWN TO PITTSBURGH

Siebert states that there were two Underground Railroad routes leaving Uniontown, both ultimately reaching Pittsburgh, and his map shows two avenues of escape heading out of Uniontown. One of them goes to Brownsville and then heads north along the Monongahela River; the other extends to Washington and then divides into two branches, one heading northeast and ending in Pittsburgh, and the other proceeding northwest to Ohio.[1] But Siebert's map does not show where other stations were located along the way, and raises many questions. Did runaways actually come from Ohio to Washington and then backtrack all the way to Pittsburgh? Were there any other escape paths not mentioned by Siebert that allowed fugitives to reach Pittsburgh?

UNIONTOWN–CENTERVILLE ROUTE

Siebert's book contains no mention of a work written by Howard Wallace, an active black agent on the Uniontown–Pittsburgh branch of the Underground Railroad. Wallace wrote a pamphlet at the end of the nineteenth century entitled *Historical Sketch of the Underground Railroad from Uniontown to Pittsburgh,* in which he provides specific details of the journey fugitives took between these two locales and the names of the agents who provided them with aid and comfort. While the work is very informative, the pamphlet was

self-published and lacks a publication date. Based on the brief autobiograph-
ical narrative given at the beginning of the work, however, one can assume
that it appeared sometime after the year 1888.[2]

Howard Wallace tells us much about himself in the introduction to his
work:

> I was born in a small house near wat is known as Moffit's Mill in West Pike
> Run Township February 24, 1831. My father's name was William Wallace.
> I attended the common schools in the vicinity and acquired a common
> education. I followed farming and gardening until I reached manhood,
> then I learned the cooper trade. which I followed for sevral years until paper
> sacks and other things took the place of barrels. I then followed butchering,
> farming and huckstering which I have worked at more or less ever since. I
> have spent nearlly all of my life in Centerville and vicinity.
>
> During the year 1854 i went to Canada and spent some time there
> employed at railroad repairs. I returned in a few years and married and set-
> tled down again in this vicinity. I was elected Jury Commisioner for Wash-
> ington County in 1888 and served a term of three three years I have been a
> member of the A. M. E. Church at Pike Run for nearly sixty years. I now
> reside on the old Smith farm near Taylor's Church.[3]

After this personal background information, Wallace tells why he wrote
this pamphlet:

> I shall write a history of the Under Ground Railroad from Uniontown to
> Pittsburgh. It was in the forties, the route beginning at Uniontown and
> ending at Pittsburgh. . . . It was always a mystery to many people just how
> the Under Ground Railroad was carried on. I find that I am the only one
> living that aided in helping the slaves through. So, therefore, I will give a
> full account of the route.[4]

The account Wallace gives is a classic tale of travel at night, secret hiding
places, narrow escapes, brave people, and an escape route filled with zigzags
and cutbacks. Wallace and Siebert are in agreement on the issue of where the
first stop was after leaving Uniontown. This was Brownsville, a pioneer town
about eleven and a half miles to the west of Uniontown. This community was
on both the National Road and the Monongahela River, and because of its
location, it was very active on the Underground Railroad. A number of citizens in the community formed a local Anti-Slavery Society on August 19,
1826. At about the same time, the Bowmans, one of the leading families in

the area, opened their home, the magnificent Bowman's Castle, to runaways. This house was located at Second Avenue and Front Street and took up an entire block.[5] Swetnam identifies another station at the Presbyterian Manse in the heart of Brownsville.[6]

The next stage of the journey, according to Wallace, entailed going upstream on the Monongahela River to the little town of Denbo. Lloyd Demas and several other unnamed agents escorted the travelers on this leg of the journey. At a spot near the former town of Malden, the runaways turned to the northwest and, cutting overland, came on the National Pike near Centerville. Once there, they found refuge at the farm of William Wallace, Howard's father.[7]

Wallace gives a detailed account of the role his family's farm played on this escape trail:

> It was considered the best stopping place on the route. I cannot tell just how long the under ground railroad was carried on, but this place was on the main route for a number of years. It was mostly through the Summer season that they would travel. this was a house having a large cellar where slaves liked to stay during the day. Some of them would venture out at night and walk around while others were very much afraid of white people and would stay very close. Sometimes they were almost worn out when they arrived and were glad to have an opportunity to rest. We generally made it a point to solicit aid from the farmers and neighbors who were always willing to help, especially the Quakers. I do not think I ever had one to refuse me. their contributions were always liberal.[8]

Wallace names Nathan Pusey and Samuel Taylor as two Quakers who were always ready to provide horses for moving the runaways. He adds that his neighbors Benjamin and Sam Wheeler, Joseph Steward, and Henry Smith were always ready to help whenever needed.[9] Once they left the farm in Centerville, the travelers had two paths from which to choose, one to Ginger Hill and the other to Maple Creek.

Ginger Hill–West Newton Route

The trail to the small community of Ginger Hill took fugitives eleven miles almost due north. The resident agent there was Milton Maxwell, and Wallace says that it was his job to forward the travelers on to Pittsburgh.[10] Swetnam also lists Ginger Hill as a station, but adds that Mingo Church, an area near Ginger Hill, likewise had a station. From these two spots, Swetnam has the route heading east across the Monongahela River to West Newton and then on to Pittsburgh.[11] However, the distance between these sites was over nineteen miles, a distance not typically covered in one night. Between Ginger Hill and West Newton lies the town of Monongahela. In their *Guidebook,* Swetnam and Smith record that an Underground Railroad station existed here in the Bethel A.M.E. Church, which was originally built in 1842. The church acted as a refuge for runaways traversing the Monongahela River for many years. The present site of the church is at 715 Chess Street.[12] There is also evidence that the Taylor family hid fugitives in their home at the northern edge of the town. In addition, the local Quakers and Methodists may have provided aid and shelter.[13]

Maple Creek–West Newton Route

The path from the Wallace farm to Maple Creek, in Washington County, involved a journey nine or ten miles to the northeast. According to Wallace, runaways stayed with George Norris or the Bowman family there. These individuals guided their guests to a spot near present-day Donora on the Monogahela River. With the aid of small boats, they crossed the river and proceeded to a community of blacks who lived near Belle Vernon, where families named Rosse, Basier, and Minney helped them. Wallace says that they left here after a brief stay and made their way to West Newton and then to Pittsburgh.[14]

UNIONTOWN–MONONGAHELA RIVER VALLEY ROUTE

There was another pathway runaways could have taken from Uniontown to Pittsburgh, following the contour of the valley cut by the Monongahela River. Brewster has a trail running from Uniontown to the town of California, located four miles downstream from the more well-known Brownsville.[15] Blockson fleshes out this route, identifying stations in the towns of Charleroi, Monessen, Donora, and Fellsberg.[16] Of these, Charleroi, Monessen, and Donora are in a line extending from California, along the Monongahela River, toward Pittsburgh and are only a few miles apart. Fellsberg, though not on the river, lies between Donora and West Newton and would have provided a much-needed hiding place for those not stopping at the black community near Belle Vernon.

UNIONTOWN–WASHINGTON ROUTE

Siebert's map shows yet another branch of the Underground Railroad going from Uniontown through Brownsville and ultimately ending at Washington.[17] If the Monongahela River Valley Route indicated on the map was the first of the two routes that Siebert said eventually went to Pittsburgh, could this route through Washington have been the second one?

That a route would have gone from Uniontown to Washington via Brownsville is a logical deduction, as the National Road traversed this same track and it is well established that runaways used the road as a highway to freedom. Likewise, the National Road, after it left Brownsville, passed close to Centerville and the refuge at the Wallace farm. Once they made it to Washington, the escapees would have entered the well-organized Washington County Underground Railroad network.

PITTSBURGH

Because of the importance and the extent of the Underground Railroad organization in the city of Pittsburgh, an entire chapter later in this work is devoted to a discussion of the network there.

PITTSBURGH NORTHWARD

As with every other major center on the Underground Railroad, there were several paths a runaway could take to exit Pittsburgh and continue on a journey to freedom. These pathways included escaping by railway, by travel up the Ohio River, by proceeding up the Allegheny River, or by heading overland in a northerly direction toward the town of Butler.

TRAVEL BY RAILWAY

Several sources mention the use of the rails as a means of leaving Pittsburgh for points north on the Underground Railroad. Levi Coffin describes how conductor John Fairfield of Virginia used the trains to help his charges get to freedom. Fairfield bought wigs and makeup to disguise fugitives as white Southerners. At Harpers Ferry, he purchased railroad tickets for them and, in their disguises, sent them on to Pittsburgh.[18]

Between 1843 and the Civil War, a number of rail lines connected Pittsburgh to several sites important to the operation of the Underground Railroad. In 1843, the Baltimore & Ohio rail line reached Pittsburgh, thus linking the city to Maryland and points south. By 1849, Pittsburgh shared a line with Wheeling, and in 1850, a line reached Erie. Pittsburgh and Cleveland were joined by rail in 1851.[19] This last connection was of special importance, and a number of runaways gained their freedom by traveling by train to Cleveland.[20]

THE OHIO RIVER ROUTE

The Ohio River Route involved transporting fugitives via the river or along-side of it from Pittsburgh to Beaver County. As early as 1809, a road linked these two locales, thus providing a means for overland transport.[21] In addition, there was ample traffic on the Ohio River, which made it easier to move runaways by boat to Beaver County.[22] The first stage of such a journey was to go by road or river through the town of Sewickley. In Sewickley, refuge could be found in the St. Matthew's A.M.E. Church. From there fugitives would leave Allegheny County and cross over into Beaver County.[23]

Beaver County had an extensive network of Underground Railroad routes and stations. The best information on this network comes from an address given at the Beaver County Centennial Celebration of June 19–22, 1900, by Rev. Paul Weyand, entitled "The Anti-Slavery Movement in Beaver County." Weyand began his talk with an exposition of the three escape routes that passed through Beaver County:

> There were three well-defined routes of escape through Beaver County. Fugitives from the vicinity of Morgantown, Virginia [West], and Cumberland, Maryland, stopped at Uniontown; thence they came to Pittsburg. From there they seem to have been sent by rail to Cleveland, Ohio, or to have been directed to follow the Allegheny or Ohio River to their tributaries northward. Many would follow the west side of the Ohio to the mouth of the Beaver, thence northward to the shores of Lake Erie and thence by steamer directly across the lake or northeasterly along its shores till Niagara Falls was reached and across it the Promised Land. More frequently, however, their trend was a little westward to the better worn tracks and the more numerous and more experienced master mechanics of the road in the Western Reserve. Some of these fugitives crossed directly from Washington County into Beaver County, following the course of Raccoon Creek to the Ohio, which they crossed, proceeding through Black Hawk out to Achor, Columbiana County, Ohio, where meetings were often quickly improvised in the schoolhouse and a greeting given to the escaping Slaves.
>
> But the greatest number were from Kentucky and Virginia. The Ohio River as a part of the Mississippi was a great natural route between slavery and freedom. Slaves would smuggle aboard steamboats at Louisville among the freight and when the more hospitable shores of Pennsylvania were reached they would leave the boat and guided by the North Star would strike for freedom.
>
> Many came on foot up the Ohio, and crossing at Wellsville, Ohio, and Wellsburg, Virginia, found their way to the Quakers of New Brighton who

fed them and took them by night in wagons—sometimes nine or ten in a group—on to the next station.[24]

In the county, there also existed a cadre of people who were more than willing to assist runaways in any way possible. The abolitionist sentiment found an early expression in the county when a group of citizens banded together and on January 28, 1836, formed the Beaver County Anti-Slavery Society. In his speech at the celebration of the Beaver County Centennial, Reverand Weyand stressed the fact that almost all of the churches in the county were opposed to slavery. He said that the Reformed Presbyterians, or Covenanters, were probably the first abolitionists in the area and that the Quakers as a unit were against slavery. He specifically mentioned Rev. James Haggerty and Rev. William McElwee, both from United Presbyterian churches in Hanover and Franklin Springs, as having prayed and preached almost every Sunday for years against the evils of the institution of slavery. Weyand also cited another United Presbyterian minister, Rev. Markus Ormand of Hookstown, as having preached many sermons against slavery. He concluded his remarks on the activity of the churches in Beaver by stating that the Methodist itinerant preachers who passed through the county also spoke out against the concept of human bondage.[25]

Siebert records the names of only three agents in the entire county: Rev. Abel Brown, Joshua Gilbert, and a person named Rakestraw.[26] Of this group, Reverand Brown left a written record of the state of the fugitives making their way to freedom through Beaver County. In a letter to Rev. C. P. Grosvenor, the editor of the *Christian Reflector,* Brown observed:

> I almost daily see the poor heart-broken slave making his way to the land of freedom. A short time since, I saw a noble, pious, distressed, spirit-crushed slave, a member of the Baptist Church, escaping from a (professed Christian) bloodhound, to a land where he could enjoy that of which he had been robbed during forty years. I saw a Baptist sister of about the same age, her children had been torn from her, her head was covered with fresh wounds, . . . she too, was going to the land of freedom.[27]

Weyand, in his address, however, cited twenty-seven people who provided assistance to runaways in Beaver. This list includes the three agents named by Siebert.[28]

Three major routes passed through Beaver County, as described by Weyand.

Pittsburgh–Beaver River Route

This route involved the majority of stations and agents found in Beaver County. According to Blockson, once the runaways left Sewickley in Allegheny County, they would pass through a succession of small river towns, only a few miles apart, until they came to New Brighton on the Beaver River. Ranging in order from Sewickley, these towns were Leetsdale, Baden, and Rochester. Across the Ohio River and located on the western bank just south of Baden was the town of Aliquippa. Blockson has Rev. Andrew MacDonald providing shelter for escapees there.[29] Weyand also names MacDonald and identifies yet another agent, Thomas Todd, who lived on the bluff overlooking Aliquippa.[30] He adds another town to Blockson's chain leading to New Brighton: West Bridgewater, which lies across the mouth of the Beaver River from Rochester. Apparently there was a station there operated by a Dr. Montana. Weyand names several other agents in the vicinity: Robert Bradshaw, James Wilson, and Andrew Watterson.[31]

New Brighton was a town of special significance in the Underground Railroad system. Weyand reports that throughout the South, New Brighton had a reputation as a haven to which fugitives could flee and expect to find refuge. The main reason for this prominent standing was that the town had a large community of Quakers. Weyand does not stint in the praise he heaps on these dedicated individuals for their courageous efforts to help runaways move northward.[32] He identifies eight agents in the town who were renowned for their activities. Four of them belonged to the Townsend family. David Townsend, the owner of a linseed oil plant and a cotton spinning mill in the area, hid runaways on an island in the middle of the Beaver River. His brother Benjamin, a real estate developer, used a cave at the corner of Penn Avenue and Allegheny Road as his hiding place. Evan Townsend had a secret trapdoor in his home that opened to a cellar specially designed for concealing fugitives. Lewis Townsend, along with James Erwin, Timothy B. White, E. Elwood Thomas, and his wife, round out the list of agents in New Brighton.[33] After a brief stay in the town, the travelers moved along the Beaver River to Beaver Falls. Blockson says that Geneva College, located in the town, may have housed fugitives.[34] At this spot, the route seems to have broken into several alternate paths: a route to New Castle, one to the small town of Enon, and one that ran along the Little Beaver Creek.

Beaver Falls–New Castle Route. From Beaver Falls, some runaways chose to head north to the town of New Castle in Lawrence County. A route depicted on Siebert's map joins the two towns.[35] Supporting this assumption is that

Weyand has an agent named Taylor on the Beaver-Lawrence County border. Taylor had been an associate judge in Lawrence County at one time and knew many people there.[36] If fugitives made it that far, the only logical place for them to go to continue their journey was to New Castle. Blockson further supports the existence of this escape path by citing an agent named William McAuliss, who, like Mr. Taylor, lived in Big Beaver Township. McAuliss lived on a farm and transported runaways to New Castle hidden in his hay wagons.[37]

When the fugitives reached New Castle in Lawrence County, they came upon an organized escape system. At New Castle, the White Homestead on North Jefferson Street was an important station.[38] Joseph White and his wife were ardent abolitionists who worked with great vigor helping escapees on their way north. They hid their visitors overnight in such unusual places as their fireplace or a large oven, and moved them the next day to Mercer County.[39] Judging by the number of agents listed by Siebert, Lawrence County had an elaborate network. The list contains twenty-two names: Alex Anderson; A. B. Bradford; Rev. Wells Bushnell; Cadwalader, Daniel, and John N. Enwer; Dr. A. G. Hart; Judge McKeever; Mathew McKeever; White McMillen; James Minich; S. W. Mitchell; Anizi C. Semple; Ewli Semple; Benjamin Sharpless; E. M. Stevenson; W. W. Walker; Joseph S. White; Alexander Wright; and David, John, and William Young.[40]

Leaving New Castle, the refugees most likely would have followed the road to Mercer, in the county of the same name. Originally built in 1807, this road extended from Beaver, through New Castle, to Mercer.[41] It also passed through the community of New Wilmington. This town was on the Lawrence-Mercer County border. Robert Ramsey, a cabinetmaker and undertaker, operated a safe house in the town for fugitives. After a short stay, Ramsey would send them on their way to Mercer. On the journey, he often hid them in boxes or crates of his own making.[42] Local legend has it that another station existed in the home of Dr. Seth Poppino. Currently, the house is a restaurant in New Wilmington called the Tavern.

Mercer County also had a rather sizable escape organization, with at least fourteen stations and a contingent of abolitionist sympathizers dating back to the 1830s, when Rev. Nathaniel North, a Presbyterian minister, and John Hoge, an activist abolitionist, formed the Mercer Anti-Slavery Society.[43] Siebert lists fourteen agents operating in the county: a Mr. Bishop, John Gilbert, Rev. George Gordon, Robert Grieson, John I. Hogue, Wesley Hogue, Mathew Jansan, James Minich, John Squires, Wilson Thorn, Richard Travis, a Mr. Ward, George Wilson, and John Young.[44] James Minich and John Young appear on both his Lawrence County and Mercer County lists.

Perhaps they moved from one county to the next, continuing their work on the Underground Railroad.

The town of Mercer was strategically situated about sixteen miles from New Castle and was connected to Beaver, New Castle, Butler, Franklin, and Meadville by a cluster of roads before the year 1807, when the Pennsylvania State Legislature allocated $3,000 for improving these roads.[45] Before reaching the town of Mercer, runaways, upon crossing the county line from Lawrence County, would have found themselves in friendly territory. In 1854, Dr. Charles Everett of Charlottesville, Virginia, purchased land in this area in order to relocate the slaves he owned and whom he was emancipating. The land was near Lackawanock, Springfield, and Wilmington Townships in southern Mercer County. Weary travelers found ready comfort among these people.[46] Blockson states that the home of Robert Hanna served as a station in the town of Mercer. He also adds the names of three other Mercer County agents not on Siebert's list: James Kilgore, Rev. Edward Smalls, and Mrs. Elizabeth S. Breckenridge.[47]

Once they left Mercer, the fugitives had three possible routes from which to choose. The majority of sources state that the most of the travelers chose the route to Erie from here. If so, they would have taken the Meadville Road, which joins Mercer to Meadville. This would have been a journey of thirty miles, and once there, they would have encountered the vast Crawford-Erie County network of escape trails. The runaways also could have taken the road to Franklin from Mercer, stopping on the way at Stoneboro, another station in Mercer County located near Sandy Lake.[48] They may even have stayed in a community of runaways that Siebert mentions was near that lake.[49] Reaching Franklin would have put them on the northern segments of the Bedford–Clearfield and Uniontown–Indiana Routes. A third option was to go due west from Mercer to the state of Ohio. Siebert has a route leaving Mercer that heads straight for the Ohio border.[50]

Beaver Falls–Enon Route. The second option leading from Beaver Falls went northwest to the towns of Darlington and New Galilee. The station master in New Galilee was William Scott.[51] In Darlington, the station master was one of the most famous agents in Beaver County, Rev. Arthur B. Bradford, pastor of the Mount Pleasant Presbyterian Church. As a religious figure, he was already famous, having broken away from the established Presbyterian Church and formed the Free Presbyterian Church in Beaver County. Weyand describes him as being very intense in his antislavery views and having lectured throughout the state on the evils of slavery. In Darlington, both he and his wife hid fugitives. When the Fugitive Slave Law of 1850 was passed, a penalty of $1,000 was to be levied on anyone convicted of helping slaves escape. Bradford, very active in the Underground Railroad and wishing to protect his wife and children from financial ruin, temporarily transferred all of his property to a friend. Mrs. Bradford was so dedicated to the cause that she often took the clothes from her own children and gave them to runaways as they passed through her home. Reverand Bradford was often threatened with tar and feathers by some of his proslavery neighbors, but nothing happened to him.[52] After fugitives stayed at his house, Bradford would have his son, O. B., escort them into Lawrence County to the town of Enon. From Enon, they would travel, frequently hidden in wagons, to Salem, Ohio, and the house of Jacob Heaton.[53]

Beaver Falls–Little Beaver Creek Route. Blockson reports a third pathway leading from Beaver Falls to the home of Jonathan Morris. Morris lived on Little Beaver Creek, which was in an area to the southwest of Darlington. Today it would be near State Gamelands No. 285 in Beaver County. Morris would take his guests to Salem, Ohio, much in the manner employed by Rev. Arthur B. Bradford in Darlington.[54]

Washington County–Beaver Route

The second route to Beaver County mentioned by Weyand came from Washington County. There were no Indian paths linking the two counties. This meant that to traverse this region, fugitives had to follow country roads or streams, or cross farmland and woodlots.

Weyand describes two tracks that runaways could follow to get to Beaver. One path followed the streambed of Raccoon Creek.[55] This brought the runaways to the Ohio River at a point between modern-day Monaca and Shippingport, slightly downstream from West Bridgewater. From here they crossed the river and went to the station located in West Bridgeport. The second path led through Hookstown, only eight miles from Washington County. Fugitives could have come there from Middletown on the old Washington Road, traveling the road on foot or hidden in wagons driven by Underground Railroad agents. From Hookstown, they went northward through the Black Hawk area of Beaver County and eventually on to Achor, Ohio.[56]

Ohio River–New Brighton Route

Weyand's third Beaver County route involved traveling up the Ohio River or walking from Wellsville, Ohio, or Wellsburg, Virginia, the ultimate goal being the Quaker community at New Brighton.[57]

Escapees choosing the water route would have found their way from Alabama, Mississippi, and southern Kentucky to the city of Lexington. A regular steamboat service ran between Lexington and Pittsburgh. Some runaways disguised themselves as white Southerners, bought tickets, and openly rode on the boats; others hid somewhere on board and made the trip in great discomfort. Upon reaching Pennsylvania, some disembarked at the town of Beaver and made their way up the Beaver River to New Brighton; others continued their journey to Pittsburgh and entered the escape paths there. William Still, in describing his work on the Underground Railroad, says that fugitives regularly traveled up the Ohio River to Pennsylvania from Cincinnati and that he considered this to be a major escape route.[58] Whether the runaways chose the New Brighton path or continued on to Pittsburgh, this was a major step in gaining their freedom.

ALLEGHENY RIVER ROUTE

Not much is known about the escape pathway that followed the Allegheny River northward, and even though Siebert asserts that it was a major escape route from Pittsburgh, his map does not show a line of march to support it.[59] Blockson gives the only other hint of a route in this direction when he says that New Kensington, in Westmoreland County, had an Underground Railroad station.[60] If the fugitives did take this route from Pittsburgh, they would have had two options. They could have made their way up the river all the way to Franklin, where they would have encountered the Bedford–Clearfield Route and, traveling on it, entered the Crawford–Erie County network. The other possibility was to travel up the Allegheny River as far as the town of Brady, leave the river at that point, and go a short distance east to the town of Rimersburg, where they would have come upon the Uniontown–Indiana Route emanating from Marion Center. Following this line of march, they also would have come to Franklin.

BUTLER ROUTE

The fourth possibility from Pittsburgh was to head due north. There is a good bit of confusion in the literature over this route, however. Siebert's map traces a route proceeding north from Pittsburgh for several miles, but then it suddenly turns sharply to the west and goes on to Ohio.[61] In his article on the Underground Railroad in Pittsburgh, Jerry Byrd describes a pathway that leaves Pittsburgh and goes to the town of Butler via the Butler Plank Road. From there, Byrd states that the runaways made their way to Erie and then to Canada.[62] Siebert also depicts a route starting just north of Butler at the town of Harrisville and passing through Millbrook to Franklin, but he has no description of how the fugitives got to Harrisville.[63] There is a possible explanation, however. There is evidence that a road existed as early as 1807 linking Butler with Mercer.[64] Siebert's route that leaves Pittsburgh, goes north, and then turns sharply to the west and Ohio could depict the route to Butler and then on to Mercer. The two lines of march are almost coincidental. This would also support Byrd's contention that runaways went to Butler on the Butler Plank Road. Also, another road was built in 1807 that tied Butler to Franklin.[65] This road ran through the town of Harrisville and may have been how fugitives got to Harrisville via Siebert's route. Though Millbrook, which is about eight miles north of Harrisville, is not on this road, the town is only a few miles west of it and could have provided a night's shelter for escapees using this route. Therefore, if fugitives chose to turn west at Butler and go to Mercer, they would have found freedom by going through Ohio; if they chose to go north after Butler, they would have come to Franklin and the convergence of three major Underground Railroad routes and freedom in Canada.

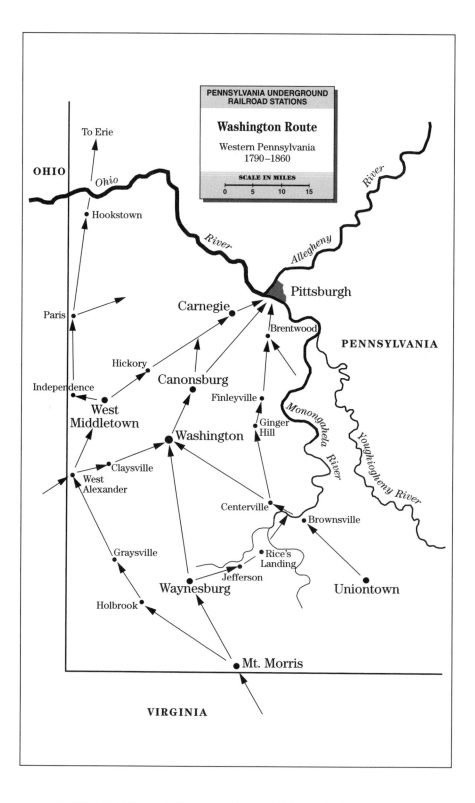

Washington Route

Washington County played a crucial role in the operation of the Underground Railroad in western Pennsylvania. Its proximity to a number of critical locations made it a natural crossroads through which many runaways traveled seeking freedom. Within the county were numerous stations and a large number of men and women who served as station masters, agents, and conductors. It was one of the major areas for funneling fugitives to Pittsburgh and to New Brighton.

The settlement of Washington County began in 1767. Pioneers chose to build homesteads along the banks of Ten Mile Creek in the county's southeastern corner. By 1774, most of this potentially rich farmland was under the control of the colony of Virginia. Settlers flocked to the area throughout the late 1770s and 1780s in order to farm the land. Because of its continued growth, Washington became a county in 1781. Within its boundaries lay land that would later become Greene County and part of Beaver County. By 1790, the population in the county reached 23,892.[1] Greene County broke away and became independent in 1796, and the modern boundaries of Washington County were established in 1800, when the parcel of land in its northwestern corner was given to the newly created Beaver County.[2]

The population of the county continued to expand in the early nineteenth century. While the population of the entire western Pennsylvania region was 210,000 in 1810, 36,289 of this number lived in Washington County. This increased to 40,038 by 1820.[3] Six groups of people dominated this population: the English, Welsh, Scots, Irish, Scots-Irish, and Germans. The English were the largest group, and the Germans the smallest.[4] The settlers of the county also employed slave labor on a limited scale. Of the 880 slaves listed on the Federal Census of 1790 as living in western Pennsylvania, 21 of them lived in Washington County. They were owned by only two slaves holders: Herbert Wallace, who had eleven, and Frederick Cooper, who had ten. By 1820, only 70 slaves were listed on the census for western Pennsylvania. This decline in the number of slaves was largely due to the passage by the state legislature of the Gradual Abolition of Slavery Law.[5]

Washington County had the two conditions needed for a successful Underground Railroad network: a cadre of sympathetic supporters and pathways over which fugitives could travel. Although Siebert only lists two agents for the county, a "Dr. Lemoin" and Mathew McKeever, many others played active roles in this escape route.[6]

The county was the scene of one of the earliest recorded attempts of a slave attempting to gain her freedom by fleeing her bondage. The following advertisement appeared in a 1796 Washington newspaper:

TWENTY DOLLARS REWARD
RUNAWAY from the House of James SEATON, living on Little Whitely
in Washington County, on the Night of Sunday the 6th of December last,
A NEGROE WENCH
about two or three and twenty years of age, named CATE, very black, short,
well made, and very active. The Wench is the property of JENNETE
PRATHER. Whoever takes up the said Wench, and delivers her to CHARLES
PRATHER, at the Mouth of Buffaloe, shall receive the above Reward.
Washington, January 4th 1796[7]

Organized efforts to aid blacks living in western Pennsylvania occurred even earlier. On February 17, 1789, a number of citizens in the town of Washington banded together to form the Washington Society for the Relief of Free Negroes. They elected a slate of officers that included Thomas Scott, president; Daniel Reddick, vice president; Alexander Addison, secretary; and Absalom Baird, treasurer.[8] This organization was the forerunner of others that would play a direct role in aiding runaways to escape bondage. The next major step in the helping of enslaved blacks came on January 26, 1824, when Dr. Francis Julius LeMoyne, a physician and professor at Washington College, helped inaugurate the Western Abolition Society in Washington.[9] This is the "Lemoin" on Siebert's list and his name surfaces in any discussion of the Underground Railroad in western Pennsylvania. Other proabolitionist groups also emerged in the county after this. The following is a notice for a meeting of one such group, appearing in the May 1, 1830, edition of the Washington paper *The Examiner:*

Notice
The Western Anti-Slavery Convention will hold an annual meeting in the
Methodist meeting house, in Brownsville, on the Fourth Tuesday in May
next, at 11 o'clock A. M. It is expected that a Discourse will be delivered on
the occasion by the Rev. John Waterman.
A. Conrad, Sec.[10]

The many abolitionist organizations eventually merged into the much larger Washington Anti-Slavery Society, which the citizens of the county formed on July 4, 1834. Joseph Henderson was elected the first president of the society, and they held their meetings in the Methodist Episcopal church in the town of Washington.[11] Even though these organizations were active throughout the early nineteenth century, not all of the citizens of the county were sympathetic to the abolition movement and the aiding of runaway slaves. The general popular sentiment of Washington County was antiabolitionist. In July 1836, Rev. Samuel Gould, a traveling minister who spoke against slavery, gave a talk at the Cumberland Presbyterian Church on West Wheeling Street in Washington. Dr. Francis LeMoyne presided over the gathering. A proslavery mob gathered outside the church and pelted the building with stones, sticks, and eggs. No one was injured, and Gould got to finish his talk. On leaving the building, the mob attacked Reverend Gould, but he was quickly taken to LeMoyne's house. Eventually the mob dispersed and Gould left town. This strong antiabolitionist feeling may be due to the fact that the institution of slavery had existed in the early days of the county. Because of this sentiment, those assisting runaways did so under great personal peril and had to conduct their passengers with greater than usual secrecy and guile.[12]

Physical routes abounded in Washington County over which escapees could travel. In the early days, three major Indian trails passed through the county, providing a ready means of traversing the wilderness in southwest Pennsylvania. These were the Catfish Path, running from the Warriors Path in southern Greene County through the future site of the city of Washington; the Mingo Path, connecting Brownsville with Washington; and the Glades Path, linking the Monongahela River with the Ohio River near Wheeling, passing through the city of Washington.[13] There were also a number of roadways over which the fugitives could travel. An examination of the 1792 map of Howell shows that at least a dozen roads linked Washington with Virginia to the east, Greene County (and Virginia) to the south, Fayette and Allegheny Counties to the west, and Allegheny and Beaver Counties to the north.[14] By 1817, the county had a complete network of roads, including the National Road, which linked all of the settlement sites with one another.[15]

While there were several routes into the county, there appear to have been only two major escape paths exiting it. Those leading into Washington County consisted of one from Wheeling to the east, two from Greene County to the south, and one from Brownsville to the west. Those departing the county took runaways either to Beaver County or to Pittsburgh.

WASHINGTON COUNTY ENTRY ROUTES

FROM WHEELING TO WASHINGTON COUNTY
AND WEST MIDDLETOWN

Swetnam states that a major escape route ran from the city of Wheeling to Washington, Pennsylvania, and that the escapees made the journey between the two cities by way of the National Road.[16] The road had connected the two communities in 1818 and made travel between the two much easier.[17] In 1805, a road and stage line covered the same ground, but it was neither as well constructed nor as efficient as the National Road.[18]

Near the Virginia and Pennsylvania border was the town of West Alexander, which was situated right on this escape route. Robert Humphrey had founded the town in 1796 and named it after his wife, Martha, whose maiden name was Alexander. When the National Road opened, West Alexander became a major stopover for coaches and travelers.[19] Forrest states that a certain "Old" Naylor, an African-American, conducted the fugitives over this route.[20] Naylor would take his passengers to a safe haven near the town on the farm of Kenneth McCoy. From here the runaways could choose from two alternatives, terminating either in the city of Washington or in the town of West Middletown.[21]

West Alexander to Washington

A number of escapees chose to continue traveling on the National Road westward to the city of Washington. About three miles from the McCoy farm, they would come to a station called Coon Island, just west of the town of Claysville.[22] From here it was a relatively short trip of eight miles to Washington. Once there, the fugitives would then be channeled toward Pittsburgh.

West Alexander to West Middletown

According to Forrest, the majority of runaways chose to take the trail that led to West Middletown, leaving the McCoy farm and making the twelve-mile journey through the Washington countryside.[23]

West Middletown appears in all of the sources as a major center on the Underground Railroad route running through Washington County. Founded about 1790, the town grew quickly. William McKeever, a maker of hats, was one of the town's first settlers. By 1797, the town had several gristmills, distilleries, and taverns. It also became the polling place for the entire Hopewell Township in that same year. By 1802, it had a post office, with David Craig, another original settler, as its postmaster.[24] In 1816, David Thomas, a traveler going from Erie to the west, described the town, in a journal entry dated June 15, as being quite large, having some thirty to forty houses.[25]

Many of the residents of West Middletown made an early commitment to fight against slavery. They formed an abolitionist group early in the nineteenth century, as evidenced by the following notice of a meeting for that group from the Washington newspaper *The Examiner* on May 26, 1827:

Notice

The Annual Meeting of the West Middletown Auxiliary Abolition Society will be held in the borough of West Middletown, on Saturday the 2d of June next at 1 o'clock P.M. As the election of officers for the ensuing year, and other important business will attended to on that day, it is hoped that members will be punctual in their attendance. By order of the standing committee.

J.M'Fadden, RS [26]

One source has no less a figure than John Brown helping establish the town as an Underground Railroad station. Posing as a buyer of sheep and wool, Brown frequently came to the town to conduct railroad business.[27] No other source corroborates this assertion, however. There are ample references to other agents in West Middletown, the most famous of whom were the Thomas, William, and Matthew McKeever families, who hid their guests in barns, attics, and cellars.[28] Thomas McKeever even had a secret panel built into the wall of his home where he could hide fugitives. An undated letter written by Matthew McKeever reveals a number of details about the operation of the Underground Railroad in West Middletown. The following is an excerpt from that letter:

Dear Sir:—You wish to know something of my experience with the "Underground Railroad." I was a director of that road for 40 years. The kind of cars we used was a good spring wagon, with a chicken coop at each end and the darkies in the middle, with a good cover over them. The highest number of slaves I ever shipped at once was eight. They came to our house about daybreak one morning before any of us were up, except a colored man, John Jordan. He took them and hid them in the sheep loft and kept them there four weeks and although we had a family of eighteen or twenty, not one of them knew they were there, not even my wife.[29]

Matthew McKeever also wrote that he used to receive fugitives from his brother-in-law, Joseph Bryant, who lived in Bethany, Virginia. The runaways were brought to West Middletown by Campbell McKeever, Matthew's son. Campbell went to college in Bethany and would often come home escorting fugitives. McKeever said that he then shipped the escapees to the city of Pittsburgh.[30]

Other individuals also helped in the town. The local United Presbyterian Church gave sanctuary to runaways. A black resident of the town, "Peachy" Herron, is cited as having helped runaways.[31] Blockson also identifies James McElroy as an agent.[32] One of the leading conductors in the area was Bill Asbury, another black person who frequently took fugitives to Hickory, a town to the east of West Middletown.[33] From Hickory, the travelers would make their way to Pittsburgh.

FROM GREENE COUNTY TO WEST MIDDLETOWN

Forrest, in his history of Washington County, states that the first station of the Underground Railroad found north of the Mason-Dixon Line in western Pennsylvania was at Crowe's Mills on the Greene County/Virginia border. After crossing into Pennsylvania near this site, runaways would travel northward from here to the home of Isaac Teagarden, who lived on Wheeling Creek. Today the area of his homestead would be just to the southeast of Ryerson Station State Park.[34] After staying with him, the fugitives would continue north to the farm of Joseph Gray, near modern Graysville and then to the home of Kenneth McCoy in West Alexander.[35] At this point, the runaways would follow the trail to West Middletown.

FROM GREENE COUNTY TO THE CITY OF WASHINGTON

There was a second route that began in Greene County and went northward, extending from southern Greene County to the city of Washington. Brewster includes it in his description of the two routes that crossed the Mason-Dixon Line near the town of Mount Morris. One of these routes ended at Uniontown. The second route, according to Brewster, went to the community of Leonardsville and then north to the city of Washington.[36] The description of this second route is rather scanty in Brewster's work and needs further elaboration.

Mount Morris, in Greene County, was a major entry port into Pennsylvania on the Underground Railroad. Once they crossed the Virginia-Pennsylvania border here, the fugitives took one of two possible trails. One of these ran along Dunkard's Creek to the Monongahela River and Uniontown. The second followed Hargus Creek toward Washington County. Those who chose the Hargus Creek trail would eventually come to the home of Rev. M. Leonard and the town of Leonardsville, mentioned by Brewster. The modern town of Holbrook has replaced the older community of Leonardsville and is about sixteen miles from Mount Morris.[37]

Leaving the home of Reverend Leonard, the travelers had another choice to make. They could go to the northwest for about six miles to the farm of Joseph Gray, located near Graysville, and from there proceed to West Alexander and West Middletown. Or they could travel about the same distance northeast to Waynesburg. Forrest mentions a black agent named Ermine Cain, who worked as a janitor in the courthouse there.[38] Upon reaching Waynesburg, the escape route again split in two, one path leading almost due northward, and the other heading northeast.

The route that went north ran along either the remnants of an old Indian trail or an old road all the way to Washington. The Indian trail was the Catfish Path, which cut through the wilderness from Brant Summit in southern Green County near the Virginia border, through Washington, to the Ohio River near Pittsburgh.[39] The road traversed the same area going from Waynesburg to Pittsburgh by way of Washington. Later it became U.S. Route 19.[40] Although no hard evidence exists of stations along the twenty-seven-mile stretch between Waynesburg and Washington, because of its length, fugitives must have found aid somewhere along it.

The route to the northeast led to the town of Jefferson, where the home of Thomas Hughes was a refuge for runaways. Hughes had come from Maryland in 1767 and was responsible for laying out Jefferson, which was later incorporated into a town in 1827.[41] Hughes built a stone house there in 1814 and turned it into an Underground Railroad station. He had the further distinction of being the first Roman Catholic in Greene County and was one of the few Catholics mentioned as an agent on the Underground Railroad.[42] From the Hughes house, the fugitives might have gone to Washington, but it is more log-

The home of Thomas Hughes in Greene County. PHOTO BY WILLIAM J. SWITALA

ical that they traveled the four short miles to Rice's Landing and entered the Uniontown–Pittsburgh Route along the Monongahela River.

FROM BROWNSVILLE TO WASHINGTON

The final entry route into Washington County was the one mentioned by Brewster running from Cumberland to Uniontown and then on to the city of Washington via the town of Brownsville.[43] It was only natural for runaways to choose to go from Brownsville to Washington. Early in the history of the Underground Railroad, escapees could have followed the well-known Mingo Path, which ran between these two towns.[44] Later, they could have taken a road described on Howell's map of 1792 that united Brownsville and Washington.[45] In 1817, the National Road reached Washington.[46]

THE CITY OF WASHINGTON

The centerpiece of the Washington County Underground Railroad network was the city of Washington. It became an important logistical center as early as 1769, when a Delaware Indian named Tingoocque, more commonly called Catfish, established a hunting camp at the site where the city later developed.[47] The presence of settlers was felt in the area when David Hoge purchased one thousand acres of land at the site of Catfish's camp in 1780. On March 28, 1781, the state legislature created the county of Washington, and by October of that year, Hoge directed David Redick, a surveyor, to lay out a town on his one thousand acres. Originally he called the place Bassett Town, after Richard Bassett, a relative of Hoge's who was a politician and a statesman in the federal government.[48] Within a few years, however, the town was renamed Washington in honor of the first president. James Eliot, a soldier in the army that came to western Pennsylvania to put down the Whiskey Rebellion in the November 9, 1794, entry in his journal, describes the town of Washington: "Washington is a considerable town, consisting of framed buildings, clapboarded, and chiefly painted red, except the court house and two or three other buildings, which are of stone. The appearance of this place was very pleasing to me, as it resembled a *New England* town."[49]

By 1816, the town had grown to more than a hundred houses, most of which were made of brick, and had paved streets. It was also the county seat.[50] In 1820, the city had 1,687 inhabitants and was by far the largest urban center in the county.[51]

It was in this early period of the city's history that the most famous figure of Washington's Underground Railroad network appeared. This was Dr. Francis Julius LeMoyne. His father, Dr. John Julius LeMoyne, came to America in

The LeMoyne House in Washington, Pennsylvania, the major station in the city.
PHOTO BY WILLIAM J. SWITALA

1797. He was a French physician who wanted to escape the turmoil of the French Revolution. In 1812, he built a magnificent stone house at 49 East Main Street in the city of Washington. The house served as a family residence and his office. His son Francis succeeded him as both a doctor and owner of the house.[52] Francis went on to become very involved in the abolition movement, helping establish the Western Abolition Society in 1824, and he even ran for vice president of the United States on the Abolitionist ticket.[53] Throughout the history of the Underground Railroad, the LeMoyne house was a haven for fugitives trying to escape bondage. It is reported that Dr. LeMoyne hid as many as twenty-six runaways at a time in a secret room on the third floor of his home.[54] Even Mrs. LeMoyne actively participated in hiding fugitives. On occasion, when slave catchers came to the house looking for runaways, she hid them under her bed and then lay in it feigning illness. The hunters did not dare disturb the lady in her bed and would not search under it. When they left, the runaways would come out of their hiding place.[55]

Dr. LeMoyne worked tirelessly for many years aiding fugitives. Later in his life, he endowed a college in Memphis, established for the education of freed blacks.[56] It was originally name LeMoyne College but today is known as the LeMoyne-Owens College.

Even though Dr. LeMoyne was such a gigantic figure in the operation of the Underground Railroad in Washington, he could not have been successful in passing fugitives on to freedom without the help of many others. Not many names of agents there are known, except for two blacks, Samuel W. Dorsey and Tar Adams, a barber.[57] Most likely the others who helped in this effort were the same people who helped Dr. LeMoyne form the Western Abolition Society and its predecessor, the Washington Society for the Relief of Free Negroes.

EXIT ROUTES FROM WASHINGTON COUNTY

There were two major terminal points for runaways leaving Washington County and heading north: the one that went to Pittsburgh and the one that took fugitives to the Beaver County network.

WASHINGTON COUNTY–PITTSBURGH ROUTE

When fugitives left Washington County for Pittsburgh, they had three escape paths from which to choose: from West Middletown, from the city of Washington, or an eastern trail through the town of Finnleyville.

West Middletown to Pittsburgh

The main road between West Middletown and Pittsburgh passed through the town of Hickory. The town was established in 1800 under the name of Mount Pleasant, but the name was changed to Hickory in 1830 because of post office confusion between this Mount Pleasant and the Mount Pleasant near Uniontown.[58] Bill Asbury, a free black, used to conduct escapees from West Middletown to Hickory. The town was located on a road (later PA Route 50) that ran all the way to the Ohio River and reached the river just below Pittsburgh. Fugitives traveling over this road would have to proceed a good twenty-one miles from Hickory before reaching Pittsburgh. There is some sketchy evidence that the town of Carnegie, which is on this route and closer to Pittsburgh, had an Underground Railroad station. The likely candidate for the station would have been the Mansfield B. Brown house. Professor V. Robert Agostino of Duquesne University, the author of a history of Carnegie, Pennsylvania, believes that Brown opened his home to fugitives. Brown had a reputation for aiding free blacks and even donated money for the building of an African Methodist Episcopal church in Carnegie.[59] Further research needs to be done to verify this possibility and to identify any other stations that must have existed along this route.

Washington City to Pittsburgh

Another route proceeded northward from the city of Washington to Pittsburgh via either the Catfish Path or an early road identified on Howell's map.[60] Taking either trail, the fugitives would have come upon a safe haven in the town of Canonsburg, located about eight miles from the city of Washington.

Col. John Canon acquired twelve hundred acres of land along Chartiers Creek north of Washington on the Catfish Path in 1773. He built a gristmill there, and within a few years, a number of settlers arrived and started to farm the area. On April 15, 1788, Canon set up the town that was named after him.[61] In 1805, the road and stage line that had connected Wheeling to Washington reached Canonsburg.[62] Eventually, because of its critical location on the route to Pittsburgh, Canonsburg became a station on the Underground Railroad.[63]

When fugitives left Canonsburg, they had a choice: They could return to the road (modern U.S. Route 19) that ran between Washington and Pittsburgh and journey on into Allegheny County, or they could continue on the Catfish Path and link up with the road that brought runaways from Hickory to Pittsburgh (modern PA Route 50). Either way, they could have reached Pittsburgh.

Finleyville to Pittsburgh

Most sources have the fugitives leaving the Mingo Church and Ginger Hill stations, in eastern Washington County, and proceeding to the Monongahela River and West Newton. However, local legend has stations in or near the Washington County town of Finleyville, which is only four miles from Ginger Hill and even closer to Mingo Church. Runaways would have easily reached it by following the road that became Route 88, which was only a mile from Ginger Hill. From Finleyville, the escapees could have continued on this road all the way to Pittsburgh.

WASHINGTON COUNTY–BEAVER COUNTY ROUTE

The second major exit route from Washington County proceeded northward to Beaver County and New Brighton. After leaving West Middletown, some fugitives journeyed northwest to the small town of Independence. From there they would move on to Paris, a small town on the Pennsylvania-Virginia border.[64] Modern U.S. Route 22 runs through the town today. Upon leaving Paris, some runaways went northward to Hookstown in Beaver County; others took the subroute that headed northeast to Raccoon Creek. Once there, they simply followed the creek to the Ohio River and arrived at a spot on the river a few miles below the town of Beaver. In either case, once they crossed the Ohio, they entered the Beaver County escape network and headed north.

The Washington County network differed from most other escape routes in that though it did possess several alternate escape paths, they did not backtrack on themselves or zigzag as much as the others. The routes in this county were more linear and northward oriented.

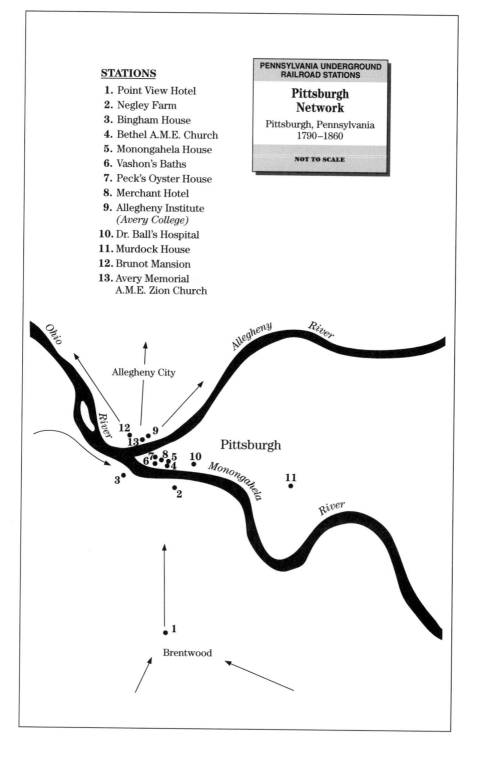

STATIONS

1. Point View Hotel
2. Negley Farm
3. Bingham House
4. Bethel A.M.E. Church
5. Monongahela House
6. Vashon's Baths
7. Peck's Oyster House
8. Merchant Hotel
9. Allegheny Institute
   (Avery College)
10. Dr. Ball's Hospital
11. Murdock House
12. Brunot Mansion
13. Avery Memorial
    A.M.E. Zion Church

PENNSYLVANIA UNDERGROUND
RAILROAD STATIONS

Pittsburgh Network

Pittsburgh, Pennsylvania
1790–1860

NOT TO SCALE

Pittsburgh Network

Pittsburgh occupied a strategic position on the Underground Railroad in western Pennsylvania. The city was a natural junction for fugitives trying to escape bondage, as it was located at the confluence of the Allegheny, Monongahela, and Ohio Rivers; was on several rail lines; and had numerous roads leading in and out. Because of its physical size and the number of people active in the escape apparatus, Pittsburgh had an extensive Underground Railroad network.

The settlement of the area, which later became the city of Pittsburgh, began with the French erecting Fort Duquesne in 1754 at the point where the three rivers of the area met. The dream the French held of dominating trade on the Ohio and Mississippi Rivers required them to occupy this key locale. This dream was dashed, however, when the British army led by Gen. John Forbes captured the fort in 1758. The foundation of the city was laid on November 27, 1758, when the soldiers of Forbes's army, having erected a fort, named it Fort Pitt.[1]

People settled on the land around the fort, and by 1788, the population in the city and on the land around it had grown to the degree that the state legislature created a new county there called Allegheny and established Pittsburgh as the county seat.[2] Trade on the three rivers developed quickly, and Pittsburgh soon became known as the "Gateway to the West."

The presence of blacks in Pittsburgh began with the building of Fort Pitt. General Forbes had fifty black soldiers in his army when he left Bedford on his march to Fort Duquesne in 1758.[3] These men helped construct and staff the new fort. More blacks came with the settlers moving into the area, most of them slaves, although some were free men and women. The census of 1790 showed that there were 159 slaves and 12 free blacks living in Allegheny County. As more and more black Americans migrated or fled to Allegheny County and Pittsburgh, the number of free blacks in the county had grown to 3,431 by 1850. Meanwhile, the number of slaves in the county dropped from 159 in 1790 to 0 by 1860.[4]

A sentiment to improve the lot of slaves emerged early in the history of the city. Hugh H. Brackenridge, one of the citizens of note in early Pittsburgh history, successfully defended a black woman brought back from Kentucky in 1793, thus restoring her freedom after slave hunters had kidnapped her in Pittsburgh and taken her south.[5] Another example of this sentiment occurred on September 25, 1826, when a number of prominent citizens gathered in the First Presbyterian Church to form the Pittsburgh Colonization Society. This was a branch of the American Colonization Society, which had as its goal the return of all enslaved peoples to their homes in Africa. The officers they elected at the meeting read like the social register for the city at that time. They included Henry Baldwin, president, and for vice presidents, Francis Herron, D.D.; Robert Bruce, D.D.; Rev. Elisha P. Swift; John Black, D.D.; Rev. C. B. Maguire; Rev. John H. Hopkins; Rev. Charles Avery; Rev. Joseph Kerr; Rev. Joseph Stockton; and Walter Forward.[6] This society remained active for another fifteen years.[7]

The blacks living in Pittsburgh also formed their own organizations to improve their conditions. They realized almost immediately that the key to improving their lot lay in education. As early as 1818, Robert Smith opened a small school to educate blacks in western Pennsylvania.[8] Under the leadership of black activist John B. Vashon, the community formed the African Education Society in 1832. Its goal was to see to the education of blacks, both young and old. Vashon became the group's first president, Rev. Lewis Woodson its first secretary, and A. D. Lewis its treasurer.[9] The headquarters for this group was in a building located between Wood and Market Streets.[10] The following year, on October 4, 1833, Vashon helped inaugurate another organization that would prove vital to the success of the early Underground Railroad in Pittsburgh: the Anti-Slavery Society of Pittsburgh.[11]

Two other societies began operating in Pittsburgh that assisted in the cause of the Underground Railroad. One was the Pittsburgh and Allegheny Ladies' Anti-Slavery Society, made up of women who were dedicated to the abolition of slavery and the emancipation of all those currently enslaved in the country.[12] The other was the Union Anti-Slavery Society of Pittsburgh and Allegheny, which began to operate in January 1839 as an attempt to combine the efforts of several smaller antislavery groups in the county. Samuel C. Cole became the first secretary of the society.[13]

Newspapers also played a role in the antislavery movement in Pittsburgh. One of the first abolitionist papers to appear on the scene was the *Christian Witness*. The Anti-Slavery Society of Pittsburgh purchased the paper in May 1837 and used it as the society's voice in the community.[14] By 1841, three other abolitionist papers flourished in the area: the *Christian Advocate, Pres-*

The Vickless-Point View Hotel in Brentwood. PHOTO BY WILLIAM J. SWITALA

byterian Advocate, and *Daily Advocate,* which all circulated editions filled with antislavery sentiments.[15] The first newspaper owned and operated by an African-American in the city was Martin Delany's *The Mystery.* Operating out of an office on Third Street, Delany began publishing his paper in 1843. Later, in 1847, he joined Frederick Douglass in coediting one of the most famous abolitionist newspapers of the era, the *North Star.*[16] Also in 1847, a woman dedicated to the cause of ending slavery assumed the editorship of a local newspaper called the *Saturday Evening Visiter.* This was Jane G. Swisshelm, and she quickly changed the agenda of the paper, making it a vehicle for promoting her ideas against slavery and for women's rights.[17] Even the leading newspaper in the city, the *Pittsburgh Gazette,* supported the colonization policies of some of the antislavery groups.[18]

Underground Railroad escape routes entered the city at various points. The previous two chapters detailed how they came from Washington and Westmoreland Counties, as well as from the Ohio River and by rail from Harpers Ferry. More elaboration is needed at this point on how the runaways got to Pittsburgh from West Newton on the Uniontown–Pittsburgh Route and from Finleyville on the Washington County Route.

The quickest way to the city, for those coming from West Newton, was to take the old Pittsburgh Road, which ran from Uniontown to Pittsburgh. This road is now the heavily traveled PA Route 51. From Finleyville, the fugitives would have taken the road that became PA Route 88. Both roads passed through or came near the community of Brentwood, a suburb of

Pittsburgh. This community had one of the few identifiable Underground Railroad stations within Allegheny County and outside the city of Pittsburgh. A station operated out of the Point View Hotel, which was on Brownsville Road. This road ran from the city limits to PA Route 88 in Library, Pennsylvania. The hotel is in existence today and still operates under the name Point View. Built in the 1820s, the Point View Hotel was a favorite stopping place for those coming to Pittsburgh from the South. In the hotel, beneath its sitting room, was a secret cellar leading to an extensive tunnel system that opened to the woods on the other side of Brownsville Road.[19] Fugitives who stayed there made their way to the south side of the city and hid in the Underground Railroad station on the Alexander Negley farm there. The runaways stayed in barns on the property next to the Monongahela River. At night, conductors took them across the Monongahela River near the point where the Ohio River begins and helped them enter the escape network in the city proper.[20] Other fugitives coming to the city from the South found refuge in the Thomas Bingham house, on the heights of Mount Washington overlooking the city. Mr. Bingham, a lawyer and journalist, had a staff of free black servants who frequently hid escapees in the house with his approval.[21]

Many individuals who were among the most famous personalities in the city's early history played important roles in Pittsburgh's Underground Rail-

The house of Thomas Bingham, on Mount Washington in Pittsburgh. PHOTO BY WILLIAM J. SWITALA

road. The four most illustrious agents of the railroad were John B. Vashon, Martin R. Delany, Rev. Lewis Woodson, and Rev. Charles Avery.

John B. Vashon was a black man who in 1829 came to Pittsburgh,[22] where, along with Lewis Woodson, he founded the Pittsburgh African Education Society. He served as that group's first president, and the following year he played a major role in organizing the Anti-Slavery Society of Pittsburgh. In 1833, he opened two commercial enterprises that brought him fame and wealth. One was a barbershop that he called his Shaving, Hair Dressing, and Fancy Establishment, located in a building at 59 Third Street, between Market and Ferry Streets. The other was his City Baths, the first public bathhouse in western Pennsylvania.[23] The shop became a center for news and information, some of which benefited the operation of the Underground Railroad in the city.[24] An incident involving Vashon directly in an escape attempt occurred in 1850, when a Mr. Rose, from Wellsburg, came to Pittsburgh on a business trip. While at Vashon's barbershop, he recognized George White, a young mulatto man, as his runaway slave. White was apprenticing with Vashon at that time and had been with him for over two years. To avoid a legal problem and the recapturing of White, Vashon paid Rose $200 for the purchase of White, and he then set him free.[25]

Martin R. Delany was a man of prodigious abilities. Delany was born in Charleston, Virginia, on May 6, 1812. Later, his family moved to Kerrstown, Pennsylvania, a small community of about forty African-American families attached to the larger town of Chambersburg. While there, Delany attended school until he reached the age of fifteen. A few years later, seeking greater opportunities, he struck out across the Allegheny Mountains toward Pittsburgh. Arriving in Pittsburgh at the age of nineteen, he became the protégé of John B. Vashon. Realizing that education was the key to success for an African-American, he enrolled in the Bethel African Methodist Episcopal Church's school and became one of its brightest students. One of the dreams he had was to become a physician. In 1832, he began to study medicine with Dr. Andrew McDowell, a white doctor who also had come from Chambersburg. After also apprenticing with Dr. Francis J. LeMoyne in Washington County and Dr. Joseph P. Gazzam in Pittsburgh, he applied for admission to the Harvard School of Medicine. He gained entrance to the school, but after only one year of study, the administration of the school forced him to leave because of complaints lodged by some of his bigoted classmates. Returning to Pittsburgh in 1851, he opened an office on Smithfield Street, where he specialized in the treatment of female and childhood illnesses. During the Civil War, President Lincoln commissioned Delany as a major in the Union army. In addition to practicing medicine, he also published *The Mystery,* the first black-owned newspaper in Pittsburgh, and coedited the abolitionist paper the *North Star* with the legendary Frederick Douglass.[26] Always assisting the Underground Railroad network in the city, Delany helped start the Philanthropic Society in Pittsburgh, which reportedly aided as many as 269 fugitives in escaping to freedom in one year alone.[27] Delany also held the opinion in the 1850s that the blacks in the United States might consider resettlement in Central America, where they might live free of discrimination and have a chance to prosper.[28]

Rev. Lewis Woodson arrived in Pittsburgh in 1815. A short time later, he helped establish and charter the Bethel A.M.E. Church at the corner of Water and Smithfield Streets in the heart of the city.[29] This was the first black church west of the Allegheny Mountains. Under his pastorate, the church became the spiritual, educational, and cultural focal point for blacks living in the Pittsburgh area. The church and its members readily provided help to fugitives passing through their community.[30] Woodson was also a strong advocate of blacks owning land and pursuing their livelihood in agriculture. He believed that this would give them more self-esteem and recognition as being industrious. It would also move them away from the overcrowded conditions they faced living in cities.[31]

Rev. Charles Avery was born on December 10, 1784, in Westchester County, New York. Avery came to Pittsburgh in 1812 and is the only white of the four famous local agents. Due to the success of his cotton mill and pharmaceutical business, Avery quickly became one of the wealthiest individuals in the city.[32] Charles Avery was a devout Methodist and a minister, and from his early life onward, he was also a dedicated opponent of slavery and a proponent of the Underground Railroad's actions. During the trial surrounding the *Amistad* incident, Avery was one of the financial backers who saw to the legal representation of the Africans held captive on the ship when their case came before the Supreme Court of the United States.[33] Like Delany and other leaders, he was convinced that the key to advancement of black people in this country rested in education. To this end, he founded the Allegheny Institute and Mission Church for black students in March 1849. The school was in Allegheny City at Nash and Avery Streets, across the Allegheny River from the heart of Pittsburgh.[34] Later the school became known as Avery College. He also assisted runaways passing through the city. There are rumored accounts of his driving a carriage with fugitives hidden inside while he sat in the driver's seat in disguise. When he died, Avery left $800,000 in his will to various black societies and to schools that were educating young black people.[35]

There were many other agents active on the Pittsburgh Route who aided fugitives in their quest for freedom. Siebert lists only one name for Allegheny County: Charles Taylor.[36] None of the more famous activists in the county

The memorial statue of Rev. Charles Avery in Pittsburgh. PHOTO BY WILLIAM J. SWITALA

appear on his list, which also should have included Alexander Negley, who had a station on the south side of the city; John C. Peck, who ran a station out of his Oyster House restaurant on Market Street; and "Daddy Ben" Richards, a successful African-American butcher who used his meat wagon to transport runaways.[37] Samuel Bruce and Bishop Benjamin Tanner, the father of artist Henry O. Tanner, also belong on that list.[38] And Lucast Dudt, the original owner of the Point View Hotel in Brentwood, Dr. John Ball, Charles Brewer, Thomas Bingham, George Black, and a Mr. Murdoch all opened their homes to fugitives.[39]

The Underground Railroad had many stations in the Pittsburgh region, including the previously mentioned stations operating at the Point View Hotel, the Negley farm, and the Bingham house on Mount Washington. Blockson found a few other stations, including the Avery Memorial A.M.E. Zion Church, on Nash and Avery Streets, which he said had a tunnel in its basement leading to a former canal and then to the Allegheny River (now the site of the Allegheny Center Mall); the home of abolitionist Charles Brewer; and the Murdock House, which was at the corner of Darlington Road and Murdock Street in the Squirrel Hill section of the city. Blockson also says that many runaways found safety in the homes of black residents living in the Arthurville (Upper Hill District near Roberts Street) and Hayti (Lower Hill District, now covered by the Civic Arena) sections of Pittsburgh.[40] Tunnels under the Felix R. Brunot mansion at 216 East Stockton Avenue provided a hiding place for escapees. In the very heart of the downtown region of the city, the City Baths of John B. Vashon and John C. Peck's Oyster House were also stations.[41] Although not officially a station, the Monongahela House certainly was the scene of many a daring rescue. Built in 1840 and situated on the northwest corner of Water and Smithfield Streets, it was the premier hotel in the city. Although the owners of the Monongahela House were European Americans, the staff of over 300 were blacks. Many a slave staying at the hotel with a Southern master found freedom after the staff there spirited him or her out of the hotel and around the corner to Vashon's Baths or Peck's Oyster House.[42] A station also existed at the hospital of Dr. John Ball on Boyd's Hill overlooking the city. Later, in the 1870s, this hospital became St. Mary's Hall of the newly formed Duquesne University.[43] Today it is the site of the university's Bayer Learning Center. Yet another station having a tunnel structure operated from the George Black mansion of Western Avenue. Like the Avery Memorial Church, these tunnels gave the fugitives access to the Allegheny River.[44] The other black churches in the area also likely aided runaways and acted as stations.

There are many accounts of attempts to rescue slaves from their masters while they were staying in Pittsburgh. Most of them involved the Monongahela House and the Merchant's Hotel, at the corner of Third and Smithfield Streets in the downtown section of the city. The men and women rescued from these two places were taken to Vashon's Baths or Peck's restaurant; given a new hairstyle, clothes, and shoes; and then spirited out of the city on one of the escape routes heading northward. In July 1850, John Drennen of Van Buren, Arkansas, stopped at the Monongahela House. While at dinner with his wife, his fourteen-year-old female slave disappeared from the hotel. An investigation by the hotel owner showed that the girl was induced to escape by the black employees there.[45] In another case, Wilson recounts the tale of a Southerner with two female slaves who stopped for lodgings at the Merchant's Hotel. The staff there managed to persuade one of the two to escape. In a daring effort, she left the building, entered the escape network, and gained her freedom.[46] In January 1847, several white slave owners from Virginia tried to kidnap a black man named Briscoe from Allegheny City. They enlisted the help of several police officers in their attempt. A group of other blacks came to Briscoe's aid, and he managed to escape from the Virginians.[47] Another incident was so celebrated that it was reported in the April 17, 1847, edition of the *Pittsburgh Daily Gazette:*

CASE OF KIDNAPPING—Our city was yesterday morning the scene of much excitement in consequence of an attempt made to carry off a slave belonging to JOSEPH LOGAN, of Winchester, Va. It seems that the slave has been for some weeks a fugitive from his master, and during that time has been a resident of this city. Last evening his master, accompanied by two other persons from his town, James Johnson and George Kramer, arrived in town, and put up at the Monongahela House. By some means the officers, with aid received in the city, decoyed the slave into one of the chambers in the third story of the Hotel, where he was confronted by his master. The scene here, we are told, was a most exciting one. He cried loudly for relief, when seized by the officers, and was heard all over the immense establishment. The noise caused much alarm and excitement amongst the numerous inmates. In the mean while, the colored population of the city became by some means apprised of what was going on, and a large body of them gathered around the entrances of the Hotel, ready to rescue the slave from the grasp of the owner and officers, who shortly afterwards made their appearance with the slave in custody, at the private door of the Hotel, intending to convey him on board the steamer Clipper No. 2, then ready to leave the wharf. The moment the man appeared, a regular rush was made to his rescue. One of the officers (Kramer) was knocked down, though but slightly injured. Mr. Johnson also received a blow. In the meantime, the slave made his escape and has not since been seen. His name is Daniel Lockhart, and his friends have sent him far beyond the reach of master or overseer.[48]

The passage of the Fugitive Slave Law of 1850 caused a great stir in Pittsburgh. The law passed through Congress in September 1850, and by September 26, a steady stream of blacks were leaving the city and the county and heading for Canada.[49] As a result of these departures, the population of black residents in Allegheny County, which was 3,431 in 1850, had dropped to 2,725 by 1860.[50]

Reaction to the passage of the law was swift. On Saturday evening, September 28, 1850, a large crowd gathered in Pittsburgh at a public meeting to discuss the law. The meeting was chaired by Rev. Charles Avery, who, along with many others present, pledged to oppose the law with all of their might.[51] Two days later, on September 30, another huge crowd gathered, this time at the Market House in Allegheny, across the Allegheny River from downtown Pittsburgh. The mayor of Allegheny City, Hugh Fleming, presided over the meeting and delivered a fiery speech denouncing the law and calling for its repeal.[52] In the end, the Fugitive Slave Law of 1850, while causing some blacks to depart, only prompted the supporters of the Underground Railroad in Pittsburgh to redouble their efforts.

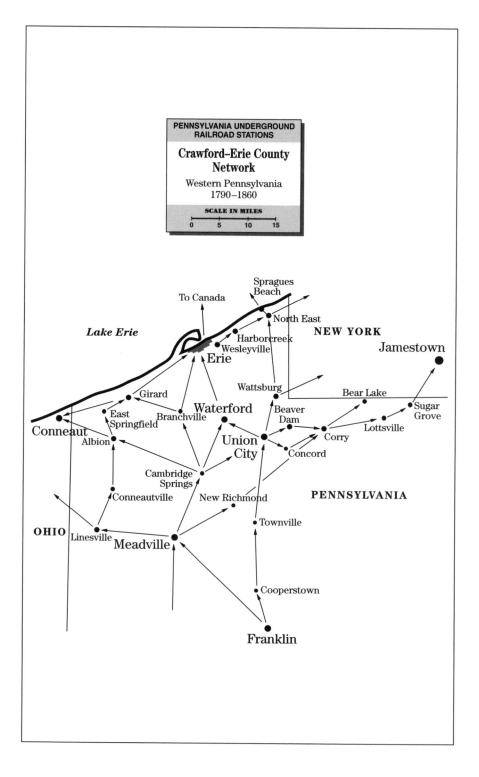

PENNSYLVANIA UNDERGROUND RAILROAD STATIONS

Crawford–Erie County Network

Western Pennsylvania
1790–1860

SCALE IN MILES

0   5   10   15

Spragues
Beach

To Canada

North East

Lake Erie

NEW YORK

Harborcreek
Wesleyville

Erie

Jamestown

Wattsburg

Bear Lake

Girard

Beaver
Dam

Sugar
Grove

East
Springfield

Branchville

Waterford

Lottsville

Conneaut

Albion

Union
City

Corry

Concord

Cambridge
Springs

Conneautville

New Richmond

PENNSYLVANIA

OHIO   Linesville

Townville

Meadville

Cooperstown

Franklin

Crawford–Erie
County Network

Each of the major western routes examined in this study led to Crawford and Erie Counties in northwestern Pennsylvania. This is only logical because of their proximity to Lake Erie, Ohio, and Canada. Both counties had extensive and complicated railroad networks, and scores of towns and individuals participated in the effort. In many cases, the towns had multiple entry and exit subroutes. The Underground Railroad in this area was much more complex than in the rest of western Pennsylvania, possibly because Erie was so close to freedom for the runaways, and slave catchers frequented the area.

CRAWFORD COUNTY

The French briefly inhabited this area in the early and mid-1700s. After the French and Indian War, they lost their foothold in western Pennsylvania, and British settlers began to appropriate the land. The state legislature created Crawford County on March 12, 1800. Shortly thereafter, the Holland, Pennsylvania, and North American Land Companies purchased extensive tracts of land in the county in the hope of selling parcels of them to settlers.[1]

Several major Underground Railroad routes converged in Crawford County. The Bedford–Clearfield Route reached there after passing through the town of Franklin, which was also a critical junction on the Uniontown–Indiana Route, and both the Uniontown–Pittsburgh and the Washington County Routes approached the town from the south via Beaver, Lawrence, and Mercer Counties.

The main pathways of these major routes traveled over roads built through funding appropriated by the state legislature in 1807. This construction effort linked Meadville directly to Mercer and Franklin, both of which were tied to Beaver, Butler, and Clearfield by similarly funded roads. Also in that same year, Meadville gained direct access to the town of Waterford in Erie

County by a new road.[2] From Waterford, one could take a well-constructed turnpike to the town of Erie as early as 1811.[3] Runaways also could have reached Meadville by traversing the Kuskusky Indian Path from the southwest or the Venango Path from the southeast. When leaving Meadville, they could have taken a road or one of several Indian trails. The Conneaut Path, heading northwest, allowed one to travel to Ohio; the Cussewago Path tended northeast and ultimately reached New York; and other branches of the Venango Path led to Fort LeBoeuf (later Waterford) and then on to Lake Erie.[4]

MEADVILLE

The most prominent town in the county was Meadville. It had its beginnings in a settlement established by David Mead in 1788. There was a steady influx of new people, and Mead decided to lay out a town on the site of his settlement, which he did in 1793.[5] Shortly after this, blacks began to make their appearance in the area. Free blacks set up a small community in the town, and it grew quickly. Between 1830 and 1850, the black population in Meadville doubled in size. This enabled them to make a contribution to the success of the Underground Railroad active in the town.[6]

Several sources provide information on the Underground Railroad in Crawford County. The oldest of them, Siebert's work, contains the least amount of data. He mentions only one station in Meadville, the Unitarian Seminary, and only three agents active in the entire county: Jonathan Benn, M. M. Brown, and someone named Churchill.[7] His map records three towns with stations—Meadville, Linesville, and Townville—but he provides no information about two of them.[8] Other sources, however, provide much more information on activity in the county.

Blockson gives numerous details about the stations and agents in Meadville. He reports that Levi Barton, owner of the Barton House Hotel, was a station master in the town and often gave refuge to escapees in his hotel, hiding them under straw mattresses. Richard Henderson, a member of the free black community who came to Meadville in 1824, was also an agent. A friend of John Brown, he was a staunch abolitionist. Opening a barbershop at 371 Arch Street, Henderson used his shop as a station, reputedly helping over 500 fugitives reach freedom, along with the aid of his brother, Edward. Next to Henderson's barbershop was a livery stable operated by Robert and James Hanna, who also assisted Richard Henderson in his Underground Railroad activities, turning their stable into a safe haven for runaways. Ardent abolitionist Taylor F. H. Randolph opened his home to fugitives, and the Bishop, Barton, and Powell families were agents with stations in their homes in Meadville.[9]

The Unitarians exhibited a solid commitment to the Underground Railroad cause in Meadville. The Unitarian Church at the corner of Main and Chestnut Streets was a station from the time of its founding in 1836 through the Civil War. The Meadville Theological Seminary, mentioned in passing by Siebert, was also a station. Established in 1844, on Chestnut Street, the seminary served two different religious denominations: the Unitarians and the Disciples of Christ. The first president of the school, Dr. Rufus P. Stebbins, opened the doors of the seminary to fugitives and cared for their needs until they were ready to move on to the next stop on their journey.[10]

FROM MEADVILLE TO ERIE COUNTY

There were several alternate escape paths leading out of Meadville. Siebert's map shows a trail from Meadville to Linesville, on the Pennsylvania-Ohio border, and a second route going from Meadville to Union City in Erie County.[11] Linesville was a natural terminus for a route. A subsidiary branch of the Conneaut Indian Path passed through this area and proceeded on to Sandusky, Ohio. Escapees could have taken this trail from Meadville to Linesville and then on to Sandusky.[12] When Lucas Line established this community in 1825, he did so to provide land for a Quaker community that wished to settle there.[13] Blockson agrees with Siebert on both Linesville and Union City, but he also has an intervening station at Cambridge Springs, which was about halfway between Meadville and Union City. This would make sense because of the distance a fugitive would have to travel from Meadville to Union City. Blockson has several routes proceeding in a fanlike fashion from Cambridge Springs to the Erie County towns of Albion, Branchville, Waterford, and Union City. A third route leaving Meadville went to the small community of Conneautville, which lay about fourteen miles northwest of Meadville. This route eventually led to the town of Girard in Erie County.[14] Siebert agrees with the Girard destination, but on his map, the route goes from Meadville, through Linesville, to Girard.[15] A fourth route took fugitives to New Richmond in Crawford County. From there the runaways would have had to go northeast along what was to become PA Route 77 until they came to Corry in Erie County, Sugar Grove in Warren County, and ultimately, Jamestown, New York. In New Richmond, the travelers could have spent the night at the home of George Dalamater. In the late 1820s, they could have stayed with another station master—none other than John Brown, who had opened a tannery in New Richmond in 1825 and operated it there for a number of years. Like so many of his other businesses, the tannery was a cover for his Underground Railroad activities.[16] At the tannery, he hid fugitives in his cellar or nearby barn.

ERIE COUNTY

The terminal network of the Underground Railroad in western Pennsylvania was in Erie County. From here the next stop for many fugitives was Canada. Hundreds made their way across Lake Erie in boats of all sizes. Those who did not go directly across the lake went to Ohio or New York, and then to Canada.

The history of Erie County and the town of Erie goes back to the mid-1700s. The French were the first Europeans to arrive, and on May 15, 1753, French troops began to erect a small fort near the site of the present-day city of Erie. They named it Fort Presque Isle, and with this fort, they hoped to begin gaining control of western Pennsylvania.[17] Their dream of an empire came to an end, however, with their defeat at the hands of the British in the French and Indian War. After the war, settlers from the British colonies in North America began to arrive in the area. The Moravians established a presence near Lake Erie, in the area around Mill Village, in the year 1791. Shortly after this, the Holland Land and Pennsylvania Population Companies began to buy large tracts of land near the lake, intending to attract more settlers who would buy parcels of land from them. By 1795, the population along the lakeshore had increased to the point where Gen. William Irvine and Andrew Elliot, the first U.S. surveyor general, decided to lay out the town of Erie. The state legislature also recognized the dynamic growth of the region when, on March 12, 1800, they elevated the status of the land near Lake Erie to that of a county. The town of Erie continued to expand in territory and population, and in 1851 it was designated a city.[18]

Few counties in Pennsylvania contained a network of Underground Railroad stations and routes as intricate as that in Erie County. There were several reasons for this. Erie was the final area in western Pennsylvania from which fugitives could depart for Canada; five different Indian trails over which runaways could travel converged here; a well-developed road system existed; and there were numerous towns and dedicated agents willing to assist escapees on their journey north.

INDIAN TRAILS

The five Indian trails crisscrossing the county were there well before the arrival of the French. The westernmost trail of this group was the Conneaut Path. It had its beginnings at Meadville and ended in the town of Conneaut, Ohio. In between these two sites, it passed through or by several towns with Underground Railroad stations. After leaving Meadville, runaways proceeded along this path about eight miles westward to the town of Harmonsburg.

From there they turned almost due north, passed by the community of Conneautville, and went to Albion. Both of these towns had stations. At Albion, which was also an Underground Railroad depot, the fugitive headed northeast along the trail to a final destination in Conneaut, Ohio.[19] For those who left Meadville with the intention of going to Ohio, this was a major thoroughfare.

The Brokenstraw Path was the easternmost of the five paths, linking Warren with old Fort LeBoeuf, which became the town of Waterford. On this trail, the fugitive went through the towns of Corry and Union City,[20] which, along with Waterford, had Underground Railroad stations.

The Venango Path connected Meadville in Crawford County with Waterford in Erie County. Two branches of the Venango Path left Meadville, one running along French Creek and the other paralleling it a few miles to the east, both terminating in Waterford. Fugitives could follow either one over the twenty miles that separated the two towns.[21]

The Presque Isle Portage was an extension of the Venango Path that covered the fifteen miles between Lake Erie and French Creek near Waterford.[22] This was an alternative route for runaways heading north from Waterford toward Lake Erie.

The Lake Shore Path ran northeast-southwest along the Lake Erie shoreline from Sandusky, Ohio, to Buffalo, New York. The city of Erie lay in the middle of the path.[23] From Erie, escapees could follow this trail in either direction to reach sanctuary.

ROADWAYS

A network of roads also linked the many small communities in the county. In 1753, the French widened the Presque Isle Portage path into a military road. Years later, it became known as the Old French Road, and modern U.S. Route 19 parallels it today.[24] In the early 1800s, a road followed the trace laid down by the Brokenstraw Path between Warren and Waterford. Eventually this road became U.S. Route 6 and linked all the counties along the northern tier of Pennsylvania.[25] Meadville and Waterford shared a road as early as 1807, and a turnpike joined Waterford to Erie in 1811. Buck states that by 1812, the whole of western Pennsylvania contained an interlocking system of roads. These roads were not the well-developed roads of today, and many of them were not much better than the Indian trails they followed, but they served to link the many settlements and towns.[26]

TOWNS AND PEOPLE

The system of escape routes that ran between the many towns in the county was quite complicated. Siebert's map shows only three pathways entering the county: one from Meadville to Girard, one from Meadville to Union City, and one from Townville to Erie.[27] Evidence found in the research of Blockson and other writers shows that there were many other escape trails as well.

Meadville–Linesville–Girard Route

Siebert has a trail beginning at Meadville, progressing westward to Linesville, and then abruptly turning north to Girard in Erie County. On the way, the trail passes by East Springfield before it reaches Girard.[28] To get from Linesville to Girard, runaways likely headed northwest along Conneaut Creek until they joined the Conneaut Path, which they followed to Albion. Here they left the path and turned north, passing within a mile of East Springfield. From here it was only four miles to Girard. Blockson identifies stations in Conneautville and Albion.[29] Siebert cites a station in East Springfield.[30] An alternative to this route was for the fugitives to go from Meadville to Linesville, and then simply cross over into Ohio a mere five miles to the west.

Once the escapees reached Girard, they would have come under the protection of Rev. Charles L. Shipman, pastor of the Universalist Church in the town and an ardent abolitionist. He was reputed to have organized the Underground Railroad route that stretched from the Ohio River to Lake Erie.[31] Girard, due to its physical location, would have been on the escape route that went east and west along the Lake Erie shore. Fugitives could have gone in either direction, but since the Ohio border was so much closer, it is safe to assume that they would have chosen to go west.

Meadville–Cambridge Springs–Albion Route

One of the escape routes fanning out from Cambridge Springs is the one that heads to the town of Albion in Erie County. To get there, travelers probably took the road that linked Meadville to Waterford. Upon reaching Cambridge Springs, approximately halfway between the two communities, they turned northwestward to Albion. After Albion, Blockson has the route go on to Girard, near the shore of Lake Erie.[32] As was the case with the Meadville–Linesville–Girard Route, from this point the runaways most likely made their way to Ohio. There was another possible route involving Albion. The old Conneaut Path traversed the town and headed off to the northwest. It ended in the Ohio town of Conneaut, only eight miles from Albion. Agents in Albion might have taken their charges to Conneaut instead of shipping them on to Girard.

Meadville–Cambridge Springs–Branchville Route

An alternate escape path involved Meadville and Cambridge Springs. This one wends its way almost due north to the community of Branchville in

McKean Township, Erie County. From Branchville, runaways apparently made their way to Girard.[33] Another possibility takes the fugitives to the town of Erie instead of Girard. The Edinboro Road ran from Edinboro, through Branchville, to Erie. It would have been easy to move the runaways over this road to the more closely situated Erie than to Girard, which was farther away and harder to reach.

Meadville–Cambridge Springs–Waterford Route

Siebert depicts another route on his map that starts at Meadville, proceeds to Union City, turns westward to Waterford, and ends in Erie.[34] Blockson has separate escape routes heading to Union City and Waterford from Cambridge Springs.[35] Instead of taking Siebert's more convoluted path, a direct route from Meadville, through Cambridge Springs, to Waterford seems more logical, as a major road connected these three locales and then went on to Erie. After leaving Waterford, fugitives following the Erie–Waterford Road would have passed through the community of Summit. Stephen C. Lee was an agent there who helped travelers on the railroad. He would have led them to their next stop, the town of Millcreek. This was a small community right outside of Erie, and runaways would have found refuge there in the homes of Giles and Hamlin Russell. It was the task of the Russells to see that their charges got into the town of Erie.[36]

Meadville–Cambridge Springs–Union City Route

Blockson has another route that emanated from Meadville–Cambridge Springs and went to Union City. In addition to this, he has an alternate route that came from Townville in Crawford County and also went to Union City.[37] Townville appears on a line of escape that Siebert drew beginning at Franklin, passing through Cooperstown, reaching Townville, and then jumping on to Erie.[38] Most likely, the actual route from Townville more closely matched the description given by Blockson than that of Siebert. The leap from Townville to Erie is just too great, considering the normal distances between stops on the railroad in Pennsylvania. Blockson's assertion that the travelers went from Townville to Waterford or to Union City before reaching Erie makes more sense.

There appear to have been multiple escape routes from Union City. Siebert's map shows divergent lines leaving that town, one going to Erie, and the other to Wattsburg. The line splits again on leaving Wattsburg. One route heads to Erie, and an alternate goes into New York.[39] Blockson states that there was a third escape pathway from Union City. Farmers in this and the Wattsburg areas hid runaways in their hay wagons and conveyed them to the community of

North East, near the shores of Lake Erie.[40] There is still another possibility. Based on the existence of stations to the east of Union City, leading to Sugar Grove in Warren County, it is highly possible that a route went in that direction.

Union City to Erie. This is the route described by Siebert on his map. Runaways departing from Union City would have needed to travel only eight miles to the northwest to reach Waterford. Once there, they would have taken the Erie–Waterford turnpike and reached the lake. This would have been a very direct route between the two points and is quite logical.

Union City to North East. Another route went from Union City to North East on the Lake Erie shore. To get there, runaways took the road that left Union City and moved on to the town of Wattsburg in Venango Township. Eventually this road became PA Route 8 and extended all the way from Pittsburgh to Erie. After staying with farmers in Wattsburg, there were two options open to the fugitives. They could go three miles to the east, enter New York, and continue their journey to Jamestown or, turning north, go on to Westfield on Lake Erie. Or they could proceed along another road leaving Wattsburg to the north (modern PA Route 89) and head for North East.

North East had several agents, of which Reed names three: Philetus Glas, Truman Tuttle, and a Dr. Smedley.[41] The nearest direct method of escape existed a short distance outside of North East, at the mouth of Sixteen Mile Creek. The creek emptied into Lake Erie at this point, and located nearby was the fishing village of Spragues Beach (Orchard Beach today).

James Crawford and John Glass were the two station masters in the village. It was their job to send the freedom seekers in small boats across the lake to Canada.[42] Glass was famous for having built the first iron foundry in Erie County. He also built a house near the beach, which was later bought by the Sprague family, after whom the village was named. The house stands at the junction of modern Route 89 and Old Lake Road.[43]

Union City to Sugar Grove. Recent research has revealed yet another line of escape emanating from Union City. This one headed eastward into Warren County through the towns of Lottsville and Sugar Grove.[44] Sugar Grove was an alternate pathway from the town of Warren to New York. The evidence now shows that a line of escape also reached the town from Erie.

The trail the runaways followed from Union City to Sugar Grove entailed traveling about twenty-seven miles, with several known stations along the way where they could have gotten assistance. Upon leaving Union City, there were two roads over which the fugitives could make their way.

One was the main road in that area, which went to Warren and then on to the east. This became the current U.S. Route 6. It traveled through the town of Beaver Dam in Wayne Township before entering Warren County. The town was reputed to have had an active Underground Railroad system, with William Gray as its chief agent.[45] From here the wayfarers would go to Corry on the Erie County–Warren County border. The other road from Union City took escapees to the town of Concord, in the township of the same name. Rev. T. H. Burroughs provided shelter while they stayed in Concord.[46] Leaving Concord, the next stop would have been Corry. Both Beaver Dam and Concord were equidistant from Union City.

There is some disagreement as to where the fugitives went next after leaving Corry. One source has them going off the main road to the town of Bear Lake, in Warren County near the New York border, and then to Lottsville, which was back on the road from Corry to Sugar Grove.[47] Another source has them going directly to Lottsville from Corry.[48] In either case, when they left Lottsville, and before they reached Sugar Grove, the fugitives found a safe rest stop in the home of James Carter, who lived on the road between these two communities.[49]

Sugar Grove was the point of departure for many fugitives trying to enter New York. Once across the border, they would head for the town of Busti and then to Canada through the New York Underground Railroad system. The activities of the railroad in Sugar Grove were well documented by two of its citizens, Richard B. Miller and his wife, Cynthia Catlin Miller, who kept diaries of their work as agents on the Underground Railroad in their community. They wrote about other agents, stations, and general practices of the network. In addition to the Millers, other agents in the town included Dr. James Catlin and his wife, Dr. Martha Van Rensilaer, and Abijah Abbot.[50] Blockson's research turned up the name of another agent, William Storum.[51] Stations existed in several homes in the area. The main one flourished in the home of Richard and Cynthia Miller on Big Tree Road. Not far away was the home of Abijah Abbot, which was built in 1840 and is now called the Sherwood Home. The house had several tiny rooms hidden in the walls for the purpose of keeping runaways from detection. There was even a secret hiding place built under the bed in the Abbot bedroom. The Humphrey Pratt House on Lauder Road served as yet another station. It had a false floor under the pantry where fugitives could hide.[52]

City of Erie

Erie was a major center on the Underground Railroad in western Pennsylvania for several reasons: It was located on the shore of Lake Erie, several major roads intersected within its boundaries, and it had a large number of aboli-

The home of Daniel Dobbins in Erie, circa 1930. ERIE COUNTY HISTORICAL SOCI-
ETY & MUSEUMS, ERIE, PENNSYLVANIA

tionist sympathizers. The roots of Erie's commitment to the cause of aiding
fugitives began with the forming of the Erie Anti-Slavery Society in 1836.
Among the founders of the society were William Himrod, Alex Mehaffey,
and Aaron Kellogg, of Erie; Philetus Glas, Truman Tuttle, and Dr. Smedley, of North East; and Col. J. M. Moorhead, Samuel Low, and a Mr. Jessup, of nearby Harborcreek. Himrod was the main Underground Railroad
agent in Erie.[53]

Most of the major stations in Erie were located in the harbor area.
William Himrod built a house at the corner of French and Second Streets
shortly after the War of 1812. Later, John Dickson opened the Dickson Tavern and Inn in part of the building. Among the guests was Oliver Hazard
Perry, the hero of the Battle of Lake Erie during the War of 1812. Because of
this, the building later acquired the title of the Perry Memorial House. When
Himrod built the house, he incorporated many secret passageways within its

walls where runaways could hide. One of them opened on the waterfront, and through it, fugitives would leave the house and board boats for the trip across the lake to Canada.[54]

Daniel Dobbins also opened his home, on the northeast corner of State and Third Streets, to fugitives. Dobbins moved into the house in 1816 and opened a tavern in it. The Dobbins family occupied the house continuously until 1885.[55] The site of the house is now part of the Hamot Medical Center.

Fugitives not departing for Canada directly from the harbor in Erie traveled eastward to North East. From there they either went to Spragues Beach and took a boat across the lake or continued on to New York and Buffalo. After leaving Erie, in their journey toward North East, runaways found shelter in the town of Wesleyville, where the belfry of the local Methodist Episcopal church on Buffalo Road offered a hiding place.[56] After Wesleyville, the next stop was Harborcreek. Here they got aid from the Moorhead, Low, and Jessup families.[57] From Harborcreek, the journey to North East was a short one.

Siebert lists a few additional Erie County agents: Frank Henry, a Dr. Judson, Jehiel Towner, James Reeder, and Job Reeder.[58]

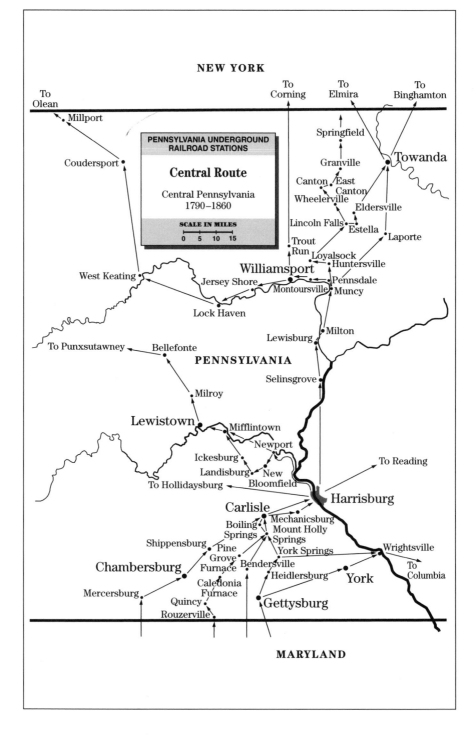

NEW YORK

To Olean

To Corning

To Elmira

To Binghamton

Millport

PENNSYLVANIA UNDERGROUND RAILROAD STATIONS

Central Route

Central Pennsylvania
1790–1860

SCALE IN MILES

0   5   10   15

Coudersport

Springfield

Granville

Towanda

Canton   East Canton

Wheelerville

Eldersville

Lincoln Falls   Estella

Laporte

Trout Run

Loyalsock

West Keating

Williamsport

Huntersville

Jersey Shore   Pennsdale

Montoursville   Muncy

Lock Haven

Milton

Lewisburg

To Punxsutawney

Bellefonte

PENNSYLVANIA

Selinsgrove

Milroy

Lewistown

Mifflintown

Newport

Ickesburg

Landisburg   New Bloomfield

To Hollidaysburg

To Reading

Carlisle

Mechanicsburg

Harrisburg

Boiling Springs

Mount Holly Springs

Shippensburg

Pine Grove Furnace

York Springs

Wrightsville

Chambersburg

Bendersville

Heidlersburg

To Columbia

Caledonia Furnace

York

Mercersburg

Quincy

Gettysburg

Rouzerville

MARYLAND

Central Route

Pennsylvania had an Underground Railroad route that ran from Maryland to New York through the heart of the state. The Tuscarora Ridge of the Appalachian Mountains bounded the route on the west, and York County and the Susquehanna River bordered it to the east. Although this route was narrow geographically, it had four possible exitways through which an escaped slave could find freedom. One of these ran the entire length of the corridor; two veered to the west, joining the Uniontown–Indiana and Bedford–Clearfield Routes; and another turned eastward and linked with the great Eastern Route in Pennsylvania. Each of these pathways involved dozens of sites and agents.

There were four major pathways over which fugitives traveled from Maryland to the Central Route in Pennsylvania. In southern Pennsylvania, they involved the towns of Mercersburg, Rouzerville, Bendersville, and Gettysburg. Most of the routes that emanated from these towns led to Harrisburg. From Harrisburg, runaways could choose to follow escape avenues that took them to Hollidaysburg, Bellefonte, Reading, or Elmira, New York. Those choosing to go to Hollidaysburg or Bellefonte entered the Western Route of the Underground Railroad. Fugitives going to Reading got on the Eastern Route. Those deciding to follow the path to Elmira took the Central Route. From Elmira, they usually went on to Niagara and Canada.

MERCERSBURG–HARRISBURG ROUTE

This route was a mirror image of the Bedford–Clearfield Route, but on the eastern side of the Tuscarora Ridge. It began at the border where Maryland touched Fulton County, Pennsylvania. Although Siebert's map does not include this route, this area was a very desirable spot for a crossover. The dense forests that ran along both sides of the Cumberland and Shenandoah Valleys provided ample cover in which escapees could lose pursuers.[1]

The first town of any size on this route that fugitives would encounter was Mercersburg. Located only eight miles from the Maryland border, and two miles to the east of Cove Mountain on the Tuscarora Ridge, it offered sanctuary to weary travelers.[2] In addition to its proximity to Maryland, a well-traveled Indian trail passed right by it. This was the Warm Springs Path, which ran to the northeast of Hancock, Maryland, crossing the Pennsylvania line between the Two Top and Claylick Mountains. From here it followed a course eight miles northward to Mercersburg. In modern times, PA Route 75 paralleled the trail.[3]

Mercersburg was settled around 1730 and was named after Gen. Hugh Mercer, who served in the Revolutionary War.[4] The town was a key station on the Underground Railroad during the 1840s and 1850s.[5] After resting in Mercersburg, runaways continued their journey in several stages toward Harrisburg.

MERCERSBURG TO CARLISLE

The route from Mercersburg to Carlisle involved several intermediate stations. After leaving Mercersburg, escapees headed northeast to Chambersburg, most likely following the Warm Springs Indian Path. This trail heads out of Mercersburg and runs due north toward Fort Loudon. About six miles from Mercersburg, the trail intersected a more famous and more traveled trail, the Raystown Path, which ran all the way to Harrisburg, first passing by Chambersburg and Carlisle. In later times, the trail became U.S. Route 30.[6] It was twelve miles to Chambersburg from the place where the Warm Springs Path joined the Raystown Path.

Chambersburg was a sizable town and the seat of Franklin County. Originally settled and laid out by Benjamin Chambers in 1764, it lay fifty miles southwest of Harrisburg.[7] Abolitionist John Brown owned a house in the town on King Street, just east of Second Street. A black man, Harry Watson, was the Underground Railroad agent in Chambersburg.[8]

Shippensburg was the next stop for freedom seekers after leaving Chambersburg.[9] To reach Shippensburg from Chambersburg, fugitives had several options. One was to proceed the ten miles that separated the two towns on the road that linked them. This road was built in the early 1800s, and by 1803, it was developed enough to permit regular stage service with Harrisburg.[10] Another possibility was to travel by railway, which also connected the two towns. Completed in 1837, this line opened Fulton and Franklin Counties to further development.[11] A third option was to avoid these more public methods of travel and take one of two Indian trails that ran through less populated areas between the two towns, either the Raystown Path or the Virginia

The home of John Brown in Chambersburg. PHOTO BY WILLIAM J. SWITALA

Path, which originated near the town of Williamsport on the Potomac River in northern Virginia. It paralleled Conococheague Creek all the way from there to Chambersburg, and then continued northeast to Shippensburg and Carlisle, eventually ending at Harrisburg. Ultimately this trail became the foundation for modern U.S. Route 11.[12] From Shippensburg, using one of these means of travel, the fugitives continued on to Carlisle.

CARLISLE TO HARRISBURG

Carlisle was the seat of Cumberland County. Nicholas Scull, the surveyor general of the Pennsylvania colony, laid out the town in 1751 and named it after the capital of Cumberland County back in England.[13] Located only fifteen miles west of Harrisburg, it figured prominently as a storage area for munitions during the Revolutionary War. Carlisle was linked to Harrisburg by both road and rail, as well as the two Indian trails, the Raystown and Virginia Paths. Although Siebert does not include Carlisle on his map, there is sufficient evidence that an Underground Railroad station existed there. Several individuals in the town were active in helping runaways advance on their journey to freedom. Chief among these were agents Dr. John McClintock, John Peck, Richard Woods, John Morison, John Harder, and Michael Bush. Peck was a black barber in Carlisle during the 1830s. Later he moved to Pittsburgh and continued to play a role in the Underground Railroad.[14] McClintock was the most famous of the group. He was a professor at Dickinson College and was involved in an incident that later became known as the Carlisle Riot of 1847. He and a group of abolitionists in the town tried to prevent the recapture of some escaped slaves in Carlisle. A fight broke out, and he was arrested, along with several others. Later he was acquitted, because of his position at the college. The incident made all of the newspapers.[15] Research also shows that the Shiloh Baptist Church in the town was a refuge for fugitives.[16]

Carlisle was also the destination for another escape route that began at the towns of Rouzerville and Quincy on the Maryland border and passed through Boiling Springs, just south of Carlisle.[17]

Runaways leaving Carlisle went to Harrisburg, either directly or stopping first at Mechanicsburg, which was situated halfway between Carlisle and Harrisburg.[18] A stopover at Mechanicsburg offered two advantages: It would provide additional rest for weary or ill travelers before reaching Harrisburg, and it might allow fugitives the opportunity to better avoid slave catchers, who often patrolled the road and rail line that ran between Carlisle and Harrisburg.

ROUZERVILLE–HARRISBURG ROUTE

Another escape path running from Maryland to Harrisburg began in the area where Adams and Franklin Counties of Pennsylvania border Maryland. Siebert makes no mention of it on his map, but there is evidence to support such a route. Like the Mercersburg–Harrisburg Route, this one proceeded in several stages to its ultimate destination.

ROUZERVILLE TO QUINCY

Blockson speaks of runaways crossing from Maryland and heading for Rouzerville, in Franklin County. Before they reached the town, they would receive assistance at the Shockey family farm, an active Underground Railroad station located just south of Rouzerville.[19] This was a good place to enter Pennsylvania, because an Indian trail known as the Georgetown Road cut through Nicholas Gap on the western slopes of South Mountain near the hamlet of Monterey here. From this point, the trail turned westward and headed to Rouzerville. At this town, it split into two arms, one continuing west to Waynesboro and Mercersburg, and the other running northwest to Quincy.[20]

Hiram Wertz was the agent near Rouzerville. He or a member of his family would meet the escapees and guide them to his farm eight miles to the north of

Rouzerville. The farm was near Quincy, a small hamlet about three miles to the north of the much larger Waynesboro. Wertz remained active on the Underground Railroad in the region for many years and later said that he and his family had aided forty-five to fifty fugitives on their quest for freedom.[21]

QUINCY TO BOILING SPRINGS

The next leg of the journey leading to Harrisburg began with Wertz guiding the fugitives about eight miles northward to the small black community called "Little Africa," near Caledonia Furnace, an ironworks owned by antislavery crusader Thaddeus Stevens.[22] From "Little Africa," they took a road, now PA Route 233, to the next destination, Pine Grove Furnace. Passing through this area, they encountered a wooded region, which later became known as the Michaux State Forest, and proceeded to the town of Mount Holly Springs.[23] At this point, Blockson has the trail continuing to Boiling Springs, a town situated four miles northeast of Mount Holly Springs.[24] However, Carlisle lies only six miles to the north of Mount Holly Springs, and a good road, the Holly Pike (modern PA Route 34) linked the two towns, so it would seem reasonable to assume that at least some of the runaways went directly from Mount Holly Springs to Carlisle.

BOILING SPRINGS TO HARRISBURG

While in Boiling Springs, some of the fugitives stayed at the Bucher Hill mansion, built in 1776 and located at 108 Bucher Hill in the town. The house was an Underground Railroad station, where escaped slaves hid in a secret chamber above a large closet in the main bedroom of the home.[25] Others went to an area called Island Grove, where Daniel Kaufman and his friends Stephen Weakley, Philip Brechbill, and Karl Mode Griggith gave them shelter and assistance.[26]

Once the fugitives left Boiling Springs, they had two possible escape routes, one leading to Carlisle and from there to Harrisburg, and the other proceeding northeast to Greenwood, near Harrisburg, and from there to the city.[27]

BENDERSVILLE–HARRISBURG ROUTE

Like the fugitives on the Rouzerville–Harrisburg escape path, who entered Pennsylvania after traveling from Maryland along the western slopes of South Mountain, there is evidence that some escapees proceeded along the eastern slopes of this same mountain into Pennsylvania.[28] At a spot opposite the town of Bendersville, they descended from the mountain and sought help there. Bendersville is approximately twelve miles north of Gettysburg. Because no Indian trails or roads ran in this direction, it would seem that this path was a secondary route and not used by many. Bendersville is only a mile from the main road that linked Gettysburg to Mount Holly Springs. Once runaways left Bendersville, it is almost certain that they took this road to Mount Holly Springs and then on to Harrisburg.

GETTYSBURG–HARRISBURG ROUTE

The fourth major line of march on the Central Route crossed from Maryland into Pennsylvania just south of Gettysburg. This is the only escape system on the Central Route that Siebert includes on his map.[29]

THE BORDER TO GETTYSBURG

Smedley states that Gettysburg was one of the most active stations nearest Maryland. He further elaborates that once fugitives reached the town, half were sent to Harrisburg, via the Central Route, and the other half went to Columbia, via the Eastern Route.[30] Escaped slaves left the counties of Frederick, Carroll, Washington, and Harford in Maryland and found their way to Adams and York Counties in Pennsylvania. Once they crossed the state line, Smedley states that "many Quakers and Abolitionists" were waiting to help them.[31] Blockson says that in addition to the Quakers, free blacks and Mennonites also provided aid and comfort to the freedom seekers.[32]

Most of the escapees, upon crossing the border, made their way to a mill on Rock Creek operated by James McAllister. The mill lay between Cumberland and Mount Joy townships, about five miles from Gettysburg. A black woman named Meg Palm guided them at this point. Her nickname was "Maggie Bluecoat." She got this title because she always wore a War of 1812 blue officer's coat. Once at the mill, McAllister hid them under the floorboards. Between 1850 and 1858, he aided about 100 runaways in this manner.[33] After they stayed with McAllister for a brief period, he saw to their transportation to Gettysburg.

GETTYSBURG

James Gettys laid out the town named after him in 1790. Later it became the Adams County seat.[34] Smedley cites several individuals as active on the Underground Railroad in the town, the key agent being a black man named Hamilton Everett. Thaddeus Stevens, the famous lawyer, state legislator, and

The law offices of Thaddeus Stevens in Gettysburg. PHOTO BY WILLIAM J. SWITALA

congressman from Gettysburg, is also listed as an agent.[35] Stevens was a member of a colonization society for slaves in 1835, a member in the Pennsylvania Anti-Slavery Society in 1836, and by 1837 was an outspoken critic of slavery and an agent on the Underground Railroad. He often defended fugitive slaves in the courts of Adams County. As a legislator, he worked hard to eliminate the institution of slavery through the passage of abolitionist-inspired laws.[36] He also opened his ironworks at Caledonia Furnace to runaways. Smedley says that a number of the faculty members at Gettysburg College and Theological Seminary secretly aided fugitives.[37] Blockson expands on the list of agents with the names Benjamin Walker, A. Heberling, and

This inn was the home of Mathew Dobbin in Gettysburg. It was a major station in the town. PHOTO BY WILLIAM J. SWITALA

William Wright and says Henry Butler was the most famous conductor in the area, guiding the fugitives from the town. He also states that the Bethel A.M.E. Church and the home of Mathew Dobbin were active stations in the town.[38]

GETTYSBURG TO HARRISBURG

Opinions vary among the sources as to where the fugitives went after they left Gettysburg. It appears that most of them went to Harrisburg by various escape trails. A few, however, went to the city of York, and from there to Columbia in Lancaster County and the Eastern Route, as depicted on Siebert's map.[39]

Gettysburg to York Springs

Underground Railroad conductors in Gettysburg frequently took runaways, hidden in wagons, toward Harrisburg on the Old Harrisburg Road (modern Route 15). About ten miles from Gettysburg, they came to the town of Heidlersburg, where William Piper, a black resident, assisted them. It is reported that Piper took many of his guests directly to Carlisle from Heidlersburg.[40] This was a journey of at least eighteen miles, more than could be covered in a single night. The more logical destination would have been York Springs, as Smedley has in his work.[41] Perhaps the direct trip to Carlisle was taken because slave catchers were in pursuit or were blocking the road to York Springs.

Fugitives arriving in York Springs found a well-organized Underground Railroad network. Smedley states that the town was second only to Gettysburg in importance for the Underground Railroad in Adams County. He names William and Phebe Wright and Phebe's brother William Wierman as the main agents in York Springs.[42] In addition, another relative, Isaac Wierman, the magistrate of Latimore Township, the site of York Springs, helped the Wrights and provided some official clout to their efforts.[43]

Farms South of Gettysburg to York Springs

Some escaped slaves crossed into Pennsylvania and found aid on the Wertz and Scheffer farms, just south of Gettysburg. Evidence suggests that members of these families guided their charges northward along White Run to Shriver's Mill, thus avoiding the town of Gettysburg. From the mill, they proceeded to Latimore Township and went to the Wrights in York Springs.[44]

York Springs to Harrisburg or Wrightsville

There are three possible avenues of escape from York Springs. Only one of these appears in a documented source, however. The other two are based on logical deductions.

York Springs to Wrightsville. Smedley has the Wrights taking their fugitives all the way to Wrightsville.[45] This was the site of a ferry and, later, a bridge that crossed the Susquehanna River to the town of Columbia and the great Eastern Route of the Underground Railroad. However, Wrightsville lay thirty miles to the east of York Springs, and the road system between the two sites was less developed. Though some runaways may have taken this route, two other possibilities are more logical.

York Springs to Mount Holly Springs. Mount Holly Springs is only seven miles to the northwest of York Springs. A good road connected the two, and only a single night's journey would have been required. A well-organized escape network existed in Mount Holly Springs, and it seems likely that some fugitives would have gone in this direction.

York Springs to Harrisburg. Harrisburg lies about as far from York Springs as does Wrightsville. A well-established thoroughfare, the Old Harrisburg Road, connects the two towns. Harrisburg was also a major center on the Underground Railroad and a spot through which the majority of the travelers on the Central Route passed. These factors would have made it very attractive to fugitives leaving York Springs, and there is a good possibility that some of them went there.

HARRISBURG NETWORK

The hub of the Central Route of the Underground Railroad in Pennsylvania was the city of Harrisburg. Originally settled in the early eighteenth century by John Harris, the site quickly grew from a trading post and ferry landing to a town by 1785. John Harris, Jr., laid out the town around the settlement his father had begun. Called Harris' Ferry at first, the town received its new name of Harrisburg in 1791. In 1812, it became the state capital. Located on the eastern bank of the Susquehanna River, the town became a center for the canal and railroad transportation in Pennsylvania.[46]

Blacks were living in Harrisburg and Dauphin County as early as 1790. In the federal census of that year, 59 free blacks and 210 slaves are listed for the county.[47] By the census of 1860, the number of blacks had risen to 1,709 out of a total of 45,047 for Dauphin County. Of these, all were free; there were no more slaves in the county.[48] The first black church there, the Wesley Union Church, opened its doors in 1829. Affiliated with the African Methodist Episcopal Church, it was located at the corner of Third and Mulberry Streets. In 1836, the Harrisburg Anti-Slavery Society began, with many black residents as members. Most of the black population lived in the city's Sixth and Eighth Wards.[49]

A Slave Commission office opened in Harrisburg after the passage of the Fugitive Slave Act of 1850. Its commissioner was Richard McAllister, a local attorney. He and his deputies became notorious for seizing blacks, both fugitives and free, and sending them south to be resold into bondage. Eventually, McAllister was forced to resign because of the scandal surrounding him and his operations. The Slave Commission office closed in 1853, and bias against blacks in Harrisburg began to abate.[50]

Harrisburg was a strategic hub on the Underground Railroad system for several reasons. First of all, the large black population in the city provided a ready source of aid to escaped slaves. The Wesley Church played a major role in this effort. William Jones, a black doctor and teamster, hid fugitives in his home on South Street. Likewise, George Custer and his wife used their restaurant at 305 Chestnut Street as a refuge for runaways. Blockson adds other names to the list of agents in the city, including Joseph Bustill, a schoolteacher and the grandson of Cyrus Bustill, the black baker who took bread to Washington's troops when they wintered over at Valley Forge; Harriet McClintock Marshall, who hid runaways in her home near Front and Calder Streets; and Dr. William Rutherford and his neighbor Wilson Kelker, who hid escapees in their homes on South Front Street or in a barn in Paxtang. Blockson also says that the local Bethel A.M.E. Church and the Presbyterian church in Harrisburg were active stations.[51]

A second reason for Harrisburg's prominence on the Underground Railroad was the existence of several possible escape routes leading into and emanating from the city and the various means of transportation for traveling over them. Major roads linked Harrisburg with Chambersburg, Carlisle, Gettysburg, and Columbia. A stage line connected the city with Lancaster and Philadelphia.[52] A major Indian trail, the Paxtang Path, left the city and ran along the banks of the Susquehanna River all the way to Shamokin (modern Sunbury).[53] The Susquehanna and Juniata Rivers provided escape routes for those heading north and northwest, and the Pennsylvania Canal joined Harrisburg to the Juniata River in 1832, thus providing yet another possibility.[54] Railroads linked Harrisburg with points to the west, east, and north. By the 1850s, the city had rail connections with Philadelphia, Reading, Pittsburgh, and Elmira, New York.[55] Because of all these options, four major exit routes emerged by which fugitive slaves could reach freedom.

HARRISBURG TO HOLLIDAYSBURG

William Still, in his recollections of the Underground Railroad, states that an escape route ran from Philadelphia, through Harrisburg, to Hollidaysburg. From here, Still says the route turned northward.[56] The only passageway between Harrisburg and Hollidaysburg at that time was the Pennsylvania Canal, which, by 1832, extended from Philadelphia to the mouth of the Juniata River, just fifteen miles north of Harrisburg. In November of that same year, the section connecting Hollidaysburg to the mouth of the Juniata was completed. This produced a continuous waterway covering the 142 miles between the two towns.[57] It took the typical canal barge about two days to complete the journey over this section of the canal.[58]

Once fugitives reached Hollidaysburg, they received assistance from one of several people there. Daniel Williams and his family opened the doors of their home, the Russ family hid them in their home on Union Street, and Rev. James Graham, pastor of the A.M.E. Zion Church, also offered refuge.[59] Leaving Hollidaysburg, runaways would have entered the Western Route network and gone to western New York or across Lake Erie to Canada.

HARRISBURG TO BELLEFONTE

McKnight, in *A Pioneer History of Jefferson County,* makes reference to an escape pathway that began in Baltimore and eventually passed through Harrisburg, Bellefonte, and Punxsutawney to Erie.[60] The trail from Punxsutawney to Erie was one of the branches of the Uniontown–Indiana Route. The challenge with McKnight's assertion is to explain how the runaways got from Harrisburg to Bellefonte.

A number of towns between Harrisburg and Bellefonte had Underground Railroad stations. The most logical line of march between these two places was to leave Harrisburg and proceed for fifteen miles along the eastern bank of the Susquehanna, following the Paxtang Path, to the mouth of the Juniata River. From here, fugitives could travel up the Juniata, through Perry County, to the small town of Newport. Blockson says that there was a station here, as well as in several other towns in the general area. A review of his positioning of stations suggests two possible avenues for fugitives to follow. One was to backtrack to the southwest through New Bloomfield and Landisburg, each having a station, and then turn northward through Ickesburg to Mifflintown. Blockson says that this route contained less important stations. Perhaps it was a secondary route used when a problem existed on the primary one, which ran more directly from Newport to Mifflintown.

Each of the towns on the route from Mifflintown onward had agents and stations to assist runaways. Mifflintown had a black agent named Samuel Imes, who would guide the fugitives to the next stop, Lewistown, on the Juniata River. Once there, he would entrust his charges to Rev. William Grimes, an itinerant black preacher and Underground Railroad agent. Grimes would take them along as he rode on his preaching circuit. The circuit ended at the town of Milroy, about seven miles from Lewistown. In Milroy, Rev. James Nourse, pastor of the Milroy Presbyterian Church, took them into his home. Nourse had formed the Milroy Anti-Slavery Society and was an ardent abolitionist. Helping him in Milroy were Dr. Samuel Maclay, John Taylor, and Samuel Thompson. These agents guided the runaways from Milroy to Bellefonte over the Seven Mountains. Blockson also mentions a woman named Esther Fellows, of nearby Wellsborough, as well as two black conductors, Samuel Molston and Philp Roderis, as helping the cause in Milroy.[61] The trail that they took from Milroy to Bellefonte most likely was the Kishacoquillas Indian Path. This old trail ran over the Seven Mountains and linked the two towns.[62] From Bellefonte, the trail to freedom led to Punxsutawney and the Western Route of the Underground Railroad in Pennsylvania.

HARRISBURG TO READING

A third avenue to safety went from Harrisburg to Reading. Siebert talks about the practice of sending fugitives to Reading via the Reading and Philadelphia Railroad.[63] This rail line linked the two cities in the 1850s. William Still supports this contention when he cites two coded letters that he received from Joseph C. Bustill in Harrisburg. The terms "packages" and "hams" were code words for fugitives, and "Reading Road" meant the Reading and Philadelphia Railroad. Once in Reading, the escapees would have entered the Eastern Route.

> HARRISBURG, March 24, '56
>
> FRIEND STILL:—I suppose ere this you have seen those five large and three small packages I sent by way of Reading, consisting of three men and women and children. They arrived here this morning at 8½ o'clock and left twenty minutes past three. You will please send me any information likely to prove interesting in relation to them.
>
> Lately I have formed a Society here, called the Fugitive Aid Society. This is our first case, and I hope it will prove entirely successful.
>
> When you write, please inform me what signs or symbols you make use of in your despatches, and any other information in relation to operations of the Underground Rail Road.
>
> Our reason for sending by the Reading Road, was to gain time; it is expected the owners will be in town this afternoon, and by this Road we gained five hours' time, which is a matter of much importance, and we may have occassion to use it sometimes in future. In great haste,
>
> Yours with great respect,
>
> JOS. C. BUSTILL

> HARRISBURG, May 31st, 1856.
>
> WM. STILL, N. 5th St.:—I have sent via at two o'clock four large and two small hams.
>
> JOS. C. BUSTILL[64]

HARRISBURG TO ELMIRA, NEW YORK

Siebert describes a route stretching from Harrisburg all the way to Elmira, New York. He states that escapees traveled this route from Harrisburg, through Williamsport, to Elmira via the Northern Central Railroad.[65] William Still, most likely Siebert's source for his assertion, mentions this manner of escape when he refers to a letter he received from G. S. Nelson of Reading dated May 27, 1857. In the letter, Nelson informs Still that he had sent his "charges" to Elmira, New York, via Harrisburg and the railroad.[66]

Rail travel was not the only method open to runaways for reaching New York from Harrisburg. There is evidence of Underground Railroad activity and stations all the way up the Susquehanna River valley. Blockson's research shows that there were a number of stations scattered throughout the counties in this

The Governor Snyder Mansion in Selinsgrove. PHOTO BY MICHAEL J. SWITALA

direction. An ample number of Indian trails, roads, and waterways existed in this same area that fugitives could have used in their quest for freedom.

Harrisburg to Muncy

Fugitives leaving Harrisburg could have followed the Paxtang Indian Path northward along the east bank of the Susquehanna River all the way to old Shamokin (modern Sunbury). From this town, an extension of the Paxtang Path continued north to Muncy.[67] Local tradition has stations at Selinsgrove, Lewisburg, and Milton along this particular route.[68] The station in Selinsgrove was located in the mansion of former Pennsylvania governor Simon Snyder. The basement of the mansion had a tunnel in which runaways hid. The tunnel also extended some 350 feet to a house built on the banks of the Susquehanna. Escaped slaves could enter or depart via the tunnel.[69] The mansion still stands today and is located at 121 North Market Street in downtown Selinsgrove. The upstairs portion of the mansion is now a gift shop, and the basement area, where the tunnel existed, is a brewpub. The tunnel is now covered by a new floor.

Several stations were located in Lewisburg. The house built by Professor George R. Bliss of Bucknell University at 63 University Avenue is cited as a station. Bliss, along with Professors Thomas F. Curtis and Howard Malcolm, are credited with having opened an Underground Railroad depot in Lewis-burg. At the Bliss house, fugitives were secreted in the carriage house built on the property.[70] Oral tradition cites two other homes in the town as having hidden runaways. The house at 27 South Water Street, built by Robert Irwin in 1791, had a small area under the floor of the kitchen where fugitives were purportedly hidden. Another home, at 17 Market Street, built in 1857 by Jonathan Nesbit, had a crawl space above the bedroom in which runaways hid while passing through the town.[71]

Muncy was an old town founded in 1797 and named after the Munsee Indians.[72] Two black residents of the town, Henry Harris and John Warner, were conductors here. Many runaways stayed at the McCarty-Wertman house in the town itself. Built in 1779, the house had a large cellar in which fugitives hid.[73] Upon leaving Muncy, escapees had two options: head west to Williamsport or go east and to the town of Towanda. In either case, they would have eventually reached New York.

Muncy to New York via Williamsport

Williamsport lies about twenty miles to the west of Muncy. The most likely route between the two towns was through the hamlets of Pennsdale and Montoursville, which were situated on the Susquehanna and were a single night's journey apart. Blockson has a route that follows this line of march. He

The carriage house at the Bliss Home in Lewisburg. PHOTO BY WILLIAM J. SWITALA JR.

says that Montoursville had a large fugitive slave community that aided run-aways. Pennsdale also had an identified station called "The House of Many Stairs." This particular house had a number of false stairways to mislead slave catchers. One of the stairways did lead, however, to a secret room in the attic in which runaways could hide.[74]

The next stopover on this route was Williamsport. The town had a thriv-ing Underground Railroad organization, and many of the runaways who reached it did so by traveling, hidden, in one of the lumber barges operated by Daniel Hughes. He would pick them up in Muncy, or even farther south, and hide them as he made his way up the Susquehanna. After arriving in Williamsport, Hughes or a member of his family would conduct them to the next stop. Another key agent in the town was Robert Faries, superintendent of the Williamsport and Elmira Railroad. Hiding fugitives in baggage cars, he helped hundreds of escaped slaves reach New York on his railroad. Other agents in Williamsport included Joseph M. Grafius, David and Philip Rodrich, Thomas Undegraff, and his son Abraham.[75] Three choices lay open to run-aways as they left Williamsport: They could go east to Towanda; head directly to Corning, New York; or go to Olean, New York, via Coudersport, Pennsylvania.

Williamsport to Towanda. Runaways could have headed due north from Williamsport on the Tioga Path Indian trail, guided by a member of the Hughes family.[76] About ten miles from Williamsport, the Tioga Path inter-sected the Sheshquin Path. This trail ran all the way from Trout Run to a point just southwest of Towanda in Bradford County.[77] Because of its prox-imity to New York and its seclusion in the forested area of the North Branch of the Susquehanna River, Towanda was an ideal jumping-off station from Pennsylvania. The escapees had a short journey from Towanda to either Elmira or Binghamton, New York.

Williamsport to Corning, New York. Fugitives leaving Williamsport on the Tioga Path also had another option. They could have stayed on this trail and gone the 50 miles it ran through Tioga County, until they reached the New York state line.[78] Near the border with New York, they received help from the Perkins family, who hid runaways in a false chimney.[79] From here the escaped slaves would cross the state line and make their way to the town of Corning.

Williamsport to Coudersport. A third possible line of escape was to take the road that followed the trace of the old Indian trail known as the Great Shamokin Path from Williamsport, through Jersey Shore, to Lock Haven. At Lock Haven, fugitives then took the Sinnemahoning Path westward along the banks of the West Branch of the Susquehanna River. This trail traversed the northern bank of the river to West Keating. At this point, it turned northward, passing near Coudersport and continuing on through Ceres Township, in McKean County, to Olean, New York.[80] Blockson has identified a number of Underground Railroad stations along this route, in Jersey Shore, Lock Haven, West Keating, Coudersport, and Millport. Millport was the stop after Coudersport and was on the New York–Pennsylvania border. In Coudersport, John S. Mann hid escapees in his home. John's brother, Joseph, and his business partner, Rodney Nichols, aided fugitives who reached Millport. Sometimes runaways left Coudersport and went through Ceres Township, in the northwest corner of McKean County, instead of going to Millport. From here they crossed into New York. Aiding them along this route were Nelson Clark, Ephraim Bishop, LeRoy Allen, and John King.[81]

Muncy to New York via Towanda

Some fugitives did not go to Williamsport from Muncy, but headed in a northeasterly direction to Towanda. They could have done this following one of two Indian paths.

Muncy to Towanda via the Genesee Road. One Indian trail that ran from Muncy to Towanda was called the Towanda Path. It was also known as the Genesee Road and was well traveled in the early 1800s. The road ran through Huntersville and near Loyalsock, Elk Creek, Lincoln Falls, Estella, and Eldersville to Towanda.[82] In Huntersville, the agent was Abraham Webster. In Lincoln Falls Nelson Pardoe aided runaways. At times, he took them hidden in his hay wagon all the way to Towanda. Those not going directly to Towanda followed an alternate route from Lincoln Falls northward to Wheelerville, where Samuel Ruebens opened his farm to runaways. The next leg of the journey took fugitives through Canton, East Canton, Granville, Springfield, and finally, across the state line to New York.[83]

Muncy to Towanda via the Wyalusing Path. The Wyalusing Path was another trail between Muncy and Towanda. This trail ran from Muncy, through the town of Laporte, to Sugar Run. From here it turned northward to Towanda and on into New York.[84]

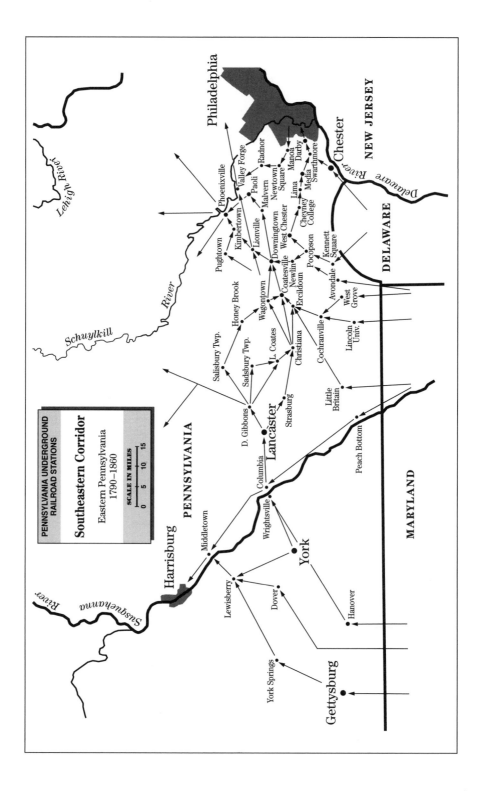

PENNSYLVANIA UNDERGROUND
RAILROAD STATIONS

Southeastern Corridor

Eastern Pennsylvania
1790–1860

SCALE IN MILES

0 5 10 15

Southeastern Corridor

Many slaves escaping from bondage fled the South through the states of Maryland and Delaware. Their goal was to reach the free state of Pennsylvania and the Underground Railroad system, which would eventually take them all the way to Canada, either through New York or New England. The majority of these escapees entered the southeastern corridor of the state, which consisted of York, Lancaster, Chester, and Delaware Counties. These counties were part of the third large Underground Railroad system in Pennsylvania, the Eastern Route. This route channeled fugitives to the east and the northeast, and finally to Canada. Each of the counties had complex Underground Railroad networks and many active agents.

YORK COUNTY

The traffic of escaped slaves through York County was especially heavy between 1820 and 1850. Even the celebrated Harriet Tubman brought runaways through the county.[1] Research shows that York had four escape routes, all leading to Lancaster County. Two were extensions of routes that began in Adams County, and two originated in Maryland.

GETTYSBURG TO COLUMBIA

Siebert's map shows a route that runs from Gettysburg, in Adams County, through the city of York, to Wrightsville on the Susquehanna River. Here the route crosses the river and enters Lancaster County at the town of Columbia.[2] Journeying from Gettysburg to York, runaways may have used the Lincoln Highway to travel from Chambersburg to Gettysburg, York, and Columbia. Built in the early 1800s, this road was the major highway linking Philadelphia with the counties of southeastern and southern Pennsylvania.[3]

Once fugitives entered York on this path, they encountered a fairly large Underground Railroad operation. Smedley lists Joel Fisher, Samuel Willis, and

William Goodrich as key agents in the city. Goodrich was a wealthy man of mixed racial ancestry who facilitated the passage of escapees to Columbia. He arranged with a black teamster named Cato Jourdon to carry them, concealed in his wagon, across the bridge over the Susquehanna River to Columbia. The system in York also received help from a powerful local politician, William Yokum, the city's main constable. When sending messages to one another concerning Underground Railroad business, the agents in York used code words such as "baggage" for fugitives and "William Penn" in place of an agent's name.[4]

Blockson expands on Smedley's description of the network in York. He says that Goodrich was a barber and a businessman who used his home on Philadelphia Street as a safe haven, hiding fugitives in a special trench with a roof of straw which he had constructed in his backyard. Blockson also mentions that there was a section of York where black residents lived, called Crotie's Row, and many runaways found refuge there. He adds another agent to the list originally given by Smedley—Amos Griest, who lived on Market Street near Penn—and two other black agents who helped conduct runaways across the Susquehanna River to Columbia, Thomas Bessich and Robert Loney.[5]

Although Columbia is often mentioned as the destination for fugitives leaving York, there actually were two escape routes emanating from the city. Smedley says that one of these went to Lewisberry, a small town about twelve miles north of York, and only two miles from the Susquehanna. Unfortunately, Smedley does not tell us where the runaways went from there.[6]

Blockson helps clear up the mystery, saying that the agent in Lewisberry, Dr. Webster Lewis, sent them either to Boiling Springs, on the Central Route, or to Middletown on the eastern bank of the Susquehanna River.[7] Blockson does not say where the fugitives went from Middletown. Since the town is located between Harrisburg and Lancaster, it is logical to assume that they went to one of these two places. Harrisburg is closer to Middletown than is Lancaster, so the majority likely went there. The second route from York proceeded east to Wrightsville and then to Columbia. Wrightsville is only eleven miles east of York, and Cato Jourdon would have traveled there from Columbia to carry runaways across the river to safety.[8]

YORK SPRINGS TO COLUMBIA

York Springs was second in importance only to Gettysburg as a station on the Underground Railroad in Adams County. Two major escape routes went from the town to either Carlisle or Harrisburg. Smedley mentions a third route, however. William Wright or his brother-in-law, Joel Wierman, took fugitives from York Springs to Wrightsville. From here they crossed the river to Columbia and Lancaster County.[9]

HANOVER TO COLUMBIA

Escaped slaves entering York County directly from Maryland did so at two locations. One of these was just south of Hanover. Meeting the runaways as they went over the state line were members of the Durr, Kyle, and Bradley families, who then guided them to Hanover.[10] Col. Richard McAllister originally founded this town, and it was called McAllister until 1755, when the name of the town was officially changed to Hanover by the state government in order to please the German settlers who lived there.[11] Upon arriving at Hanover, the escapees were met by and received aid from Jacob Wirt, who conducted them, after allowing them to rest for a while, to the next stop on the escape route, Columbia.[12] How Wirt got the fugitives from Hanover to Columbia is not described in any of the sources. One possibility is that he made use of the road that followed the trace of the Monocacy Indian Trail, an old footpath that led from Hanover to York, and from there to Wrightsville and on to Columbia.[13]

DOVER TO MIDDLETOWN

The final Underground Railroad route through York County ran from Dover to Middletown. This route most likely followed a branch of the Monocacy Path from Maryland to the vicinity of New Oxford. Near this town, runaways then went along the banks of Conewago Creek all the way to Dover.[14]

Dr. Robert Lewis was the agent in Dover, and he saw to the care of runaways reaching him at his home there. Lewis sent escapees to his father, Dr. Webster Lewis, in Lewisberry, who then forwarded them to either Boiling Springs or Middletown.[15]

LANCASTER COUNTY

The complexity of the Underground Railroad network and the number of stations and agents increased in Lancaster County. Though many stations and agents are listed in the sources, the links between them are tenuous or, in some cases, completely absent. Establishing the exact locations for stations is made even more difficult because most of them were on farms or in townships, and not towns. Although Siebert's map offers some assistance, it does not record all of the sites which are mentioned in the source material. What follows is an attempt to provide connections among the many sites found in the various sources.

MIDDLETOWN TO HARRISBURG OR COLUMBIA

Middletown is a site with no exit described in the sources. It is likely that most of the runaways reaching the town would have gone on to Harrisburg. The city is only ten miles to the north of Middletown and, because of its position on the Central Route, would have been very attractive to fugitives. A single night's journey over the major highway that ran from Harrisburg to Columbia, and passed near Middletown, would have taken escapees to the city.

The other possible option for runaways was to take the road from Harrisburg south to Columbia. This was also a famous Underground Railroad site, but it lay over twenty miles to the south—the wrong direction for escaping slaves. Runaways may have taken the Columbia route when the road to Harrisburg was blocked by slave catchers.

COLUMBIA TO LANCASTER AND STRASBURG
OR TO THE DANIEL GIBBONS HOME

Columbia was ideally located as an Underground Railroad station. Situated on the eastern bank of the Susquehanna, it was only twelve miles northwest of Lancaster. The town was originally known as Wright's Ferry, because of the ferry operated there by John Wright, but its name was changed to Columbia when Samuel Wright, John's grandson, officially laid out the town in 1787.[16] The inhabitants of the town built bridges over the Susquehanna in 1812 and in 1834 to facilitate traffic with Wrightsville, and a railroad connected Columbia with Philadelphia in 1834. This line passed through Lancaster.[17] Major roads connected Columbia with Lancaster to the southeast, and with Middletown and Harrisburg to the northeast.[18]

Columbia was also an ideal stopping place on the Underground Railroad because of the number of townspeople who acted as agents and conductors. The northeastern section of the town had a large black population, who provided a ready source of protection for escapees. The town also had many Quakers, most of whom were sympathetic to the cause and freely aided runaways passing through the town.[19]

Whenever Cato Jourdon or one of the other conductors brought fugitives to Columbia, they were cared for by a number of people. William Whipper was among the first of the townsfolk to offer help. His home was strategically located near the end of the bridge from Wrightsville.[20] He and a partner,

Stephen Smith, ran a lumber business in Columbia. They were quite successful at this and regularly sent lumber to buyers in Philadelphia. They often hid
fugitives in the false end of a special boxcar carrying their products. In this
manner, the escaped slaves reached Philadelphia and the waiting hands of
William Still.[21]

In his recollections of the Underground Railroad in Philadelphia, Still says
that at times Whipper sent fugitives all the way to Pittsburgh hidden on a
boat.[22] This was likely via the Pennsylvania Canal, the only waterway stretching from Columbia to Pittsburgh over which a boat, or actually a barge, could
travel. Whipper toured the East, speaking out against slavery. In the 1830s, he
believed that if blacks improved their moral condition through temperance,
hard work, education, and religion, white prejudice would disapper.[23] By the
1850s, he had changed his mind and concluded that racism was ingrained and
instinctive in whites.[24] Two other key agents in Columbia were Samuel W.
Mifflin and William Wright, according to Smedley.[25]

Columbia to Lancaster and Strasburg

Siebert does not have a route leading from Columbia directly to Lancaster or to
Strasburg on his map. He does have one that passes near Lancaster but does
not stop there. It was likely that both localities had stations, however.

Lancaster had two direct connections with Columbia: a major road and a
rail line. The fugitives hidden in Whipper's special boxcar would have stopped
in Lancaster on their way to Philadelphia. Since the journey to Philadelphia
was lengthy, it is possible that agents in Lancaster gave the runaways on the
boxcar additional provisions during their stop there. Using the road, the journey between Columbia and Lancaster could have been made in a single night.
Therefore, it is reasonable to assume that fugitives would have chosen to proceed in this direction from Columbia, since it quickly led to the major portion
of the Eastern Route. Smedley does make a brief reference to Lancaster's
involvement in a route, saying that an escape line ran from Columbia, through
Lancaster, to northern Chester County.[26]

Smedley also describes two Underground Railroad stations that lay to the
south and east. One was in Lampeter Township, which bordered Lancaster to
the south and was the home of Lewis Peart in the 1830s and early 1840s. Peart
was an active agent in the township during that time, and he helped many
escapees continue on their journey to the east. Peart moved to a farm near Valley Forge in 1844 and was active in the escape network in Chester County.

The other station was in the town of Strasburg, which is only ten miles
southeast of Lancaster. Dr. J. K. Eshleman was the leading Underground Rail-

road sympathizer here.[27] Strasburg was situated between Lancaster and the most famous Underground Railroad site in Lancaster County, Christiana. Fugitives could have easily gone from Columbia to Lancaster in one night and from there to Strasburg in a second night, passing through Lampeter Township, and continuing on to Christiana during a third night's journey.

Columbia to the Daniel Gibbons Home

Siebert's map shows a clear Underground Railroad line going from Columbia to the home of Daniel Gibbons. This route is amply documented in other sources as well. Daniel Gibbons appears many times in discussions of escape routes on the great Eastern Route. One major escape route reached his home, and several exited from it. He and his wife, Hannah, were ardent Quaker abolitionists and legendary in their work for the cause. Assisting them in their efforts was their son, Dr. Joseph Gibbons. The Gibbons family lived only six miles east of Lancaster, and their home was on an old turnpike that connected the city with Reading to the northeast.[28]

Siebert's map depicts five escape avenues leading from the Gibbons home: to Reading; northeast to the Speakman home in northern Chester County; eastward to the Bonsall homestead, also in Chester County; southeast to Lindley Coates, who lived in Sadsbury Township, Lancaster County; and to Thomas Whitson in Bart Township, and from there to Christiana, on the border between Lancaster and Chester Counties. Siebert links the route going from Gibbons to Coates with Thomas Whitson and with Joseph Fulton in Chester County.[29] Smedley adds that Coates sometimes sent his "visitors" to James Williams, Mordecai Hays, Emmor Kimber, and others in Chester County.[30]

Smedley includes an alternate to the Gibbons route. This may have been put into use when the Gibbons home was being too closely watched by slave catchers. Smedley says that at times, fugitives coming from Columbia went to the home of Joshua Brinton in Salisbury Township instead. He does not say where escapees went from the Brinton home.[31] It is possible that they went to either Lindley Coates or Thomas Whitson. Salisbury Township, where Brinton lived, is between the Gibbons home and those of Coates and Whitson. That they should go to one of these two well-known stations on an established route seems logical.

HAVRE DE GRACE TO CHRISTIANA

Smedley describes an avenue of escape beginning in Havre de Grace, Maryland, and going directly into Lancaster County. The path followed the

Susquehanna River northward, using it as a guide.[32] Blockson says runaways crossed into Lancaster County at the mouth of Octoraro Creek, near which an agent named William Brown operated a station.[33] From here they headed northward to the home of agent John Russell, Joseph Smith, or Oliver Furniss. Russell and Smith lived in Drumore Township, on the eastern banks of the Susquehanna, and Furniss lived in the town of Little Britain. Russell forwarded escapees on to Henry Bushong, who lived nine miles away in Bart Township; Smith sent them to Thomas Whitson or to Joseph and Caleb Hood, who also resided in Bart Township.[34] Furniss also sent some fugitives to Henry Bushong, but others he forwarded directly to the town of Ercildoun in Chester County.[35] The Hoods conveyed runaways to Jeremiah Cooper in Sadsbury Township, who sent them to Christiana.[36]

Christiana was a stopover for many escaped slaves heading into Chester County. Jeremiah Moore, the leading agent in the town, hid escapees in a furniture wagon he owned. He had a trusted black teamster drive the wagon, with its hidden cargo, to James Fulton in Ercildoun. This was a journey of only eight miles to the east.[37] Assisting in the effort to transport fugitives from Christiana to Ercildoun were two Mennonites, Christian Frantz and Dr. Augustus W. Cain.[38]

PEACH BOTTOM TO COLUMBIA

Blockson discusses a second route that ran directly from Havre de Grace, Maryland, into Lancaster County. Instead of turning eastward from the Susquehanna at the mouth of Octoraro Creek, it continued following the river to Peach Bottom, which was primarily a boat landing and not much of a town. A black conductor met runaways there and guided them along the river northward to Columbia.[39] From Columbia, they took one of the escape routes discussed above.

CHESTER COUNTY

No other county in Pennsylvania had as complex a system of Underground Railroad escape routes as that of Chester County. There were dozens of stations and agents, and the county, though not large in size, contained many routes and subroutes. Fugitives entered the county from York and Lancaster Counties, as well as directly from Maryland and Delaware. Leaving the county, runaways headed to Berks, Delaware, and Montgomery Counties, and to Philadelphia.

Perhaps the finest eyewitness account of how fugitives moved through Chester County is found in a letter written by Dr. Edwin Fussell to a friend. In the letter, Fussell describes many of the practices used by agents and conductors to convey fugitives through the county. He also paints a poignant picture of the hardships runaways faced on this journey. The following excerpts from that letter detail some of those practices:

MEDIA 2d Mo. 26th, 1880

DEAR FRIEND: I will endeavor to give a few of the facts in relation to the operations of the Underground Railroad in Chester county, so as they fell within my knowledge. Although I am a Chester county man by birth, I only lived in that county for a few years of the time when the Underground Railroad was in full operation, but knew of its workings in the West and also in Philadelphia. . . . The trains on this remarkable road nearly always ran in the night, and its success was owing to the darkness, the guidance of the North Star and the earnest souls of the men and women who loved freedom, and who recognized the rights of every man to be free, and the duty of every one "to remember those in bonds as bound to them." . . . The movements were almost always made in the night, and the fugitives were taken from one station to another by wagon and sometimes on foot; they consisted of old men and young, women, children, and nursing babes. Sometimes they came singly, sometimes by the dozen. In the middle of the night there came a low knock on the door, a window was raised softly— "Who is there?" a low, well known voice in reply—"How many?" The matter is soon arranged. Hidden away in garrets, barn, cellar, or bedroom during the next day, (or sometimes many days) and then on an auspicious night forwarded to the next station. Clothing is changed where possible, fetters removed when necessary; wounds are dressed, hungry bodies fed; weary limbs are rested, fainting hearts strengthened and then up again and away for Canada. . . . One noteworthy peculiarity of these fugitive parties was that the babies never cried. Was it that slave mothers had no time to attend to infantile wants and the children found that it did not "pay" to cry, or did the timid mothers teach their little ones to tremble and be still in horrible fear as do the mother partridges impress their young with dread of the hawk as soon as they are out of the shell?

This is a large subject, and a thousandth part of its miseries and heartbreaks can never be written, but, thanks to the Father of the poor, the horror is dead, the bloodhound is no longer on the track, the Underground Railroad is no more.

EDWIN FUSSELL[40]

Smedley speaks of three major systems of escape paths traversing the county: the Northern Route, which came from Columbia and proceeded across the northern edge of the county to Elijah Pennypacker's in Phoenixville; the Central Route, which ran from Delaware and Maryland and coursed through the center of the county to Phoenixville; and the Eastern Route, which also began in Delaware and Maryland but passed through Kennett and Williston Townships to Phoenixville or Philadelphia.[41]

NORTHERN ROUTE

Smedley describes this route as beginning in York County, going to Columbia, in Lancaster County, and extending across northern Chester County to Phoenixville. He attributes the creation of this route to William Wright. Fugitives would leave Wright's home and proceed to Christiana, cross over into Chester County, and make their way to Ercildoun, where they would stay with Gideon Pierce or James Fulton, Jr.[42]

Smedley also has fugitives leaving Lancaster County and entering northern Chester County from Joshua Brinton's home in Salisbury Township and from Lindley Coates's home in Sadsbury Township. From Brinton's, fugitives went to Thomas Bonsall in the town of Wagontown; from Coates's, they made their way to Joseph Fulton in Sadsbury Township, Chester County.[43] From these entry points, the Northern Route proceeded in two branches to Elijah Pennypacker's in Phoenixville.

Wagontown to Phoenixville

This branch of the Northern Route began at the home of Thomas Bonsall in Wagontown, West Caln Township. Smedley says that he forwarded his charges either to John Vickers, who lived near Lionville, or to Gravner Marsh in Caln Township. Both stations were about eleven miles from Bonsall's. If slave catchers were guarding the access to either of these two places, fugitives could be taken to an alternate safe house in the home of Abraham Bonsall, who lived in Valley Township, about halfway between Wagontown and Caln Township. Abraham Bonsall was Thomas's father.[44]

Caln Township had a large Quaker population that provided many willing helpers in the effort to move escaped slaves eastward to freedom. The leading agents in the township were Gravner and Hannah Marsh. Their home in Caln was only five miles west of Downingtown. Their daughter transported fugitives over these five miles and went from Downingtown, via a turnpike, to either John Vickers or Allen Wills in Uwchlan Township. Assisting in this effort was Dr. J. K. Eshleman and Zebulon Thomas, both of whom lived in Downingtown. Eshleman was active as an agent in Lancaster

County. In 1848, he relocated to Downingtown and continued to participate in the Underground Railroad.

In addition to the Marsh family, Seymour C. Williamson operated an alternate station in the township. Runaways came to him from Thomas Hambleton in Penn Township and from James Fulton in Ercildoun. Williamson conveyed his "visitors" to William and Micajah Speakman, who lived in Uwchlan Township and sent the fugitives on to Thomas Lewis in Berks County or to Benjamin Schofield, Richard Janney, or a Dr. Fell in Bucks County.[45]

John Vickers was legendary on the Underground Railroad circuit. His home near Lionville in Uwchlan Township was the destination of numerous routes from all over Chester County. He was a Quaker, and his father, Thomas Vickers, had instilled strong antislavery sentiments in John. The elder Vickers was one of the charter members of the Pennsylvania Anti-Slavery Society.[46] John, in partnership with Mahlan Brosius, operated a pottery plant near Lionville. They used an old pottery kiln there as a hiding place for escaped slaves.[47] From the plant, Vickers sent them in one of several directions. Some he conveyed in a carriage southeast the thirty miles to Philadelphia. Others he sent northeast to the home of Esther Lewis in West Vincent Township or southeast to William Trimble in West Whiteland Township. A backup station in Lionville was run by Charles Moore. Smedley says that Moore handled the overflow whenever a large number of runaways arrived at Vickers's plant.[48]

Esther Lewis's station was a family affair, with her daughters, Grace Anna, Mary, and Elizabeth, aiding in the endeavor. One of the special services that runaways received at the Lewis home was medical attention. Esther and her daughters always nursed ailing escapees back to health before sending them on to the next station. Esther's husband, John, also an ardent opponent of slavery, had died in 1824 while caring for two black neighbors suffering from typhoid fever. John also contracted the disease and died. After Esther's death in 1848, Grace Anna assumed the leadership of the station. The Lewis family took their charges either to Elijah Pennypacker, in Phoenixville, or to Lewis Peart, near Valley Forge.[49]

Fugitives leaving the Lewis house and bound for Pennypacker's passed through the town of Kimberton, where agent Emmor Kimber operated a boarding school for girls, which he used as an Underground Railroad station. Aiding him in his work were his daughters, Abigail and Gertrude, both of whom became active, in their own rights, in the Chester County network. Another Kimberton agent was Norris Maris, who lived on a farm just outside of town and often hosted runaways coming from the Lewis station. With the help of a neighbor, John A. Groff, he took them to Pennypacker in Phoenixville or, at times, to Peart in Valley Forge.[50] Blockson identifies Emmor Hunter as another person who assisted Maris in the transfer of escapees. Blockson also states that on some occasions, Maris took fugitives directly to Pottstown or Limerick in Montgomery County.[51]

Fugitives who reached Lewis Peart near Valley Forge were then conveyed in one of two directions. Some went to Norristown, in Montgomery County, and others traveled to Charles Adamson, in Schuylkill Township, Chester County. From the Adamson home, they crossed the county line and entered Montgomery County.[52]

The station run by Elijah F. Pennypacker in Phoenixville was the destination for the majority of fugitives passing through the Chester County network. A Quaker and a supporter of the abolitionist movement, Pennypacker was a critical member of the Underground Railroad in the county. He had served in the state legislature from 1831 to 1836 and was the secretary of the Pennsylvania Canal Board from 1836 to 1838. In 1840, he became a member of the Society of Friends, the religion of his wife, Hannah, and in 1842, he became a minister in that faith.[53] A well-known businessman in Phoenixville, he and Hannah owned a drugstore there.[54]

Escaped slaves came to Pennypacker from each of the three routes that traversed Chester County. He usually arranged for their movement across the Schuylkill River to Norristown, in Montgomery County, although on occasion, he forwarded escapees to Philadelphia, Reading, or Quakertown. He sent fugitives into Montgomery County in several ways, taking some in wagons across the Phoenixville bridge or the bridge at Pauling's, and transporting others across the river in canoes at Port Providence.[55] The following brief letter from Pennypacker to William Still shows that he sent fugitives to Norristown and Philadelphia:

SCHUYLKILL, 11th mo., 7th day, 1857

WM. STILL:—*Respectd Friend*—There are three colored friends at my house now, who will reach the city by the Phil. & Reading train this evening. Please meet them.

Thine, &c, E. F. PENNYPACKER

We have within the past 2 mos. passed 43 through our hands, transported most of them to Norristown in our own conveyance.

E.F.P.[56]

Sadsbury and Ercildoun to Phoenixville

Though some fugitives entered the Northern Route through Chester County at Wagontown, the majority of escapees came through Sadsbury Township or the town of Ercildoun. The leading agent in Sadsbury was Joseph Fulton. He had become an abolitionist as a young man and subscribed to all of the leading antislavery newspapers in the East. He and his family received runaways from Thomas Whitson, Lindley Coates, and Daniel Gibbons, in York and Lancaster Counties. Once they arrived at Fulton's, he usually hid them in the hayloft of his barn. His daughter, Mary Ann, would take food to them after dark. Everything was done in great secrecy, as he was always watched by his proslavery neighbors.

Fulton took his guests to Edwin Coates and Michael Meyers in Coatesville. Moses Whitson, a surveyor and civil engineer in the township, frequently aided him in this activity. Whitson often would employ runaways temporarily in his surveying work. Coates and Meyers saw to it that the runaways got to Downingtown, after a brief stay at the home of Thomas Hopkins, who lived near the town.[57]

Ercildoun was another Chester town often mentioned as a destination for escaped slaves entering southeastern Pennsylvania. Gideon Pierce and James Fulton, Jr., were the major agents in the town. They were neighbors and often collaborated in assisting runaways. Smedley says that Pierce and Fulton took escapees to Nathan Evans in Williston.[58] Though this may have been their ultimate goal, such a long and direct journey would have been highly improbable. It would have meant taking fugitive slaves completely across a county in which slave catchers were very active. A more likely scenario is that they sent them to Coatesville, and from there to Downingtown and the remainder of the Northern Route.

Blockson identifies an alternate route proceeding from Downingtown to Phoenixville rather than going to John Vickers in Lionville. Instead, some runaways went eastward to Malvern, where they turned northeast and proceeded to Paoli and then to Phoenixville.[59] They probably took this route when the normal avenue was blocked.

CENTRAL ROUTE

A second Underground Railroad route began in Maryland and Delaware, ran through the center of Chester County, and ultimately linked with the Northern Route. This pathway had four entry points into the county—three from Maryland and one from Delaware. Two of the three from Maryland converged on Cochranville, and the other went to Avondale. The route from Delaware ran to Kennett Township.

Lower Oxford Township to Ercildoun

One of the two escape paths that crossed into Pennsylvania from Maryland did so in East Nottingham Township, Chester County. This pathway was most active between 1855 and 1862. After entering the township, it ran north for about six miles to Lower Oxford Township. Here escapees found assistance either at the home of Charles Hambleton or at Lincoln University, where the faculty and students hid fugitives on campus.[60] From either of these two stations, the route continued on to Cochranville. Levi Coates had a station near the town.[61] Coates took the runaways another six miles northeast to Ercildoun. Here the fugitives entered the Northern Route.

The second route from Maryland to Cochranville had its origin at Havre de Grace. It led fugitives across the state line into Penn Township, where they went to the homes of Eli or Thomas Hambleton, the brothers of Charles Hambleton, or to a station run by Benjamin and Hannah Kent. Other escapees went to a station in the town of West Grove, in London Grove Township, which bordered Penn. Here Mahlon and Amos Preston and William Jackson aided the travelers.[62] From these various stations, fugitives were guided to Cochranville and then to Ercildoun.

Avondale to Pughtown

The third route coming from Maryland had its origin at the home of Elisha Tyson in Baltimore. Runaways leaving Tyson's home traveled north into Chester County and proceeded through London Britain Township to Avondale. This small town overlaps the borders of London Grove and New Garden Townships and is two miles directly east of West Grove, another Underground Railroad site. Jacob Lindley was the agent in Avondale, and he was responsible for transporting the fugitives to the home of Philip and Benjamin Price, in East Bradford Township. The Prices, in turn, took them in one of three directions. They took some to Abraham Bonsall in Valley Township, and then north to Isaiah Kirk, who lived near Pughtown in East Vincent Township on the Northern Route.[63] They took others northeast to Valley Forge, and still others to Darby in Delaware County.

Kennett Township to Downingtown

The final trace of the Central Route, which ran through Chester, began in Wilmington, Delaware. This route is mentioned in the following letter that Grace Anna Lewis wrote to William Still:

KIMBERTON, October 28th, 1855

ESTEEMED FRIEND:–This evening a company of eleven friends reached here, having left their homes on the night of the 26th inst. They came into Wilmington, about ten o'clock in the morning of the 27th, and left there, in the town, their two carriages, drawn by two horses. They went to Thomas Garrett's by open day-light and from thence were sent hastily onward for fear of pursuit. They reached Longwood meeting-house in the evening, at which place a Fair Circle had convened, and stayed a while in the meeting, then, after remaining all night with one of the Kennet friends, they were brought to Downingtown early in the morning, and from thence, by daylight, to within a short distance of this place.

They come from New Chestertown, within five miles of the place from which the nine lately forwarded came, and left behind them a colored woman who knew of their intended flight and of their intention of passing through Wilmington and leaving their horses and carriages there.

I have been thus particular in my statement because the case seems to us one of unusual danger. We have separated the company for the present, sending a mother and five children, two of them quite small, in one direction, and a husband and wife and three lads in another, until I could write to you and get advice if you have any to give, as to the best method of forwarding them, and assistance pecuniarily, in getting them to Canada. The mother and children we have sent off of the usual route, and to a place where I do not think they can remain many days.

We shall await hearing from you. H. Kimber will be in the city on third day, the 30th, and any thing left at 408 Green Street directed to his care, will meet with prompt attention.

Please give me again the direction of Hiram Wilson and the friend in Elmira, Mr. Jones, I think. If you have heard from any of the nine since their safe arrival, please let us know when you write.

Very Repectfully, G. A. Lewis[64]

As this route came over the Pennsylvania border, it first entered Kennett Township. Thomas Garret, in Wilmington, sent most of the runaways coming from his station on this pathway. The township had a number of stations located among its largely Quaker inhabitants. Refuge was readily found at the homes of Allen and Maria Agnew, Isaac and Dinah Mendenhall, and John and Hannah Cox.[65]

The Cox home was in Longwood, and it was one of the first stations runaways approached on entering Chester. Usually a black conductor, named Jackson, brought them there from Wilmington. On arriving at the Cox home, Jackson would rap loudly three times on the fence post. John or Hannah would call out, "Who's there?" Jackson's coded reply was "Friends." At that word, the Cox family would admit and care for the travelers.[66]

The Mendenhalls also lived near Longwood. Their home was a scant ten miles from Wilmington. They estimated that they received several hundred runaways over the years their station was in operation. One of their neighbors was the illustrious Harriet Tubman. The Mendenhalls usually forwarded their charges to John Vickers or the Barnard family via the Central Route. On occasion, however, they sent some to John Jackson in Darby, Delaware County, or to Philadelphia. The Agnews, as well as Anne Preston and Samuel Pennock of the township, also helped escapees and forwarded them northward on the Central Route.[67]

The journey from the homes of these agents began by passing through the town of Kennett Square, which, founded in 1686 by Francis Smith, rested in the northwest corner of Kennett Township and was only twelve miles from Wilmington.[68]

The town was the home of Dr. Bartholomew Fussell. Born in 1794, Dr. Fussell grew up in Chester County. As a young man, he taught slaves how to read in a Sunday school he ran in Maryland. Later, he returned to Chester and opened a medical practice. Because of his antislavery sentiments, he turned his home into an Underground Railroad station. He and his wife, Lydia, welcomed many runaways on their journey to freedom. Being a personal friend of Thomas Garrett, Dr. Fussell established a direct escape link with Wilmington. In the late 1830s, he moved to West Vincent Township. After Lydia died in 1838, he married Rebecca C. Hewes and moved to York County, where he opened a school. No matter where he lived, however, he was always active on the Underground Railroad.[69] Blockson says that a black agent named James Walker also operated a station from his home on South Union Street in Kennett Square.[70]

There were four escape routes from Kennett Township, leading to East Marlborough, West Marlborough, Newlin, and Pocopson Townships. The branch to East Marlborough led to the home of Levi B. Ward. Ward then guided escapees to Pocopson Township. Those going to West Marlborough received assistance from James N. Taylor. From here runaways were guided north to Newlin Township. Some fugitives leaving Kennett Township went directly to Newlin Township, which was quite active in the Underground

Railroad. The Barnard, Hayes, and Meredith families were agents in the township, and they aided hundreds of runaways on their journeys. The Barnards, Simon and Sarah, transported escapees in their large two-horse wagon, which they called the "Black Maria," to either Downingtown or West Chester. Mordecai and Esther Hayes also provided shelter for fugitives; their son Jacob often took them to Dr. Eshleman in Downingtown. Isaac and Thamazine Meredith operated a station from their home, which was located in a remote, secluded part of the township; They also took fugitives to Downingtown.[71] Other escapees went directly from Kennett Township to Pocopson Township, where William Barnard and his brother and sister-in-law, Eusebius and Sarah P. Barnard, kept safe havens for runaways. Frequently they hid fugitives in their Dearborn carriage and drove them the six miles northward to the home of William Sugar, in West Bradford Township, who then took them to Dr. Eshleman in Downington.[72]

EASTERN ROUTE

Smedley mentions a third route going through Chester County, which was an alternate to the other two routes. This one ran along the eastern edge of the county. Like the Central Route, it began at the borders with Maryland and Delaware and also involved the towns of Avondale and Kennett Square. The goal of this route was to reach Montgomery County or Philadelphia.

Avondale to Valley Forge

From the Price home in East Bradford Township on the Central Route, some fugitives went northeastward on the Eastern Route to Enoch Walker, who lived at Moore Hall Mill, just to the east of Valley Forge.[73] Moore Hall Mill was not far from the Montgomery County line, and it was in this direction that Walker guided his visitors.

Kennett Square to Williston

A second branch of the Eastern Route began at Kennett Square. It initially followed the same direction as the Central Route, but when it got to Pocopson Township, it proceeded to West Chester via East Bradford Township.

West Chester was an old town with an active escape network for fugitive slaves. Chandler and Hannah Darlington operated a station here. Helping them in their work were three black residents, Abraham Shadd, John Brown, and Benjamin Freeman, who conducted fugitives from West Chester to their next destination.[74] Blockson adds the name of another black conductor, John Price.[75]

The road to freedom went in two directions from West Chester. One branch went to John Vickers and the Northern Route. The other turned northeast and went to Williston Township, which bordered Montgomery County and was the home of Nathan Evans, a Quaker minister who operated a station under the greatest scrutiny of his antiabolitionist neighbors. In spite of constant harassment, Evans continued to aid those who passed through his station. He took his guests either to Elijah Pennypacker in Phoenixville or to William Still in Philadelphia.[76]

DELAWARE COUNTY

The Underground Railroad system in Delaware County was much less complicated than the one in Chester County. Essentially, fugitives came into the county from four places: East Bradford and Williston, in Chester County; Delaware; and Philadelphia. The sources give evidence of four escape routes traversing the county: East Bradford to Darby, Williston to Darby, Chester to Newton Square, and Philadelphia to Phoenixville.

EAST BRADFORD TO DARBY

Philip Price and his son Benjamin, who ran a station in East Bradford Township, Chester County, forwarded runaways to numerous agents, among them John Sellers and John Jackson, both in the town of Darby, Delaware County. Smedley says that Price sent fugitives to his cousins Philip, Isaac, and Samuel Garrett in Delaware County as well, but he does not identify specifically where they lived. Smedley also has the Mendenhalls in Longwood sending some of their guests to John Jackson in Darby.[77] Siebert's map shows just such a route coming from East Bradford and going across the center of Delaware County to Darby.[78]

The journey from East Bradford or Longwood to Darby would have been a long one, and it is likely that several stops were made along the way. Blockson identifies other Underground Railroad stations in the county. An examination of these stations shows a likely line of march. The town of Cheyney was the nearest to East Bradford. Here Blockson says that a house on the corner of Cheyney and Creek Roads was a station and that Cheyney College was a site. Faculty and students there hid runaways on the campus. From Cheyney, the route most likely went to the town of Lima, where the Honeycomb A.M.E. Church was an active station. Leaving Lima, fugitives probably passed through stations in the towns of Media, Wallingford, Rose

Valley, and Swarthmore, where large populations of Quakers aided runaways on their journey. After Swarthmore, it was but a short trip to Darby and the homes of Sellers and Jackson. From Darby, the fugitives were conveyed to Philadelphia.[79]

WILLISTON TO DARBY

Siebert's map depicts a second route emanating from Chester County and proceeding through Delaware County. It starts at the home of Nathan Evans in Williston and crosses Delaware County, through Marple Township, to Darby.[80] Smedley relates that Nathan Evans asked James Lewis, a currier and tanner in Marple Township, to establish an "intermediate station" there on the way to Darby. Lewis did so, and James T. Dannaker agreed to become the conductor who led runaways from Marple to Darby and then to Philadelphia.[81] Blockson also mentions Underground Railroad activity in Marple Township, saying that there was a station in the A.M.E. Church there.[82]

CHESTER TO NEWTON SQUARE

Blockson speaks of a route that led from the city of Chester, on the Pennsylvania-Delaware border, through Delaware County, to the town of Newton Square. Fugitives crossing from Delaware to Chester were met and aided by Joseph Schimer, who owned a cotton mill and regularly kept fugitives there. Hiding escaped slaves in bales of cotton, he shipped them northward to Newton Square, where they received help from David and Taamar Pratt. The Pratts owned and operated the Wagon Inn, which was on the southwest corner of Newton Street and Gochen Road. Blockson does not describe where the route went from here, but it likely went to Radnor, less than five miles away, where the home of the Amport family, at the corner of County Line and Gulph Roads, was a station.[83] Radnor bordered Montgomery County and was on the way to Phoenixville, making it a logical stopping place for a route leading out of Delaware County.

PHILADELPHIA TO PHOENIXVILLE

The main escape route in Delaware County, according to Blockson, proceeded along the West Chester Pike from Philadelphia to the home of Elijah Pennypacker, in Phoenixville. This route made use of intermediate stations in Upper Darby, Manoa, Broomall, and Newton Square. In Upper Darby, fugitives stayed at the Howard family home, on the northwest corner of

West Chester Pike and Pennock Avenue, or at the Black Bear Inn, run by Abraham Pennock, son-in-law of Darby's John Sellers.[84] Leaving Upper Darby, the escape path took fugitives through Manoa and Broomall to Newton Square, from where runaways likely continued to Radnor and then on to Phoenixville.

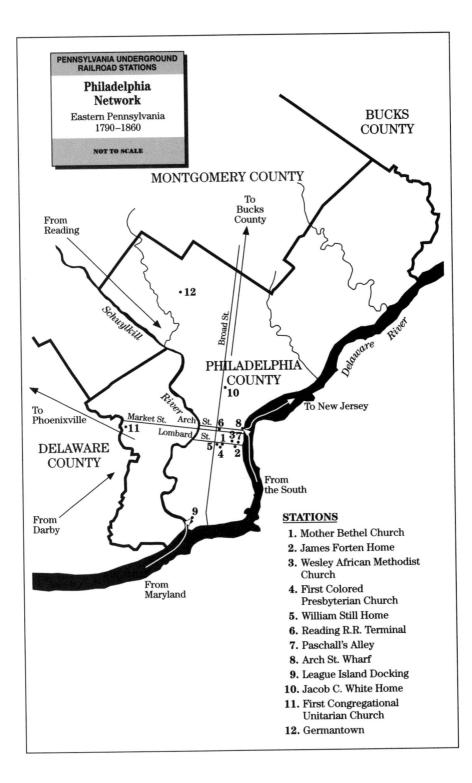

PENNSYLVANIA UNDERGROUND RAILROAD STATIONS

Philadelphia Network

Eastern Pennsylvania
1790–1860

NOT TO SCALE

BUCKS COUNTY

MONTGOMERY COUNTY

To Bucks County

From Reading

•12

Schuylkill

Broad St.

Delaware River

PHILADELPHIA COUNTY

•10

To New Jersey

To Phoenixville
•11

River

Market St. Arch St. 6   8
Lombard St. 1 3 7
5 •   • •
4 2

DELAWARE COUNTY

From the South

From Darby

9

From Maryland

STATIONS
1. Mother Bethel Church
2. James Forten Home
3. Wesley African Methodist Church
4. First Colored Presbyterian Church
5. William Still Home
6. Reading R.R. Terminal
7. Paschall's Alley
8. Arch St. Wharf
9. League Island Docking
10. Jacob C. White Home
11. First Congregational Unitarian Church
12. Germantown

Philadelphia
Network

Philadelphia was at a pivotal point on the Eastern Route of the Underground Railroad in Pennsylvania. Fugitives coming from the South arrived there over land and sea routes. In addition, many of the routes of the Southeastern Corridor converged on the city. It was also a dispersal center from which fugitives were sent northward to New York City and the towns of New England. Within the city itself, slaves had been escaping their masters on a regular basis since the mid-1700s. Without Philadelphia, the Eastern Route network would not have been as successful as it was.

Philadelphia was one of the older cities in the American colonies. Laid out by William Penn in 1683, it was the place where some of the greatest events in early American history took place. During the Revolutionary War and the early national period, the city was host to the Continental Congress, which signed the Declaration of Independence in 1776; the convention that ratified the United States Constitution in 1787; and the first capital of the country under the Constitution in 1790.[1]

The political, economic, and cultural center of the colonies, Philadelphia's population grew rapidly from 24,000 in 1765 to 70,000 in 1800. Among those living there were people from northern Europe, Africa, and the West Indies. English, German, Scots-Irish, Irish, and refugees from France and Haiti flocked to this city with its reputation for religious and political tolerance.[2] Clement Biddle gives one of the earliest descriptions of the city in *The Philadelphia Directory,* published in 1791:

> The ground plot of the city is an oblong square, about one mile North and two miles East and West, lying in the narrowest part of the isthmus between the Delaware and Schuylkill Rivers about five miles in a right line above the confluence.[3]

Biddle gives a picture of the rich religious diversity of the city, listing many churches, meetinghouses, and a synagogue with active congregations there. He says that the Quakers openly aided the black inhabitants of Philadelphia by operating a free school for blacks of all ages and sexes, both free and slave.[4] Conspicuously absent from Biddle's list is the African Methodist Episcopal Church, the church founded by Richard Allen in Philadelphia to address the religious needs of the black community, which were not being met by the other organized churches. By 1816, this church had grown prodigiously.[5] Biddle's oversight is attributed to the fact that this church did not really begin to operate until shortly after he had completed his work.

Blacks made their appearance in Philadelphia very early in its history. In 1639, a few Africans were slaves to the Swedish, Finnish, and Dutch settlers along the Delaware River Valley.[6] In 1684, the ship *Isabella* landed in Philadelphia with a cargo that included 150 African slaves. The Quakers purchased them to help clear the land in and around the city. Between 1682 and 1705, one in every fifteen families in the city owned slaves. After 1730, the slave trade tapered off, and indentured servants from Great Britain, Ireland, and Germany began to arrive in great numbers. After 1756, however, there was an upswing in buying African slaves again because they were cheaper to maintain than indentured servants. In 1754, 100 slaves were purchased, and that number increased to 500 in 1762. Tax assessor reports for Philadelphia show that there were 814 slaves between the ages of twelve and fifty in the city in 1767. By 1775, the estimated slave population of Philadelphia was 672 out of a total of 19,650 inhabitants.[7]

Not all of the black residents of Philadelphia were slaves, however. Records show that free blacks were living there as early as 1717. These records also show that the number of free blacks in the city stood at 150 in 1770 and 250 by 1776. The children of free blacks were attending Anglican and Quaker schools, and between 1756 and 1775, 68 free blacks were baptized into the Anglican Church.[8] By 1830, the black population had grown to 15,000, and of these, 1,000 were considered to be fairly wealthy.[9] By 1860, there were 57,000 blacks living in Pennsylvania, and 30 to 40 percent of them lived in Philadelphia.[10] The combination of a large black population, a rising wealthy middle class among these blacks, an organized social structure centered around the A.M.E. Church, and a number of sympathetic whites among several of the churches in the city produced a climate in which the Underground Railroad could rise and flourish in Philadelphia.

Philadelphia was a place where slaves were fleeing their owners as early as the mid-1750s. In George Washington's April 12, 1786, letter to Robert Morris, he wrote of the escape of a slave owned by a fellow Virginian and said that Philadelphia, with antislavery Quakers living there, was not a desirable place for Southerners to visit if they were accompanied by any of their slaves.[11] A review of the court records in the late 1700s shows that Philadelphia was becoming a goal for runaways. For example, in 1795, between January 3 and September 5, there were nine cases in which fugitive slaves were apprehended and detained for reclamation by their masters. In 1791, there was one case, and in 1793, four cases.[12] Another indicator that Philadelphia was becoming a magnet for runaways may be seen in the number of advertisements for escaped slaves that appeared in the *Pennsylvania Gazette* between 1795 and 1796. There were no less than twenty ads offering rewards for the apprehension of runaways. The following is a typical example of these notices:

January 21, 1795

Twenty Dollars Reward

RAN away from the subscriber, living in Nottingham, on Patuxent river, Prince George's county, Maryland, a lively, active Mullato slave, called HARRY, who since his departure has assumed the name of FLEET. He is about 22 or 23 years of age, and 5 feet 10 inches high: has grey eyes and sandy coloured hair, which he wears turned up before, and very short and straight behind. He appears confused when spoken to, but when closely examined, much embarrassed. His cloathing cannot be particularly described, as he has been gone ever since July. By a letter from him to his father, dated the 17th of Sept. last, it appears that he was then in Philadelphia, and he says he expected to sail for London in about two months. All masters of vessels are hereby cautioned against carrying off the said slave at their peril. Whoever takes him up, and secures him in gaol, so that I get him again shall receive the above reward, and all reasonable charges for bringing him home.

MATHEW EVERSFIELD[13]

Note the warning given to masters of seagoing vessels that they should not aid runaways. This was a stock warning that appears in most of the advertisements. Each year, the number of fugitive slaves passing through the city grew. One researcher estimated that by 1860, almost 9,000 runaways had entered and departed from Philadelphia.[14]

Philadelphia's Underground Railroad developed over a period of years. It had its roots in the various antislavery societies that had formed in the late 1700s and early 1800s in the city. The earliest of these was the Independent Free African Society. Founded in 1787 by Rev. Absalom Jones and Rev. Richard Allen, it originally was designed to provide assistance to free blacks who were in economic difficulties. It soon became a source of aid for fugitive slaves and was the first attempt at an Underground Railroad system in Philadelphia.[15]

The early 1800s saw the birth of several other organizations that helped solidify an Underground Railroad presence in the city. In 1830, James Forten helped organize the Convention of Free Negroes in Philadelphia. Its goal was the abolition of slavery as an institution and the granting of full citizenship to all former slaves in the United States.[16] Another early group in the fight against slavery was the Philadelphia Female Anti-Slavery Society. Formed on December 9, 1833, by Lucretia Mott, it initially had sixty female members, both black and white, including the wife and daughters of James Forten.[17] Two years later, in August 1835, the most effective of the societies that aided runaways was formed. This was the Vigilance Committee. Its purpose was to help fugitive slaves who arrived in Philadelphia reach safety. Three of the first officers of the committee were prominent members of the affluent class of the black community: James McCoummel, president; Jacob C. White, secretary; and James Needham, treasurer.[18]

The number of runaways passing through Philadelphia became so great by the 1850s that a need arose to reorganize the Underground Railroad network there. Under the leadership of Robert Purvis and William Still, the old Vigilance Committee was reconstituted as the Philadelphia Vigilance Committee on December 9, 1852. It was to be an umbrella organization coordinating the activities of all the other antislavery groups in the attempt to aid escaped slaves. Purvis was elected as the overall chairman of the group, and Charles Wise was its first treasurer. The names of the general steering committee reflected the leading members of the abolitionist movement in the city. A special committee, called the Acting Committee, was chosen to carry on the everyday work of helping fugitives find safety in the city. It consisted of five members: chairman William Still, Nathaniel W. Depee, Jacob C. White, Passmore Williamson, and Charles Wise.[19] The homes of these individuals were already serving as stations in Philadelphia. Over its existence, the Philadelphia Vigilance Committee helped over 800 escaped slaves find freedom.[20]

The three individuals who were most instrumental in organizing and seeing to the operation of the Underground Railroad in Philadelphia were James Forten, Robert Purvis, and William Still. Forten served in the fledgling U.S. Navy during the Revolutionary War. While aboard ship, he became adept at repairing sails. When the war ended, Forten opened a sail repair business near the docks in Philadelphia. His business grew, and in a short time, he became the wealthiest black person in the city. Not content with accumulating wealth, and possessing a true social conscience, Forten spent his fortune on a variety of causes, including women's rights, temperance, peace, and equal rights for blacks.[21] He was also an ardent opponent of any attempts to send blacks back to Africa. He felt that their home was now in America.[22]

Robert Purvis was the son of a wealthy white businessman and a black mother. Although his skin color was light enough that he could pass as white, he preferred to identify with his African ancestry. He received an excellent

The house of Robert Purvis in Philadelphia. PHOTO BY KEVIN
J. SWITALA

education, graduating from Amherst College, and entered the world of business. He married the daughter of James Forten and joined his father-in-law in the fight against slavery. Purvis was instrumental in founding both the American and Pennsylvania Anti-Slavery Societies. Most of his time was spent helping run the Philadelphia Underground Railroad network.[23]

The third member of this group was William Still. Born in New Jersey, he was the son of an ex-slave father and an escaped-slave mother. He developed his hatred for slavery from the stories his mother told him about her life under bondage. In 1844, Still moved to Philadelphia, where he taught himself to read and write. When Forten and Purvis realized his talents for organization and leadership, they saw to it that Still was given a position of importance in the Underground Railroad system within the city.[24] Later, in the 1870s, Still decided to record and publish his recollections of the escape network in the city.

The Underground Railroad in Philadelphia consisted of a myriad of agents, conductors, stations, and means of transportation. The basic modes of transportation used were by rail, water, and overland. Fugitive slaves arrived daily from several different directions and in various ways. They came from the town of Darby in Delaware County, from Peart in Valley Forge, from Pennypacker in Phoenixville, from Bustill in Harrisburg, from Reading, from Garrett in Wilmington, from Baltimore by train, and from various coastal towns along the Southern seaboard in steamboats and schooners. Between 1830 and 1860, Philadelphia became a great rail center and port, especially for ships and steamboats traveling northward from the Southern states of Virginia, Maryland, and Delaware.[25]

Rail travel was used to a surprising degree to bring runaways to Philadelphia. This was the favorite way of sending fugitives to William Still in the city from Harrisburg and Reading. The following letter from Joseph Bustill in Harrisburg details how this took place:

> Harrisburg, May 26, '56
>
> Friend Still:–I embrace the opportunity presented by the visit of our friend, John F. Williams, to drop you a few lines in relation to our future operations.
>
> The Lightning Train was put on the Road on last Monday, and as the traveling season has commenced and this is the Southern route for Niagara Falls, I have concluded not to send by way of Auburn, except in cases of great danger; but hereafter we will use the Lightning Train which leaves here at 1 1/2 and arrives in your city at 5 o'clock in the morning, and I will telegraph about 5 o'clock in the afternoon, so it may reach you before you close. These four are the only ones that have come since my last. The woman has been here some time waiting for her child and her beau, which she expects here about the first of June. If possible, please keep a knowledge of her whereabouts, to enable me to inform him if he comes.
>
> *I have nothing more to send you, except that John Fiery* [a slave catcher] *has visited us again and much to his chagrin received the information of their being in Canada.*
>
> Yours as ever,
> Jos. C. Bustill[26]

The train from Harrisburg and Reading arrived in Philadelphia at the railway station located at Eleventh and Market Streets. Members of the Acting Committee of the Vigilance Society would meet them there and take them to a safe house in the city.[27] Thomas Garrett made use of the railroad that ran between Wilmington and Philadelphia to convey runaways to William Still.[28]

Frederick Douglass speaks of runaways hiding on trains that came to Philadelphia from Baltimore.[29] And William Whipper forwarded fugitives to Philadelphia hidden in special lumber-carrying boxcars from Columbia.

According to Douglass, many escapees boarded steamboats coming along the coast to Philadelphia. Sympathetic steamboat captains either hid them aboard their boats or tolerated their presence among the vessel's cargo.[30] Thomas Garrett made use of this mode of travel, as is evident from the following letter he sent to William Still:

> Wilmington, 7th mo. 19th, 1856
>
> Respected Friend, William Still:–I now have the pleasure of consigning to thy care four able-bodied human beings from North Carolina, and five from Virginia, one of which is a girl twelve or thirteen years of age—the rest all men—After thee has seen and conversed with them, thee can determine what is best to be done with them. I am assured they are such as can take good care of themselves. Elijah Pennypacker, some time since, informed me he could find employment in his neighborhood for two or three good hands. I should think that those from Carolina would be about as safe in that neighborhood as any place this side of Canada. Wishing our friends a safe trip, I remain thy sincere friend.
>
> THOS. GARRETT
>
> After conferring with Harry Craige, we have concluded to send five or six of them tonight in the (rail)cars, and the balance, if those go safe, tomorrow night, or in the steam-boat on Second day morning, directed to the Anti-Slavery office.[31]

Other runaways hid aboard schooners and oceangoing steamships that plied the coastline to Philadelphia and New England. Still tells the story of three men, James Mercer, William H. Gilliam, and John Clayton, who hid in a coal hopper of a steamer. The ship sailed from Richmond and reached Philadelphia with the three fugitives, who were barely alive by the time the ship docked. Those coming aboard schooners usually got off near League Island, at the foot of Broad Street.[32] Runaways hidden on steamships disembarked at the Arch Street wharf.[33]

Underground Railroad conductors also brought runaways overland to Philadelphia, as in the case of James T. Dannaker, who brought runaways to the city over the roads linking it with Marple Township and the town of Darby. Frederick Douglass also speaks of fugitive slaves traveling by turnpike from Baltimore to Philadelphia between 1830 and 1850.[34] Another letter from Thomas Garrett to J. Miller McKim, one of William Still's associates, describes runaways walking, and possibly taking a carriage, from Maryland to Philadelphia, in this case led by Harriet Tubman:

> Wilmington, 12 mo. 29th, 1854
>
> ESTEEMED FRIEND, J. MILLER McKIM:–We made arrangements last night, and sent away Harriet Tubman, with six men and one woman to Allen Agnew's, to be forwarded across country to the city. Harriet, and one of the men had worn their shoes off their feet, and I gave them two dollars to help fit them out, and directed a carriage to be hired at my expense, to take them out, but do not yet know the expense. I now have two more from the lowest county in Maryland, on the Peninsula, upwards of one hundred miles. I will try to get one of our trusty colored men to take them to-morrow morning to the Anti-slavery office. You can pass them on.
>
> THOMAS GARRETT[35]

These same modes of transportation were also used to move fugitives from the city. Siebert speaks of William Still sending runaways by train to Elmira, New York.[36] This escape method is supported by a letter to William Still sent by John W. Jones, an Underground Railroad agent in Elmira:

> Elmira, June 6th, 1860
>
> FRIEND WM. STILL:–All six came safe to this place. The two men came last night, about twelve o'clock; the man and woman stopped at the depot, and went east on the next train, about eighteen miles, and did not get back till to-night, so that the two men went this morning, and the four went this evening.
>
> O, old master don't cry for me,
>
> For I am going to Canada where coloured men are free.
>
> P.S. What is the news in the city? Will you tell me how many you have sent over to Canada? I would like to know. They all send their love to you. I have nothing new to tell you. We are all in good health. I see there is a law passed in Maryland not to set any slaves free. They had better get the consent of the Underground Rail Road before they passed such a thing. Good night from your friend,
>
> JOHN W. JONES[37]

Blockson's research shows that Still also sent fugitives from Philadelphia to New York City and New England via train.[38]

Ships were also employed to convey runaways from the city to safety. When James T. Dannaker brought fugitives to Philadelphia from James Lewis, he often took them to the wharf at the end of Arch Street. There he would hand them over to Captain Whildon, who would hide them aboard his vessel. The ship then sailed for Trenton and Bordentown, where the runaways would disembark.[39] Still speaks of sending many fugitives to Boston by ship.[40]

There were two main highways over which the Vigilance Committee could move slaves from Philadelphia northward. One was the West Chester Pike, by which escapees were taken from the city to Phoenixville and Elijah Pennypacker. The other was the Bethlehem Pike, built in 1763, and the major highway linking Philadelphia with the Lehigh Valley.[41] This roadway became the main way to conduct escapees northward toward New York.

A great number of agents and stations were active in Philadelphia. The majority of these tended to be in the southern section of the city, especially on or near Lombard Street. The cornerstone of the agents and stations in Philadelphia was the active participation of many churches and ministers. While this included both whites and blacks, the black ministers viewed participation in the cause as a holy crusade. Blockson states that "the most vociferous organizers of networks . . . were the churchmen. This was because many black ministers felt that organized assistance to fugitives, and the commitment that meant to freedom, challenged the prevailing religious dogma of many white churches that a truly religious man was one who was patient."[42]

At the heart of the black church involvement in Philadelphia's Underground Railroad was the First African Methodist Episcopal Church. Known as Mother Bethel, this church was founded by Richard Allen. In 1831, the first black political convention in Pennsylvania to protest slavery met in the church. Delegates to the convention, most of whom were members of the clergy, were encouraged to use their churches as sanctuaries for escaped slaves. By 1838, most of the black clergy in the state were doing just that. Rev. Walter Proctor, pastor of Mother Bethel Church, became the role model for the clergyman-agent on the Underground Railroad.[43] The other two A.M.E. churches in Philadelphia, the Zoar A.M.E. and Wesley A.M.E. Churches, also served as stations and safe havens.[44]

It was at the Wesley A.M.E. Church that the Committee of Philadelphia Blacks met on October 14, 1850, to discuss the recent passage of the Fugitive Slave Act of 1850. The group passed several resolutions. The most noteworthy of these were "to resists the law at any cost and at all hazards," and "never to refuse aid and shelter and succor to any brother or sister who escaped from the prison-house of Southern bondage."[45]

Other black churches in Philadelphia not affiliated with Mother Bethel Church also opened their doors to runaways. Rev. Stephen H. Gloucester, pastor of the Central Presbyterian Church of Color, the home church of William

The First Congregational Unitarian Church in Philadelphia. PHOTO BY KEVIN J. SWITALA

Still, used his church as a sanctuary. Rev. Daniel Scott of the Union Baptist Church did the same. The Campbell African Methodist Church in the Franklin section of the city was a station, as was the First Colored Presbyterian Church.[46]

White churches and religious groups also played a role in the Philadelphia branch of the Underground Railroad. The Society of Friends congregation in Germantown readily helped runaways. Three members of their group, Abraham L. Pennock, John Button, and Samuel Rhoads, converted their homes into safe houses for fugitives.[47] William Still singles out the work of Rev. Dr. William H. Furness, the minister at the First Congregational Unitarian Church, as being instrumental in the success of the Philadelphia network.[48]

Many nonclergy individuals also played an essential role as agents and conductors in the city. William Still, as the chairman of the Acting Committee, was by far the most important of these. He was the person who received and dispatched fugitives arriving in the city and who arranged for the sheltering and transporting of the runaways as they passed through Philadelphia. He even hid fugitives in his house on Twelfth Street.[49] James Forten and Robert Purvis also hid runaways in their homes. Purvis and his brother, Joseph, frequently used the home of their mother, Harriet Judah Purvis, on Ninth and Lombard Streets, as a refuge. Later, after they had inherited a large amount of money, they purchased a farm in Byberry, Bucks County, located about fifteen miles from Philadelphia, and used the house and barn there as a station.[50]

Many ordinary people in the city also helped in the cause. Blockson lists several people who acted as agents and conductors: Mifflin Gibbs; Isaiah C. Ware; Jacob C. White, a black barber and hairdresser who hid fugitives in his house at 100 Old York Road; William H. Johnson; John Lewton, a black chimney sweep; and Mary Myers, a black woman who owned a cake shop on Lombard Street. Apparently the entire neighborhood known as Paschall's Alley, situated between Fifth and Coates Streets, served as hosts for runaways.[51] The family of the famous Cyrus Bustill worked for the railroad. One of the more fascinating agents in Philadelphia was Henrietta Bowers Duterte, who, in 1858, became the first black female undertaker in the city. Her unique way of transporting fugitives was to hide them in caskets.[52] Another professional who aided fugitives was James McCrummel, a successful black dentist who opened his home to escapees.[53] Finally, there were two major conductors who transported dozens of fugitives to and from Philadelphia: Still speaks of the untiring efforts of Samuel D. Burris, a black man, who regularly led escaped slaves from Wilmington to Philadelphia.[54] The other was Rev. Thomas Clement Oliver, who lived in Camden, New Jersey, but made regular trips to Philadelphia. This was a cover for leading fugitives from Philadelphia to Camden, Jersey City, and at times, New York City.

NEW YORK

PENNSYLVANIA UNDERGROUND
RAILROAD STATIONS

Northeastern Corridor

Eastern Pennsylvania
1790–1860

SCALE IN MILES
0   5   10   15

Susquehanna

Friendsville

Montrose

Towanda

Sugar Run

Waverly

Carbondale

River

Dunmore

Delaware River

Milford

Wilkes-Barre

East
Stroudsburg

Stroudsburg

PENNSYLVANIA

Lehigh

River

Schuylkill

Palmerton

NEW

JERSEY

Pottsville

Easton

Bethlehem

Delaware

Bingen

River

River

Quakertown

Pine Forge

Solebury

New Hope

Schaefferstown

Reading

To Philadelphia

Telford

Doylestown

Newtown

Harrisburg

Birdsboro

Pottstown

Salford
Twp

Yardley

Joanna Furnace

Hopewell
Village

Horsham

Langhorne

Warminster

Susquehanna River

Morgantown

Phoenixville

Plymouth
Meeting

Bensalem

Bristol

Daniel Gibbons

Norristown

Philadelphia

MARYLAND

DELAWARE

Northeastern Corridor

The final phase of the Eastern Route network involved escape trails passing through the counties of Lebanon, Berks, Montgomery, Bucks, and the counties to the north of these all the way to the New York state line. While this network had dozens of stations and hundreds of agents and conductors, it was especially complex as it progressed through Montgomery and Bucks Counties. There were five major escape routes in this system.

LEBANON COUNTY ROUTE

There is evidence that an Underground Railroad route went from Lancaster County, through Lebanon County, to Harrisburg and the Central Route. While the source this is based on does not say how the runaways got to Lebanon, some conjecture can be made, based on other evidence. Daniel Gibbons, who had a station in northern Lancaster County, sent escaped slaves in many directions after they had stayed at his home. One of these routes took them into Berks County. It is entirely possible that an alternate route led fugitive slaves in a more northerly direction to Lebanon County. Blockson says that Mennonites in Heidelberg Township, Lebanon County, readily aided runaways. He cites Moses Dissinger, an evangelical preacher in Schaefferstown, Heidelberg Township, as being an Underground Railroad agent. Schaefferstown was only fifteen miles north of the Gibbons home. He also states that the Bachman family in Campbelltown opened the doors of their home to runaways.[1] Campbelltown was not more than sixteen miles west of Schaefferstown and was on the road (modern U.S. Route 322) that ran directly to Harrisburg, only thirteen miles to the west. A route from Gibbons's station, through Schaefferstown and Campbelltown, to Harrisburg would be quite logical. The distance between stations is not great, it is supported by Underground Railroad stations, and it terminates at Harrisburg, a prominent depot on the Central Route.

BERKS COUNTY ROUTE

As early as 1835, fugitives coming from Lancaster and Chester Counties made their way through Berks County seeking to escape slavery.[2] There seem to have been two escape paths through that county. One came from Lancaster County and went to Reading. From here the route continued by train to either Philadelphia or Harrisburg. The other route began at Pennypacker's in Phoenixville, bypassed Reading, and proceeded to Pottsville and the northern section of the Central Route.

LANCASTER TO READING ROUTE

Fugitives leaving the station located at the home of Joshua Brinton in Salisbury Township, Lancaster County, usually went to Thomas Bonsall in Wagontown, Chester County. Equidistant from Bonsall's home was the village of Morgantown, Berks County, and Smedley has runaways passing through Morgantown to a station kept by Joseph P. Scarlett in "Robinson" (actually Robeson) Township, also in Berks County. Joseph and his mother, Elizabeth, aided escapees journeying through this area. Smedley cites another agent in the same township, Thomas Lewis, who was also active in helping runaways.[3] Smedley, however, does not say which station the escaped slaves had come from before entering Berks County. Due to its proximity, the most obvious choice was Brinton's home.

Runaways reaching Morgantown had two possible ways of moving on to Reading. One was to take the Nanticoke Indian Path, which passed through Morgantown and extended northward to Reading.[4] This trail took them by two sites with Underground Railroad stations. The first was Joanna Furnace, an ironworks located just three miles northwest of Morgantown. Many of the workers at this plant were blacks who lived nearby in their own small community. The owner of the ironworks, Levi Smith, was sympathetic to the cause, and he and his workers often aided escapees traveling to Reading. Another four miles farther on the trail, just outside of Plowville, was a place called Fingal. The Cole family sheltered runaways there as they passed through the town.[5] From Fingal, the next destination was Reading.

An alternate route ran from Morgantown, seven miles to the northwest, to Hopewell Village. The Mount Fisby A.M.E. Church in the town was a station. Its congregation helped runaways reach their next goal, Birdsboro, just four miles northwest of Hopewell Village.[6] Leaving Birdsboro, runaways followed the Schuylkill River the remaining nine miles to Reading.

Reading had several stations and agents who assisted escaped slaves. The Bethel A.M.E. and the Washington Street Presbyterian Churches were stations here. The town constable, "Bully" Lyons, was an agent and even used his jail as an overnight rest stop for fugitives. Blockson identifies C. S. Nelson, a black man, as the key agent in Reading.[7] Once the fugitives got to Reading, they were usually placed aboard trains heading either to Philadelphia or to Elmira, New York, via Harrisburg.

POTTSTOWN TO POTTSVILLE ROUTE

The second escape path traversing Berks County ran from Pottstown, Montgomery County, to Pottsville, Schuylkill County. Blockson says that this route was secondary to the Reading route. Escapees came from Pennypacker's station to Pottstown, which had several stations. The chief local agents were John P. Rutter, Henry Potts, Jesse Ives, Joseph Neide, and John Titlow. The next stop for the runaways was Pine Forge, just across the county line in Berks. There, John P. Rutter operated a station in his home, called Manor House, and he had tunnels dug in its basement in which he could hide escapees. Upon leaving Pine Forge, the escape path tended northwest to Kirbyville, a little town about six miles north of Reading in Richmond Township. The Kirbyville Hotel was the station in the town. The attic contained a hiding place for runaways. After Kirbyville, fugitives finally came to Pottsville. From Pottsville, fugitives went on to Snyder, Northumberland, and Montour Counties on the Central Route.[8]

NORRISTOWN TO NEW YORK ROUTE

A third major escape route of the Northeastern Corridor had its origins in Norristown, Montgomery County. This county had a long history of antislavery sentiment. In 1837, a number of residents banded together to form the Montgomery County Anti-Slavery Society. In 1838, two other communities in the county, Plymouth and Horsham, also established antislavery societies. Norristown instituted its own society in 1839. As many as twenty-five of the original members of the Pennsylvania Abolition Society lived in Montgomery County.[9]

Norristown was the leading city in Montgomery County, and according to Smedley, it had an Underground Railroad station as early as 1839. Among the agents in the town, Smedley says Rev. Samuel Aaron, Isaac Roberts, John Roberts, Dr. William Corson, Daniel Ross, Thomas Read, and Dr. Jacob L. Paxson were especially active in the operation of the railroad. Paxson also served as a conductor, guiding escaped slaves to several other locations once they left Norristown.[10] Blockson adds to Smedley's list and gives a better picture of the involvement of the city populace. He states that the First Baptist Church, originally at the corner of Airy and Swede Streets, under the direction of Rev. Samuel Aaron, was very active in the Underground Railroad, and that the Zion A.M.E. Church, organized by John and Jane Lewis in 1844, was another major station. A paint shop on Church Street, between Marshall and Chestnut Streets, served as a hiding place for runaways, who hid in the basement there until it was safe to move to the next stop. Blockson singles out several black residents for their participation in the effort to convey escapees to freedom: William Lewis, John Augusta, and Benjamin Johnson. Aiding them were Daniel Ross and his wife, who lived on Green Street.[11]

Fugitives came to Norristown from two places: Pennypacker's in Phoenixville and Peart's in Valley Forge. In either case, their journey took them across the Schuylkill River into Montgomery County. On the way to Norristown, they most likely stopped at a station operated by Thomas Hopkins near Arcola. From there it was only five miles to Norristown.[12]

There is evidence that some fugitives bypassed Norristown in their journey northward and took an alternate route from Pennypacker's and Peart's to the west of Norristown through Upper Providence Township in Montgomery County, just west of Phoenixville and bordering the Schuylkill River. Blockson cites stations in the township run by Abel Fitzwater and William W. Taylor.[13] Although no direct evidence exists of this, it is possible that some runaways, when they reached Upper Providence, turned westward through Limekiln Township to Pottstown. From here they could have followed the Pottstown to Pottsville Route and gone on to New York. The majority of runaways, using this alternate route around Norristown, however, proceeded northeast to Salford Township.

NORRISTOWN TO QUAKERTOWN

The first leg in the trip to New York stretched from Norristown to Quakertown. All the sources speak of Quakertown as a major depot on the Underground Railroad. Siebert's map has a route running directly from Norristown to Quakertown.[14] However, the distance between these towns was a rather lengthy twenty-five miles and could not have been covered in a typical single night's journey. More recent research has identified several stopping places along the way that gave aid to fugitives.

To reach Quakertown from Norristown, the runaways and their conductors went along the Dekalb Pike (U.S. Route 202) northeast, until they reached the Old Bethlehem Pike (PA Route 309) just outside of Lansdale. The Old Bethlehem Pike was built in 1763 and connected Philadelphia with

Bethlehem.[15] It followed the trace of an old Indian trail known as the Minsi Path.[16] Near Lansdale, Seth Lukens had a station in his home on Forty Foot Road.[17] Leaving Lukens's station, runaways went another eight miles to the town of Telford, where they spent the night hidden in tunnels dug in the basement of Gerhart's Tavern, located at 898 Allentown Road. The tavern is still there today but is now called the Rising Sun Inn.[18] It was here that fugitives who had bypassed Norristown rejoined the main route to Quakertown. The next stop after Telford was Perkasie, six miles away.[19] A trip of only seven more miles brought the escapees to Quakertown.

QUAKERTOWN TO BETHLEHEM

Smedley speaks of Quakertown as a major depot on the Northeastern Route, emphasizing the fact that Dr. Paxson in Norristown saw to the transfer of hundreds of runaways to this town. He also states that fugitives coming from Pennypacker and Peart who bypassed Norristown also made for Quakertown.[20]

The town was so named because of the large numbers of Quakers living there. Blockson identifies Richard Moore as the leading agent in the town.[21] Moore lived at Main Street and Edgemont Road, and his home was a regular stop for escapees traveling through the area.[22]

Once the fugitives left Quakertown, some of them continued on Old Bethlehem Pike to Applebachsville, about six miles to the northeast.[23] Others went northwest through Milford Township, where they found shelter at the Brick Tavern Inn.[24] Both routes then led to Bingen, five miles south of Bethlehem. William Yeager used his home as a sanctuary for runaways coming through Bingen, and he guided them the final few miles to Bethlehem.[25]

BETHLEHEM NORTHWARD

Bethlehem was the center of Moravian culture in Pennsylvania. Blockson's research shows that the Moravians opposed slavery to the point where they would actually purchase slaves from Southern masters, emancipate them, and then hire them as workers so that they could earn a livelihood.[26] After a brief stay in Bethlehem, there were three possible places to which fugitives could go: Easton, Stroudsburg, or Palmerton.

Bethlehem to Easton

There is evidence to support a route from Bethlehem to Easton. Blockson located an Underground Railroad station there, and Easton was just across the Delaware River from New Jersey.[27] The distance between Bethlehem and Easton was only ten miles and could be traveled easily in a single night.

Bethlehem to Stroudsburg

Siebert's map depicts a clear line of march from Quakertown to Stroudsburg.[28] Although Bethlehem does not appear on the map, the trace of the route passes right through where the town would be. Runaways wishing to travel to Stroudsburg could have left Bethlehem by taking the Wechquetank Indian Path northward from the town. This Indian trail, also known as David's Path, was used after 1765 by Moravian missionaries traveling north to their Indian converts. Before reaching Hecktown, the fugitives could have taken a side trail eastward for several miles, until it linked with Sullivan's Road. This was a military road originally built by Gen. John Sullivan in 1779, during his invasion of the Iroquois territories. This road went from Easton to Wilkes-Barre and passed near Stroudsburg.[29]

Bethlehem to Palmerton

Siebert's map has a dotted line beginning in the vicinity of Bethlehem and going to Wilkes-Barre.[30] The dotted line indicates that Siebert had heard of this route but was not sure of it. Blockson, however, has located a station in the town of Palmerton in Carbon County that would fall on the dotted line, about twenty miles northwest of Bethlehem.[31] Fugitives could have easily gotten to Palmerton from Bethlehem by following the shores of the Lehigh River northward until they came to the town. From there they could have taken the well-established Lehigh Indian Path all the way to Wilkes-Barre.[32]

Stroudsburg to East Stroudsburg and New Jersey

Runaways reaching Stroudsburg, the major town in Monroe County, from Bethlehem were met and assisted by Dr. Syndenham Walter, the agent in town. He determined in which direction the fugitives would next proceed. Helping him in these efforts was Jacob Singmaster, his chief conductor.[33] Walter had three possible exit routes over which he could forward his charges. One went to East Stroudsburg. Although Siebert's map does not illustrate this route, recent research has established that there was an Underground Railroad station in the town, as well as an agent, Robert Brown, one of the sons of the famous John Brown. He lived at the corner of Braeside Avenue and East Brown Street. From East Stroudsburg, fugitives would have traveled eastward for two miles to the Delaware River.[34] Blockson has some of the runaways heading north at this point, along the shores of the Delaware on the Minsi Path, to Milford in Pike County. He has identified a station in an old printing shop in that town, and from there the escapees could have gone northward, through Wayne and Susquehanna Counties to New York.[35] It makes more sense, however, to assume that most of the fugitives simply crossed the river at Milford and entered the New Jersey escape network.

Stroudsburg to Waverly via Dunmore
The second option open to Dr. Walter was to send runaways northward to the town of Waverly on a route that led through Dunmore. Siebert has the main route of the Northeastern Corridor running up the Lehigh Valley from Stroudsburg to Waverly in Lackawanna County.[36] Those heading in this direction would have traveled overland without the benefit of any Indian trails or major roads. Before reaching Waverly, some distance from Stroudsburg, Blockson has the fugitives passing through stations in the towns of Dunmore and Clark's Green. From Dunmore, he has established an alternate route that took escapees to Carbondale instead of Waverly. This route likely was used when the trail to Waverly was blocked for some reason. From Carbondale, the route turned toward the New York state line. Those staying on the main route came to Clark's Green after departing from Dunmore. In this hamlet, the Clark family gave refuge to escapees.[37] From here the next stop was Waverly.

Stroudsburg to Waverly via Wilkes-Barre
The third route from Stroudsburg also went to Waverly but passed through Wilkes-Barre. Although Siebert's map does not show a route from Strouds-burg to Wilkes-Barre, he mentions it in the text of his work.[38] Fugitives could have easily made this journey by following a well-traveled trail linking the two sites, known as the Pechoquealin Path. This trail cut a trace through the Pocono Mountains and was also called the Lower Road by some.[39]

Wilkes-Barre had a large number of abolitionist-sympathizing residents. Rev. William C. Gildersleeve was the leading agent in the town, and the Bethel A.M.E. Church was its major station.[40] It was here that fugitives who had taken the route from Bethlehem to Palmerton joined those coming from Stroudsburg.

The escape path left Wilkes-Barre and headed almost due north to Waverly. At least four individuals maintained safe havens for runaways in the town: John Stone, John G. Fell, Charles Bailey, and Leonard Batchelor.[41]

Waverly to New York
Siebert's map and text describe three possible escape routes from Waverly north to New York. They went to Sugar Run, Friendsville, and Montrose.[42]

Waverly to Sugar Run. A trail headed northwest from Waverly to La Plume. This town was only five miles from Waverly and had several stations. The agents here were Eunice Chase, Decon Pardon Tillinghast, Dr. Archa Mumford, and Rodman Sisson.[43] In LaPlume, fugitives would have taken the Great Warriors Indian Path, a major trail that began at Sunbury and followed the Susquehanna River northward through Sugar Run, Wyoming County, to Towanda, Bradford County. Modern U.S. Route 6 follows the line of the trail today.[44] Blockson has Jonathan Drake and Nicholas Overfilled as the leading agents in the area.[45] Once runaways reached Towanda, they could go to either Elmira or Binghamton, New York.

Waverly to Friendsville. Not much is known about this route. Siebert placed it on his map and refers to it in the text of his work, but he does not elaborate on the site or any of its agents.[46]

The name Friendsville implies a Quaker settlement of some type. No Indian trail comes near it, and it appears to have been quite isolated. The New York border lies only a few miles to the north of the settlement, and this fact, coupled with the Quaker nature of the place, may have made the town attractive to escaped slaves.

Waverly to Montrose. The third possible option from Waverly was to go to Montrose in Susquehanna County. This town was to the north of Waverly, and Siebert has a line of escape going from it to Plymouth, New York.[47] Blockson states that Montrose was the main station for the Underground Railroad in Susquehanna County. He adds that a colony of black farmers, established by Dr. Robert Rose in 1836, was located in Silver Lake Township in the county.[48] That would have placed the colony directly between Montrose and the New York border, an ideal place for an Underground Railroad refuge.

NORRISTOWN TO NEW JERSEY ROUTE

There were two major escape routes that left Norristown and headed to New Jersey. One ended in the town of Bristol, and the other at the town of Yardley. Both routes proceeded through Bucks County, and the two towns were on the Delaware River across from New Jersey.

NORRISTOWN TO BRISTOL

From Norristown en route to Bristol, runaways headed east through Plymouth Meeting, Conshohocken, and Whitemarsh Township. These places were a few miles east of Norristown and had a long history of abolitionist activity. Plymouth Meeting had an antislavery society dating back to 1833, and Joseph and George Corson, two of the founders of the society, were Underground Railroad agents there.[49] Helping the Corsons was Samuel Mulsby, another agent in the town. In Conshohocken, Benjamin Harry opened his home to escapees. As they passed through Whitemarsh Township, fugitives stayed at a station kept by Peter Dager, located at the corner of Spring Mill Road and Ridge Pike.[50]

From Whitemarsh Township, the escaped slaves probably went to the farm owned by Robert and Joseph Purvis, who had moved their Underground Railroad station from their mother's home in Philadelphia to a farm in Byberry, Bucks County, only two miles from Bensalem, the next stop on this route. Blockson says that Bensalem was an important depot in Bucks County.[51] From Bensalem, escapees went to Bristol, a town on the Delaware River. Bristol had a large contingent of agents, including members of the following families: Beance, Buckman, Bugess, Doan, Hampton, Ivin, Janney, Linton, Lloyd, Longshore, Palmer, Schofield, Smith, Swain, and Twining. Charles W. Pierce also kept a station there, hiding runaways in a secret room above the linen closet on the second floor of his home.[52] Leaving Bristol, runaways crossed the Delaware and went on to either Florence or Burlington, New Jersey.

NORRISTOWN TO YARDLEY

The second route departing from Norristown tended more to the northeast, and the town of Yardley was its goal. This path went through Upper Darby Township, where fugitives were aided by Thomas and Hanna Atkinson. From here they went to Horsham. Croasdale Twining opened his home to escaped slaves in this town.[53] It was here that this route intersected with the Philadelphia–New Hope Route.

That Horsham was a place sought by fugitives can be vividly seen in the following advertisement for a runaway slave, which appeared in the *Pennsylvania Gazette:*

October 21, 1795

Forty Dollars Reward

RAN-AWAY from the subscriber, living at the head of Bohemia, Cecil county, Maryland, on the 9th of August last, a Negroe man, named NED about forty years of age, 5 feet 8 or 9 inches high, of yellowish complexsion, forward and impertinent; had on a coarse tow linen shirt and trousers, a high crown'd felt hat, and old corduroy or thick set waistcoat, a greyish mix'd cloth coat, and carries a large cane with a brass head carved, and wears a belt round his waist, on account of the rim of his belly being broke. The above Negroe worked with Jesse Holt and Samuel Torrance, in

Hiroshima township, Montgomery County near Mrs. Ball's tavern these six weeks past, and calls himself *Jack;* it is likely he will leave that neighborhood and change his name again, as he was pursued in that neighborhood on Thursday last, by one of his young masters, who got all of his clothes except the above mentioned.

Whoever takes up the said Negroe, and secures him in Philadelphia gaol, shall have THIRTY DOLLARS, or if brought home, the above reward and reasonable charges, paid by ABIGAIL RYLAND.[54]

The next leg of the journey took runaways from Horsham due east to the town of Langhorne, Middletown Township. Here the trail turned north and went to Newtown. The old Newtown Pike connected the two sites, and the four miles between them would have been quickly covered. In Newtown, fugitives received help and shelter from Mahlon Linton. The final leg of this route was from Newtown to Yardley, on the Delaware River across from New Jersey. Though most fugitives probably crossed at this point, some hid in coal barges and went up the Delaware to Easton, crossing into New Jersey there.[55]

PHILADELPHIA TO NEW HOPE ROUTE

The final escape route of the Northeastern Corridor ran from Philadelphia to the town of New Hope in Bucks County. From there fugitives crossed the Delaware River and entered New Jersey. Some took the overland route from Philadelphia and traveled northward on the Old Bethlehem Pike or the Old York Road. Those taking the Old York Road crossed into Montgomery County and entered Cheltenham Township. The first Underground Railroad station they encountered there was the one managed by the famous James and Lucretia Mott. Helping these two pioneer abolitionists were Jay Cooke and Jacob C. White.[56]

The route seems to have split into two branches on leaving Cheltenham. One branch continues northward toward Jenkintown; the other, following the Limekiln Pike, went to Jarrettown in Upper Darby. Blockson says that this branch continued all the way to Berks County.[57] There is some doubt about his assertion, however. Limekiln Pike proceeds to Perkasie after exiting Jarrettown. This town was a key link on the route to Quakertown and had a well-organized Underground Railroad. It seems more likely that once fugitives arrived there, they would go on to Quakertown, rather than to the much more distant Berks County.

The second branch of the route from Philadelphia continued northward, following the Old York Road (modern PA Route 263) from Jenkintown to Willow Grove in Moreland Township. From there it went to Horsham. The key agents along this portion of the escape path were Dr. Charles Shoemaker, Croasdale Twining, and David Newport, a justice of the peace in that area.[58] Exiting Horsham, the route went through Warminster to Doylestown. Both of these towns are reputed to have had stations, but the names of the agents are unknown.[59] It was at Doylestown that the Old York Road veered east and traversed Buckingham and Solebury Townships, ending at New Hope. Smedley speaks of the importance of Buckingham Township on the Underground Railroad and lists William H. Johnson and John Jackson as the key agents in Buckingham and Jonathan McGill as the agent in Solebury.[60] Blockson considers Buckingham Township one of the three most important stations in all of Bucks County, after Quakertown and Bensalem.[61] This branch of the escape route from Philadelphia came to an end in New Hope, on the Delaware River. Fugitives would cross there and enter Lambertville on the New Jersey side of the river.[62] The main Underground Railroad station in New Hope was in the A.M.E. church.[63]

The Mother Bethel A.M.E. Church in Philadelphia. PHOTO BY KEVIN J. SWITALA

The Role of
Organized Religion

Religion motivated many individuals to help slaves achieve freedom through the Underground Railroad. For a great number of these people, the principles of Christianity, as put forth in the Bible, almost compelled them to do whatever they could in this enterprise, even if it meant great personal risk. Men and women of conscience felt that it was their moral duty to help runaways attain the goal of freedom.

Throughout the early nineteenth century, prior to the Civil War, a number of organized religions viewed slavery as an abomination, slave holding as sinful, and the helping of slaves to escape their bondage as the right thing to do. These issues also caused serious splits within several religious groups. These schisms fell along geographic lines. The churches in the South opposed any elimination of slavery and in some cases even offered scriptural justifications for its practice. The churches of the same denominations in the North opposed slavery and called for its abolition. Even among the Northern churches, however, there was a disagreement as to how far they should go in supporting these positions. Some favored the gradual abolition of the practice; some wanted an immediate cessation of it; some thought it was morally imperative to encourage slaves to escape from their masters and to provide them with assistance in doing so; and still others felt that slavery was not a matter of concern for the churches and opposed any action taken against the elimination of slavery or the helping of runaways.

While most of the mainstream churches urged an end to slavery, they wanted this to take place in a peaceful, gradual manner based largely on encouraging individual slave holders to emancipate their slaves. These same churches often denounced the more radical actions of the abolition movement and considered the abolitionists "incendiaries, disunionists, and infidels."[1] The following discussion examines the attitudes of the major denominations on the question of slavery and reviews their participation in the operation of the Underground Railroad in western Pennsylvania.

AFRICAN METHODIST EPISCOPALIANS

One of the few religious organizations that never questioned the abolition of slavery and helping slaves escape was the African Methodist Episcopal Church. The major reason for this unified position was the simple fact that the church consisted mainly of African-Americans, and there was never any question in their minds as to the evils of slavery, the need to abolish it, or the moral obligation to assist runaways.

The A.M.E. Church had its beginnings in the late 1700s and early 1800s in Philadelphia. The driving force behind the formation of the church was the dynamic figure Richard Allen (1760–1831). Allen converted to Christianity in 1777, while still a slave. After he purchased his freedom, he attempted to be ordained a minister in the Methodist religion in 1784. Refused ordination on the ground of his race, Allen continued his involvement with the Methodist Church by traveling with some itinerant preachers and occasionally doing some of the preaching. In 1787, he and a group of fellow blacks tried to attend a religious service at St. George's Methodist Church in Philadelphia. They were asked to leave because of their race, and Allen decided to form his own denomination. In 1789, he opened his own church, the Bethel Church, in Philadelphia. Similar black churches began to appear throughout the country. Allen convened an assembly in 1816 to discuss the issue of black churches. Representatives from sixteen independent African-American Methodist congregations attended the meeting. The end result of this convocation was the formation of the African Methodist Episcopal (A.M.E.) Church and the election of Richard Allen as the church's first bishop. The church grew quickly, and by 1826, it had two bishops and 7,927 members. Almost immediately, the church got involved in the slavery question. Allen opposed the resettlement of freed slaves in Africa, as proposed by the American Colonization Society. Instead, he urged blacks to go to Canada, where they would be free, until slavery was abolished in the United States.[2]

A.M.E. churches sprang up wherever there was a community of blacks in Pennsylvania. These churches were the first places to give fugitives sanctuary on their journey to freedom. On the Eastern Route, a number of local A.M.E. churches acted as Underground Railroad stations wherever they were located. In Philadelphia, the Mother Bethel, Zoar, and Wesley A.M.E. Churches were very active in aiding runaways. On the Southeastern and Northeastern Corridors, A.M.E. churches served as stations all along escape routes, including the Zion A.M.E. Church in Norristown, the Bethel A.M.E. Church in Reading, the Mount Fisby A.M.E. Church in Hopewell Village, the Honeycomb A.M.E. Church in Lima, the Marple A.M.E. Church in

Marple, and the Bethel A.M.E. Church in Wilkes-Barre. The Central Route also had several A.M.E. churches as stations, including the Bethel A.M.E. Church in Gettysburg, the Wesley Union Church in Harrisburg, and the Zion A.M.E. Church in Hollidaysburg. The A.M.E. Church came to western Pennsylvania a few years after its establishment in the eastern part of the state. In 1834, Rev. Samuel Clingman organized the Bethel A.M.E. Church in Monongahela, Pennsylvania. Construction of the first actual church building began in 1842. The church partially burned in 1849 and was rebuilt in 1858. Throughout its existence, the church served as an Underground Railroad station.[3] Some years earlier, in 1815, Rev. Lewis Woodson came to Pittsburgh. A short time after his arrival, he established the Bethel A.M.E. Church on the corner of Water and Smithfield Streets, in the heart of the city. This church played a major role in the educational, spiritual, and social life of the African-American community in Pittsburgh, and it also served as an Underground Railroad station. Woodson was an important agent on the Pittsburgh line. St. Matthew's A.M.E. Church in Sewickley and the Avery Memorial A.M.E. Zion Church on Pittsburgh's north side were both Underground Railroad stations.

QUAKERS

The Society of Friends, or Quakers, originated in seventeenth-century England. Part of a larger movement known as pietism, the Quakers had several unique beliefs that brought about an adverse reaction from the English government. Their founder, George Fox (1624–91), had a distaste for the rigid formalism found in the religions, society, and government of his day. He felt that religion should be a deeply personal experience and that one should be guided by a divine inner light instead of external decrees given by religious hierarchies. Based on his interpretation of scripture, and a deep commitment to the idea of brotherly love, Fox was adamantly opposed to war, serving in the military, using titles, and the taking of oaths. In the England of his time, such ideas were dangerous and considered treasonable. Because of this, the government persecuted Fox and his followers.[4]

One of Fox's most famous converts was William Penn. Though he was the son of a famous English admiral and heir to a large fortune, William Penn was still subject to the same persecution as the other Quakers. Due to a particular set of circumstances, which included the death of his father, debts owed to his father by the king, and a change of attitude toward the Quakers, Penn found himself in the possession of a large colony in America in 1681.

In Pennsylvania, Penn saw an opportunity to establish a place where he and his fellow Quakers could practice their religion in peace. The Quakers flourished there, and by 1683, over 4,000 members of the sect lived in the colony. By 1760, some 30,000 Quakers resided in America.[5]

The Quakers opposed the notion of slavery based on the grounds that all human beings are brothers. They considered all people equal before God and the laws of the state. They also believed in total equality in society. Because of these sentiments, some have considered the Quakers to be the greatest antislavery activists of any nonblack religious sect in the British colonies.[6]

Although opposed to the practice of slavery, the Quakers did not seek the elimination of the institution through a general change in the laws of the state; rather, they preferred to urge individual slave holders to free their slaves.[7] Two Quakers, Ralph Sandiford and Benjamin Lay of Philadelphia, who were friends of Benjamin Franklin's, wrote continually against the practice of slavery. Lay called the keeping of slaves the "Mother of all Sins." He urged slave holders to follow a plan in which they would first educate slaves in reading and writing, teach them the principles of truth and righteousness, teach them a trade, and then set them free.[8] Another Philadelphia Quaker of the 1700s, Anthony Benezet, used every form of publication, including newspapers, pamphlets, almanacs, and books, to spread his antislavery views. His plan included two steps: first, put an end to the importation of slaves; and second, after a certain period of service, set free all of those already enslaved.[9]

As the years passed, the Quakers in Pennsylvania issued a series of regulations that eventually brought about an elimination of any slave holders from their own membership.[10] The question of opposing slavery, however, was not a simple one for the society. Levi Coffin, the great Quaker activist on the Underground Railroad in Indiana, wrote that the Quakers were divided over the question of slavery. He said that they held four different opinions on the matter: Some wanted to resettle freed slaves in Africa; some opted for gradual emancipation; others favored immediate emancipation and felt obligated to help slaves gain freedom; and still others opposed abolitionism and helping escaped slaves.[11] Coffin wrote that eventually the society split into two factions over the slavery question. One favored active involvement in opposing slavery and in aiding slaves to escape; the other opposed any role in helping slaves leave their masters. Each faction ended up holding its own annual official gathering called the Yearly Meeting of Friends.[12]

Many Quakers in Pennsylvania fell into the group that opposed slavery and aided runaways. In Philadelphia, Quakers operated a school for black children, and in the Germantown section of the city, they actively aided fugitives in their journey northward. The large Quaker populations in Adams, York, Lancaster, Chester, and Delaware Counties accounted for the majority of the Underground Railroad agents and conductors there. Names like Daniel Gibbons, Elijah Pennypacker, Nathan Evans, and Grace Anna Lewis, all of whom were Quakers, were legendary in the operation of the Underground Railroad in eastern Pennsylvania. The Quakers in Bucks and Montgomery Counties were largely instrumental for passing runaways on to the numerous exit routes along the Northeastern Corridor.

The Quakers in western Pennsylvania played no less of a role in the success of the Western Route. For example, the Quaker community of Fishertown played an important role on the Bedford–Clearfield Route. The actions of the Penrose family, the Millers, Samuel Way, William Kirk, John Albaugh, and Nathan Hammond made it possible for many fugitives to move from the Bedford area to Johnstown and Hollidaysburg. The Quaker community at St. Clairsville assisted escapees heading north to Clearfield. Isaac B. Carmalt, the Quaker stationmaster in Brookville, guided fugitives to Shippenville. The Quaker settlement near Uniontown, founded by Quaker Henry Beeson, channeled runaways to the north and west. Quaker families also played a role in helping fugitives move through the Monongahela River valley toward Pittsburgh. The Quakers in Linesville in northwestern Pennsylvania helped escapees proceed to Girard and Ohio. The Quaker town of New Brighton in Beaver County was also significant, and the hospitality shown to runaways by Quakers in the town was well known throughout the South.

PRESBYTERIANS

According to the sources, the Presbyterian Church had the greatest number of nonblack participants in the Underground Railroad. The American branch of the Presbyterian Church owes much of its formation to Francis Makemie, an Ulsterman who came here in 1684 and established a church. He traveled among the settlements of Maryland, Virginia, and the Carolinas, preaching to the colonists. By 1705, under his direction, a number of congregations sent ministers to Philadelphia, where the first American Presbytery began. They called it the Philadelphia Presbytery. With the influx of Scots-Irish immigrants in the early 1700s to the frontiers of Pennsylvania, the Presbyterian Church grew quickly.[13] In the mid-1700s, two ministers, Charles Beatty and George Duffield, went to the western frontier of Pennsylvania to preach and establish a formal Presbyterian presence there. They journeyed throughout western Pennsylvania and even preached at Fort Pitt. In the 1770s, John McMillan, James Power, Thaddeus Dod, and Joseph Smith, all ministers, arrived in western Pennsylvania and began to build the first permanent Presbyterian churches in the area. By 1781, the churches had grown so much that the Presbytery of Redstone was formed, and a few years later, the Presbytery of Erie (1801) and the Presbytery of Pittsburgh (1802) were also established.[14]

In addition to this group of Presbyterians, two other sects of that faith made their appearance on the frontier. In Scotland, the Presbyterian Church had split into two factions over theological differences. These two groups were the Associate Presbyterians, also called the Seceders, and the Reformed Presbyterians, called the Covenanters.[15] The Covenanters arrived in 1769 and settled on the land between the Youghiogheny and Monongahela Rivers. In 1800, the first Covenanter minister, Joseph Black, came and took over the duties as pastor of the Pittsburgh Reformed Presbyterian congregation. The Seceder sect began to arrive at about the same time, and within a few years, they far outnumbered the Covenanters. Matthew Henderson reached western Pennsylvania in 1775 and organized two formal Seceder congregations, one at Chartiers and another at Speer's Spring.[16]

The Presbyterian Church expressed antislavery sentiments soon after its establishment in America. In 1787, the General Assembly of the Church condemned the institution of slavery, promoted its abolishment, and called for the education of all black people, both free and slave. This action was reaffirmed by the General Assembly in 1793.[17] In 1808, the Presbyterian Church in Pennsylvania ruled that slave holding was a sin and that the practice was both morally evil and unjustifiable. Rulings in 1811 and 1831 further condemned the practice and even went so far as to exclude slave holders from membership in the Church.[18] By 1845, the Church began to experience a division in the ranks over the issue of slavery and the exclusion of slave holders from the Church. The Presbyterians in the South had serious problems with these positions. Finally, in 1859, after the General Assembly of the Church condemned slavery once more, many Southern ministers withdrew from the assembly's jurisdiction.[19]

The Presbyterian churches figured prominently in the successful operation of the Underground Railroad in Pennsylvania. Some churches opposed slavery and supported the efforts of the American Colonization Society to resettle former slaves in Africa. The First Presbyterian Church in Pittsburgh belonged to that group. Many Presbyterian congregations and ministers were more active in their opposition to slavery. They provided shelter and aid to runaways and led them to other safe havens along the Underground Railroad system. The most notable of these were the Central Presbyterian Church of Color in Philadelphia; the Washington Street Presbyterian Church in Reading; the Presbyterian Church in Harrisburg; the Milroy Presbyterian Church, under the pastorate of Rev. James Mourse; Rev. Arthur B. Bradford, and his Mount Pleasant Free Presbyterian Church in Beaver County; Rev. Loyal Young of Butler County; Rev. John Hindman and his Seceder congregation in Clarion County; Rev. David Blair and the Conemaugh and Crooked Creek congregations of the Associated Presbyterian Church in Indiana County; the Presbyterian Church in Brownsville, Fayette County; the United Presbyterian Church in West Middletown, Washington County; Rev. Nathaniel North, an agent in Mercer County; the Reformed Presbyterian Church in Allegheny City, Allegheny County; and the Presbyterian Church in Barnes, Warren County. It is apparent from this list that the Presbyterian Church in western Pennsylvania contributed greatly to the success of the Underground Railroad. Some Presbyterians in the western part of the state, however, did not believe in helping runaways and opposed the church's encouragement of such a practice. Some churches, such as the one in Indiana County, even split over the issue.

METHODISTS

Another religious denomination that opposed slavery and participated in the Underground Railroad movement in western Pennsylvania was the Methodist Episcopal Church. Founded by John Wesley (1703–91) in England, Methodism was a more moderate and popular form of pietism. Although John Wesley spent a brief time in the American colony of Georgia, the real founder of American Methodism was Francis Asbury (1745–1816), a disciple of Wesley. It was under his influence that the church in America devoted much of its time to social reform efforts. The main concerns of this reform movement were education, health, sanitation, temperance, penal reform, and the abolition of the slave trade.[20]

Soon after the establishment of the church in the colonies, the Methodists took a formal position against slavery. At the Methodist Conference in 1780, held in Baltimore, the group declared that slavery was "contrary to the laws of God, man, and nature." The conference advised the freeing of all people currently enslaved and required this of all the traveling preachers of the church. The conference further stated that the only way one could legitimately purchase a slave was with the intention of freeing the slave immediately. The very next year, however, these rules were relaxed for ministers working in the South.[21] In 1784, the decrees of the Baltimore Conference were modified. The new interpretation required all church members to free their slaves in those states that permitted emancipation. Once again, however, because of opposition from slave-holding Methodists in the South, the decree was suspended six months later. The church did take a strong position on the issue in 1816, decreeing that no slave holders would be eligible for any official position in the church if they did not liberate their slaves, while living in a state that permitted it. The end result of this rule, and others like it, led to a formal schism in the Methodist Church between a Northern Church that was abolitionist and a Southern Church that permitted slavery.[22] The controversy did not end there, however. In 1828, the General Conference met in Pittsburgh and passed a resolution approving the actions of the American Colonization Society. Up to this point, the church had not given formal support to the actions of the Underground Railroad. At the General Conference of 1836 meeting in Cincinnati, the group condemned the tactics of the abolitionists. At the Conference of 1840, the church leaders received hundreds of antislave petitions, mostly from Northern congregations.[23] Finally, in 1860, at the Buffalo General Conference, the Methodist Church issued its final proclamation on the topic, unequivocally condemning the institution of slavery everywhere in the country.[24]

Most of the involvement of the Methodist Church in the Underground Railroad took place in western Pennsylvania. The only site in eastern Pennsylvania mentioned as a station in the source material was the Campbell African Methodist Church in Philadelphia. Even in western Pennsylvania, there were not many Methodists living there during the 1700s and early 1800s. In 1793, only 151 members of the church worshipped on the Pittsburgh circuit.[25] Eventually they built a brick church for the group in Pittsburgh in 1810, on the north side of Front Street. A second Methodist church appeared in 1818 on the southeast corner of Smithfield Street and Seventh Avenue.[26] Gradually Methodist churches were built all over western Pennsylvania. Though they were not as numerous as the Presbyterians, the Methodists still participated in the operation of the Underground Railroad. Bausman, in his study of Beaver County, says the Methodist churches there were very active in the fight against slavery.[27] Methodist ministers and churches aided runaways in their quest for freedom in several other counties in western Pennsylvania. For example, Rev. Christopher Fogel was an agent at Brookville in Jefferson County, and the Methodist church on Buffalo Road in Wesleyville was a station in the Crawford–Erie County Network.

BAPTISTS

The Baptist Church in America had its beginnings in the Rhode Island colony of Roger Williams in 1638. This religious denomination gradually made its way to Pennsylvania, and in 1707, the first meeting of the Baptist Association of America took place in Philadelphia.[28] The first Baptists in western Pennsylvania, a group of settlers led by Isaac Sutton, appeared in Uniontown around 1770. Shortly after their arrival, Henry Crosbye, a Baptist minister, visited them and established the Great Bethel Baptist Church in Uniontown. He then ordained Sutton as the church's first minister. By 1808, there were thirty Baptist churches in the western part of the state.[29]

Like the Presbyterians and the Methodists, the Baptists were divided over the issue of slavery. In 1789, the General Committee of Virginia Baptists, an organization that represented all the Baptist churches in that state, approved a resolution citing slavery as a "deprivation of the rights of nature and inconsistent with a republican government." It also urged its members to take every legal means possible to put as end to the practice. That same year, the Philadelphia Baptist Association endorsed societies working for the abolition of slavery and recommended that all Baptist churches in the state form abolition societies of their own.[30] In the 1830s, however, a schism occurred in the church over the issue of slavery. Southern Baptist churches held that scriptures supported the right to own slaves, while Northern churches considered the practice sinful. Eventually the church split into Northern and Southern Associations over the matter.[31]

Three Baptist churches are mentioned in the sources as having been Underground Railroad stations: the Shiloh Baptist Church in Carlisle, the Union Baptist Church in Philadelphia, and the First Baptist Church in Norristown.

UNITARIANS

The Unitarian denomination began in New England during the mid-1700s. A dispute among the Congregational Church members over the concept of the Trinity led to the formation of an anti-Trinitarian group, who referred to themselves as Unitarians. In 1815, a formal separation of the two groups took place, and the American Unitarian Church began. The new denomination spread rapidly throughout New England and soon made its way to Pennsylvania.[32]

It was not long before the Unitarians became active in the antislavery movement. The basis for their antislavery position was the belief that all men everywhere in the world were brothers. The governing body of the Church, the American Unitarian Association, passed a resolution in May 1851 that condemned the institution of slavery and promoted the aiding of slaves in their attempts to escape from their "oppressors."[33] The first Unitarian church in Pennsylvania was the First Congregational Unitarian Church in Philadelphia. This church was an Underground Railroad station. In western Pennsylvania, a Unitarian church was established in Meadville in 1837. Eight years later, the number of Unitarians had increased in western Pennsylvania to the point where a seminary opened in Meadville to train ministers for service in the Church. The seminary was shared with another denomination, the Disciples of Christ. Its first rector was Dr. Rufus P. Stebbins.[34] The Meadville Unitarian church and the seminary both were Underground Railroad stations.

OTHER DENOMINATIONS AND RELIGIONS

Several other denominations—the Universalists, Mennonites, Moravians, Lutherans, Anglicans, and Disciples of Christ—appear in the sources as having provided aid to fugitives on the Underground Railroad.[35]

Members of the Universalist congregation in Indiana County were strong opponents to slavery, and the Universalist church in Girard, Pennsylvania, served as an Underground Railroad station.

Mennonites Christian Frantz and Dr. Augustus W. Cain were Underground Railroad agents, and the Mennonites in Heidelberg Township, Lebanon County, opened their homes to fugitives passing through their area.

On the Northeastern Corridor, the Moravians assisted fugitives going through the town of Bethlehem.

The participation of the Lutheran Church was limited to the opening of the doors of the Lutheran Theological Seminary in Gettysburg. The faculty of the seminary, along with faculty members at Gettysburg College, helped runaways reach the town.

The Anglican Church operated a school for black children in Philadelphia and also had a number of black congregation members.

The Disciples of Christ, while not having as large a group of followers as the other Protestant denominations in western Pennsylvania, did offer assistance on the Underground Railroad at the seminary in Meadville that it shared with the Unitarians.

One Catholic is mentioned in the sources as an agent on the railroad: Thomas Hughes, who also offered his home as a station in Greene County. There are no other references in any of the sources of Catholic churches or priests being actively involved in the Underground Railroad in Pennsylvania.

Regardless of the denomination, there are ample references to churches in Pennsylvania taking an active role in the operation of the Underground Railroad. Without their participation, it would have been far more difficult for runaways to successfully traverse the great distances through the state in their quest for freedom.

NOTES

THE ESCAPE OF HENRY "BOX" BROWN

1. William Still, *The Underground Railroad: A Record of Facts, Authentic Narratives, Letters, & c.* (Philadelphia: Porter & Coates, 1872; reprint, Arno Press and the *New York Times,* 1968), 81.
2. Ibid.
3. Ibid., 83.
4. Ibid., 82–84.
5. Larry Gara, *The Liberty Line: The Legend of the Underground Railroad* (Lexington, KY: University of Kentucky Press, 1967), 4.
6. Charles L. Blockson, *Underground Railroad* (New York: Berkley Books, 1987), 205.
7. Gara, *Liberty Line,* 42.

THE SETTING

1. Stanley M. Elkins, *Slavery: A Problem in American Institutional and Intellectual Life* (New York: Grosset & Dunlop, 1963), 38.
2. *The Statistical History of the United States from Colonial Times to the Present* (Stamford, CT: Fairfield Publishers, 1965), 11–12.
3. *Negro Population in the United States 1790–1950* (New York: Arno Press and the *New York Times,* 1968), 220.
4. Garret Hendrick, et al., "Resolutions of the Germantown Mennonites," *Documents of American History,* edited by Henry Steele Commager (New York: Appleton-Century-Croft, 1958), 37–38.
5. Ibid.
6. Ira V. Brown, *The Negro in Pennsylvania History* (University Park, PA: Pennsylvania Historical Association, 1970), 3.
7. Wayland F. Dunaway, *A History of Pennsylvania* (Englewood Cliffs, NJ: Prentice-Hall, 1948), 185.
8. Ira V. Brown, *Pennsylvania Reformers: From Penn to Pinchot* (University Park, PA: Pennsylvania Historical Association, 1966), 6.
9. Samuel Eliot Morison, *The Oxford History of the American People* (New York: Oxford University Press, 1965), 295.
10. Dunaway, *History of Pennsylvania,* 186.
11. Morison, *Oxford History,* 295.
12. Commager, *Documents,* 128–32.
13. Ibid., 197–98.
14. Brown, *Pennsylvania Reformers,* 7.

15. Elkins, *Slavery,* 179–80.
16. Brown, *Pennsylvania Reformers,* 8.
17. Commager, *Documents,* 278–81.
18. Brown, *Negro,* 14.
19. Julie Winch, *Philadelphia Black Elite Activism, Accommodation, and the Struggle for Autonomy, 1787–1848* (Philadelphia: Temple University Press, 1988), 49.
20. James Oliver Horton and Lois E. Horton, *In Hope of Liberty, Culture, Community, and Protest among Northern Free Blacks, 1700–1860* (New York: Oxford University Press, 1997), 209–10.
21. Winch, *Philadelphia Black Elite,* 50.
22. Wilhelmena S. Robinson, *Historical Negro Biographies* (New York: Publishers Company, 1967), 19–20.
23. Winch, *Philadelphia Black Elite,* 63.
24. Ibid., 66.
25. Ibid., 11.
26. Robinson, *Historical Negro Biographies,* 24.
27. Ibid., 120.
28. Ibid., 72.
29. Ibid., 119.

OPERATION OF THE RAILROAD

1. Gara, *Liberty Line,* 2.
2. Letter to Robert Morris, April 12, 1786, *The Writings of George Washington from the Original Manuscript Sources 1745–1799,* ed. John C. Fitzpatrick (Washington, DC: U.S. Government Printing Office), vol. 28, 407–8.
3. Washington, Letter to William Drayton, November 20, 1786, vol. 29, 78–79.
4. Washington, Letter to Robert Morris, April 12, 1786, vol. 28, 407–8.
5. Washington, Letter to the Marquis de Lafayette, May 10, 1786, vol. 28, 424.
6. Washington, Letter to John Francis Mercer, September 9, 1786, vol. 29, 5.
7. Wilbur H. Siebert, *The Underground Railroad from Slavery to Freedom* (New York: Macmillan Company, 1898; reprint, Russell & Russell, 1967), 34.
8. W. J. McKnight, M.D., *A Pioneer History of Jefferson County, Pennsylvania and My First Recollections of Brookville, Pennsylvania, 1840–43, When My Feet Were Bare and My Cheeks Were Brown* (Philadelphia: J. B. Lippincott Company, 1898), 273.
9. W. J. Bell, Jr., "Washington County, Pennsylvania, in the 18th Century Antislavery Movement," *Western Pennsylvania Historical Society Magazine* 25 (1942): 136–37.
10. R. C. Smedley, M.D., *History of the Underground Railroad in Chester and the Neighboring Counties of Pennsylvania* (Lancaster, PA: Office of the Journal, 1883; reprint, Arno Press and the *New York Times,* 1969), 25.
11. Siebert, *Underground Railroad,* 37.
12. Ibid., 45.
13. Smedley, *History of the Underground Railroad,* 34–35.

14. Rev. Calvin Fairbanks, *During Slavery Times* (New York: Patriotic Publishing Co., 1890; reprint, Negro Universities Press, 1969), 61–62.

15. Siebert, *Underground Railroad,* 341.

16. S. G. Howe, *Report to the Freedmen's Inquiry Commission 1864: The Refugees from Slavery in Canada West* (Boston: Wright & Potter, Printers, 1864; reprint, Arno Press and the *New York Times,* 1969), 15.

17. Gara, *Liberty Line,* 37.

18. Samuel Ringold Ward, *Autobiography of a Fugitive Negro: His Anti-Slavery Labours in the United States, Canada & England* (London: John Snow, 1855; reprint, Arno Press and the *New York Times*), 154.

19. Siebert, *Underground Railroad,* 341.

20. Washington, Letter Book, undated entry, vol. 30, 481.

21. Howe, *Freedmen's Report,* 12.

22. Ibid.

23. Marion Gleason McDougall, *Fugitive Slaves 1619–1865* (Boston: Fay House Monographs, 1891; reprint, Bergman Publishers, 1967), 25.

24. Ward, *Autobiography,* 292–93.

25. Howe, *Freedmen's Report,* 9.

26. Siebert, *Underground Railroad,* 27–28.

27. McDougall, *Fugitive Slaves,* 25.

28. Howe, *Freedmen's Report,* 14.

29. Levi Coffin, *Reminiscences* (Cincinnati: The Robert Clarke Company, 1898; reprint, Arno Press and the *New York Times,* 1968), 111.

30. Ibid., 111–13.

31. Ibid., 20.

32. Still, *Underground Railroad,* 201.

33. Smedley, *History of the Underground Railroad,* 28–29.

34. Col. William M. Cockrum, *History of the Underground Railroad as It Was Conducted by the Anti-Slavery League* (New York: Negro Universities Press, 1969), 13–15.

35. Ibid., 17.

36. Smedley, *History of the Underground Railroad,* 270.

37. Fairbanks, *During Slavery Times,* 11.

38. Coffin, *Reminiscences,* 111.

39. Fairbanks, *During Slavery Times,* 10.

40. Ibid., 20–23.

41. Still, *Underground Railroad,* 106–7.

42. William and Ellen Craft, *Running a Thousand Miles to Freedom; or, The Escape of William and Ellen Craft from Slavery* (London: William Tweedie, 1860; reprint, Arno Press and the *New York Times,* 1969), 42–80.

43. Fairbanks, *During Slavery Times,* 15–19.

44. Coffin, *Reminiscences,* 337–41.

45. Frederick Douglass, *Narrative of the Life of Frederick Douglass an American Slave Written by Himself* (New York: Penguin Books USA, 1986), 124.

46. Still, *Underground Railroad,* 98.
47. Ibid., 165–67.
48. Ibid., 54–55.
49. Ibid., 282–83, 607–10.
50. Smedley, *History of the Underground Railroad,* 199–200.
51. Coffin, *Reminiscences,* 173–74.
52. Ibid., 337–41.
53. Ibid., 441.
54. Fairbanks, *During Slavery Times,* 20–23.
55. Ibid., 34–44.
56. Craft, *Running a Thousand Miles,* 28–68.
57. Douglass, *Narrative of the Life of Frederick Douglass,* 125–27.
58. *American Slavery as It Is: Testimony of a Thousand Witnesses* (New York: American Anti-Slavery Society, 1839; reprint, Arno Press and the *New York Times,*1968), 62–63.
59. Ibid., 27, 85–111.
60. Still, *Underground Railroad,* 422–23.
61. Douglass, *Narrative of the Life of Frederick Douglass,* 86.
62. *American Slavery,* 88–89.
63. Smedley, *History of the Underground Railroad,* 271.
64. McDougall, *Fugitive Slaves,* 19.
65. Commager, *Documents,* 321–23.
66. Craft, *Running a Thousand Miles,* 93.
67. Fairbanks, *During Slavery Times,* 11.
68. J. C. Lovejoy, *Memoir of Rev. Charles T. Torrey, Who Died in the Penitentiary of Maryland Where He Was Confined for Showing Mercy to the Poor* (Boston: John Jewett & Co., 1847; reprint, Negro Universities Press, 1969), 126–202.
69. Smedley, *History of the Underground Railroad,* 116–23.
70. Siebert, *Underground Railroad,* 121–22.
71. Ibid.
72. Ibid., 122–23.
73. Ibid., 121.

BEDFORD–CLEARFIELD ROUTE

1. Siebert, *Underground Railroad;* E. Howard Blackburn and William H. Welfley, *History of Bedford and Somerset Counties, Pennsylvania, with Genealogical and Personal History* (New York: Lewis Publishing Co., 1906); Edward Burns, "Slavery in Western Pennsylvania," *Western Pennsylvania Magazine* 7 (1925); Charles L. Blockson, *The Underground Railroad in Pennsylvania* (Jacksonville, NC: Flame International, 1981).
2. Paul A. W. Wallace, *Indian Paths of Pennsylvania* (Harrisburg, PA: Pennsylvania Historical and Museum Commission, 1971), 181–82.

3. *Pennsylvania Atlas and Gazetteer* (Freeport, ME: DeLorme Mapping Company, 1987), 88.
4. Blackburn and Welfley, *History of Bedford and Somerset,* 376.
5. Blockson, *Underground Railroad in Pennsylvania,* 140.
6. Ibid.
7. Wallace, *Indian Paths,* 184.
8. Blackburn and Welfley, *History of Bedford and Somerset,* 375.
9. Ibid.
10. Blockson, *Underground Railroad in Pennsylvania,* 141.
11. Ibid.
12. Wallace, *Indian Paths,* 182–83.
13. William H. Clark, "Bedford County from Indian Trail to Tourist Resorts," *Pennsylvania Heritage* 12 (1986): 12–17.
14. John W. Harpster, ed., *Crossroads Description of Western Pennsylvania 1720–1829* (Pittsburgh: University of Pittsburgh Press, 1938), 46.
15. Clark, "Bedford County," 13.
16. Ibid.
17. Ibid.
18. Ibid., 14.
19. Harpster, *Crossroads,* 131–32.
20. Solon J. Buck and Elizabeth Hawthorn Buck, *The Planting of Civilization in Western Pennsylvania* (Pittsburgh: University of Pittsburgh Press, 1967), 368.
21. Blackburn and Welfley, *History of Bedford and Somerset,* 376.
22. Siebert, *Underground Railroad,* 431.
23. Blockson, *Underground Railroad in Pennsylvania,* 141.
24. Ibid.
25. Wallace, *Indian Paths,* 59.
26. Ibid.
27. Siebert, *Underground Railroad,* 434.
28. Wallace, *Indian Paths,* 35.
29. Blackburn and Welfley, *History of Bedford and Somerset,* 376.
30. Blockson, *Underground Railroad in Pennsylvania,* 141.
31. Blackburn and Welfley, *History of Bedford and Somerset,* 376.
32. Ibid., 377.
33. Ibid., 376.
34. Ibid., 377.
35. Ibid., 377–78.
36. Ibid., 377.
37. Henry Wilson Storey, *History of Cambria County, Pennsylvania,* vol. 1 (New York: Lewis Publishing Company, 1907), 188.
38. Ibid., 186; *My Pennsylvania: A Brief History of the Commonwealth's Sixty-seven Counties* (Harrisburg: Commonwealth of Pennsylvania, 1946), 25.
39. Blockson, *Underground Railroad in Pennsylvania,* 139.

40. Storey, *History of Cambria County,* 188.
41. Ibid., 186.
42. Ibid., 188.
43. Wallace, *Indian Paths,* 51–52.
44. Storey, *History of Cambria County,* 186.
45. Blockson, *Underground Railroad in Pennsylvania,* 103.
46. Siebert, *Underground Railroad,* 123.
47. Clarence D. Stephenson, *Indiana County 175th Anniversary History,* vol. 1 (Indiana, PA: A. G. Halldin Publishing Co., 1978), 365.
48. Ibid., vol. 3, 114.
49. Blackburn and Welfley, *History of Bedford and Somerset,* 379–80.
50. Ibid., 376–79.
51. Siebert, *Underground Railroad,* 431.
52. Blackburn and Welfley, *History of Bedford and Somerset,* 380.
53. Wallace, *Indian Paths,* 22–24.
54. Storey, *History of Cambria County,* 186–87.
55. Siebert, *Underground Railroad,* 432.
56. Ibid., 123.
57. McKnight, *A Pioneer History,* 275.
58. Wallace, *Indian Paths,* 174.
59. McKnight, *A Pioneer History,* 275.
60. Ruth Reitz, "Slave Escape Network Passed through Brookville," [DuBois, PA] *Courier Express* (June 1, 1987): B8–B9.
61. Ibid.
62. Ibid.
63. McKnight, *A Pioneer History,* 281.
64. Ibid., 275.
65. Wallace, *Indian Paths,* 27.
66. McKnight, *A Pioneer History,* 275.
67. Blockson, *Underground Railroad in Pennsylvania,* 126–27.
68. Wallace, *Indian Paths,* 129.
69. Ibid., 39.
70. Siebert, *Underground Railroad,* 434.
71. Ibid., map insert.
72. Wallace, *Indian Paths,* 170.
73. Siebert, *Underground Railroad,* map insert.
74. Ibid., 236.

UNIONTOWN–INDIANA ROUTE
1. Buck, *Planting of Civilization,* 149–50.
2. Harpster, *Crossroads,* 261–62.
3. Siebert, *Underground Railroad,* 122–23.
4. Ibid., 123.

5. Ibid., 113.
6. R.W. Brewster, "The Rise of the Antislavery Movement in Southwestern Pennsylvania," *Western Pennsylvania Historical Magazine* 22 (March 1939): 5.
7. Wallace, *Indian Paths,* 109.
8. Ibid., 110–11.
9. Archer Butler Hulbert, *The Old National Road: The Historic Highway of America* (originally published in the 1901 edition, vol. 9, of the *Ohio Archaeological and Historical Publication*), 1954, 421–25.
10. Thomas B. Searight, *The Old Pike: A History of the National Road with Incidents, Accidents, and Anecdotes Thereon* (Uniontown, PA: self-published, 1894), 109.
11. Siebert, *Underground Railroad,* 113.
12. Brewster, "Rise of the Antislavery Movement," 5.
13. Buck, *Planting of Civilization,* 516–17.
14. Wallace, *Indian Paths,* 165–67.
15. Pamphlet, "Youghiogheny River Lake," (Pittsburgh: U.S. Army Corps of Engineers, 1995), 1.
16. Siebert, *Underground Railroad,* 113; Brewster, "Rise of the Antislavery Movement," 5.
17. Brewster, "Rise of the Antislavery Movement," 5.
18. Blockson, *Underground Railroad in Pennsylvania,* 162–63.
19. Siebert, *Underground Railroad,* 113.
20. Buck, *Planting of Civilization,* 516–17.
21. Siebert, *Underground Railroad,* 113, 122–23.
22. Wallace, *Indian Paths,* 27–29.
23. Buck, *Planting of Civilization,* 516–17.
24. Wallace, *Indian Paths,* 184–85.
25. Siebert, *Underground Railroad,* 432.
26. Blockson, *Underground Railroad in Pennsylvania,* 162.
27. Howard Wallace, *Historical Sketch of the Underground Railroad from Uniontown to Pittsburgh* (self-published, c. 1888), 1.
28. Ibid.
29. Blockson, *Underground Railroad in Pennsylvania,* 162.
30. James Hadden, *A History of Uniontown: The County Seat of Fayette County Pennsylvania* (Akron, OH: New Werner Co., 1913), 609.
31. George Swetnam, *Pittsylvania Country* (New York: Duell Sloan & Pearce, 1951), 183.
32. Hadden, *History of Uniontown,* 610–11.
33. Ibid.
34. Blockson, *Underground Railroad in Pennsylvania,* 162.
35. Siebert, *Underground Railroad,* 123.
36. Hadden, *History of Uniontown,* 610.
37. Brewster, "Rise of the Antislavery Movement," 5.
38. Swetnam, *Pittsylvania Country,* 183.

39. Siebert, *Underground Railroad,* 113.
40. Blockson, *Underground Railroad in Pennsylvania,* 159.
41. Wallace, *Indian Paths,* 27–29.
42. Hulbert, *Old National Road,* 422.
43. Buck, *Planting of Civilization,* 516–17.
44. Siebert, *Underground Railroad,* 113.
45. Blockson, *Underground Railroad in Pennsylvania,* 159.
46. Ibid.
47. Siebert, *Underground Railroad,* 113.
48. Buck, *Planting of Civilization,* 516–17.
49. Siebert, *Underground Railroad,* 113.
50. Stephenson, *Indiana County,* vol. 3, 113.
51. Ibid.
52. Hadden, *History of Uniontown,* 610.
53. Buck, *Planting of Civilization,* 516–17.
54. Stephenson, *Indiana County,* vol. 1, 367.
55. Siebert, *Underground Railroad,* 433.
56. Stephenson, *Indiana County,* vol. 1, 371.
57. Ibid., vol. 3, 113–15.
58. Western Pennsylvania Historic Survey, *Guidebook to Historic Places in Western Pennsylvania* (Pittsburgh: University of Pittsburgh Press, 1938), 98.
59. Stephenson, *Indiana County,* vol. 3, 113.
60. *Guidebook,* 98.
61. Stephenson, *Indiana County,* vol. 3, 113.
62. Ibid., 115.
63. Siebert, *Underground Railroad,* 113.
64. Stephenson, *Indiana County,* vol. 3, 114.
65. Wallace, *Indian Paths,* 27–29.
66. Stephenson, *Indiana County,* vol. 3, 114.
67. Blockson, *Underground Railroad in Pennsylvania,* 162.
68. Siebert, *Underground Railroad,* 113.
69. *Guidebook,* 99.
70. McKnight, *A Pioneer History,* 281.
71. Ibid.
72. Siebert, *Underground Railroad,* 113.
73. Blockson, *Underground Railroad in Pennsylvania,* 102–3.
74. Wallace, *Indian Paths,* 56.
75. Blockson, *Underground Railroad in Pennsylvania,* 102–3.

UNIONTOWN–PITTSBURGH ROUTE

1. Siebert, *Underground Railroad,* 113.
2. Howard Wallace, *Historical Sketch,* 3.
3. Ibid., 2.

4. Ibid., 3.

5. Blockson, *Underground Railroad in Pennsylvania,* 161.

6. Swetnam, *Pittsylvania Country,* 183.

7. Howard Wallace, *Historical Sketch,* 4.

8. Ibid., 4–5.

9. Ibid., 4–5.

10. Ibid., 5.

11. Swetnam, *Pittsylvania Country,* 183.

12. George Swetnam and Helene Smith, *A Guidebook to Historic Western Pennsylvania* (Pittsburgh: University of Pittsburgh Press, 1976), 224.

13. Scott Beveridge, "The Fugitives," *Washington Observer-Reporter* (Sunday, February 23, 1997): B1.

14. Howard Wallace, *Historical Sketch,* 5.

15. Brewster, "The Rise of the Antislavery Movement," 5.

16. Blockson, *Underground Railroad in Pennsylvania,* 162.

17. Siebert, *Underground Railroad,* 113.

18. Coffin, *Reminiscences,* 441.

19. Erasmus Wilson, ed., *Standard History of Pittsburg (sic) Pennsylvania* (Chicago: H. R. Cornell & Co., 1898), 134–40.

20. Siebert, *Underground Railroad,* 123.

21. Buck, *Planting of Civilization,* 235.

22. Siebert, *Underground Railroad,* 123.

23. Blockson, *Underground Railroad in Pennsylvania,* 157.

24. Rev. Joseph H. Bausman, *History of Beaver County, Pennsylvania, and its Centennial Celebration* (New York: Knickerbocker Press, 1904), 1141–42.

25. Ibid., 1142–45.

26. Siebert, *Underground Railroad,* 431.

27. *American Slavery,* 88.

28. Bausman, *History,* 1144–49.

29. Blockson, *Underground Railroad in Pennsylvania,* 157.

30. Bausman, *History,* 1144.

31. Ibid.

32. Ibid., 1142.

33. Ibid., 727 and 1142.

34. Blockson, *Underground Railroad in Pennsylvania,* 153.

35. Siebert, *Underground Railroad,* 113.

36. Bausman, *History,* 1144.

37. Blockson, *Underground Railroad in Pennsylvania,* 151.

38. *My Pennsylvania: A Brief History of the Commonwealth's Sixty-seven Counties* (Harrisburg, PA: Commonwealth of Pennsylvania, 1946), 76.

39. Blockson, *Underground Railroad in Pennsylvania,* 151.

40. Siebert, *Underground Railroad,* 433.

41. Buck, *Planting of Civilization,* 235.

42. Blockson, *Underground Railroad in Pennsylvania,* 151.
43. "Slavery, Anti-Slavery, and the Underground Railroad," *Mercer County History* 4, no. 2 (Fall 1974): 33–34.
44. Siebert, *Underground Railroad,* 433.
45. Buck, *Planting of Civilization,* 235.
46. Blockson, *Underground Railroad in Pennsylvania,* 125.
47. Ibid., 125–26.
48. Ibid., 125.
49. Siebert, *Underground Railroad,* 273.
50. Ibid., 113.
51. Bausman, *History,* 1144.
52. Ibid., 1146–49.
53. Ibid., 1142.
54. Blockson, *Underground Railroad in Pennsylvania,* 152.
55. Bausman, *History,* 1141.
56. Ibid.
57. Ibid., 1142.
58. Still, *Underground Railroad,* 25.
59. Siebert, *Underground Railroad,* 123.
60. Blockson, *Underground Railroad in Pennsylvania,* 159.
61. Siebert, *Underground Railroad,* 113.
62. Jerry Byrd, "A Trackless Railroad," *Pittsburgh Press Roto* (October 17, 1982): 19.
63. Siebert, *Underground Railroad,* 113.
64. Buck, *Planting of Civilization,* 235.
65. Ibid.

WASHINGTON ROUTE

1. *Historical United States Census Data Browser* (http://fisher.lib.virginia.edu/census/).
2. Buck, *Planting of Civilization,* 214.
3. *Historical United States Census Data Browser.*
4. Buck, *Planting of Civilization,* 152.
5. Ibid., 279–80.
6. Siebert, *Underground Railroad,* 434.
7. *The Western Telegraph and Washington Advertizer* (February 9, 1796): 3.
8. W. J. Bell, Jr., "Washington County Pennsylvania, in the 18th Century Antislavery Movement," *Western Pennsylvania Historical Society Magazine* 25 (September–December 1942), 136–37.
9. Earle R. Forrest, *History of Washington County, Pennsylvania* (Chicago: S. J. Clarke Publishing Co., 1926), vol. 1, 416.
10. *The Examiner and Farmers' and Mechanics' Repository* (May 1, 1830): 3.
11. Forrest, *History of Washington,* vol. 1, 419.
12. Ibid., 419–20.
13. Wallace, *Indian Paths,* 32 and 59.

14. Buck, *Planting of Civilization,* 516–17.
15. Ibid., 236.
16. Swetnam, *Pittsylvania Country,* 183.
17. Hulbert, *Old National Road,* 407.
18. Buck, *Planting of Civilization,* 241.
19. Patrick Connors, *Pennsylvania Historic Towns of Washington County* (Monongahela, PA: Historic Towns Publishing, 1996), vol. 1, 40.
20. Forrest, *History of Washington,* vol. 1, 425–26.
21. Ibid., 424.
22. Ibid.
23. Ibid.
24. Connors, *Pennsylvania Historic Towns,* vol. 1, 42.
25. Harpster, *Crossroads,* 273.
26. *Examiner and Farmers' and Mechanics' Repository* (May 26, 1827): 3.
27. Brewster, "Rise of the Antislavery Movement," 5.
28. Forrest, *History of Washington,* vol. 1, 425.
29. Ibid., 426.
30. Beveridge, "Fugitives," B1.
31. Forrest, *History of Washington,* vol. 1, 425–27.
32. Blockson, *Underground Railroad in Pennsylvania,* 158.
33. Beveridge, "Fugitives," B3.
34. Forrest, *History of Washington,* vol. 1, 424.
35. Ibid.
36. Brewster, "Rise of the Antislavery Movement," 5.
37. Beveridge, "Fugitives," B1.
38. Forrest, *History of Washington,* vol. 1, 426.
39. Wallace, *Indian Paths,* 32.
40. Buck, *Planting of Civilization,* 516–17.
41. Rev. William Hanna, *History of Greene County, Pennsylvania, Containing an Outline of the State from 1682 until the Formation of Washington County in 1781* (self-published, 1882), 116–18.
42. Swetnam and Smith, *Guidebook,* 151.
43. Brewster, "Rise of the Antislavery Movement," 5.
44. Wallace, *Indian Paths,* 100.
45. Buck, *Planting of Civilization,* 516–17.
46. Hulbert, *Old National Road,* 407.
47. Wallace, *Indian Paths,* 32.
48. Connors, *Pennsylvania Historic Towns,* vol. 1, 35.
49. Harpster, *Crossroads,* 170.
50. Ibid., 272.
51. Buck, *Planting of Civilization,* 215.
52. Swetnam and Smith, *Guidebook,* 213.
53. Blockson, *Underground Railroad in Pennsylvania,* 158.

54. Swetnam and Smith, *Guidebook,* 213.
55. Sally Kalson, "Along the Freedom Path," *Gazette* (February 6, 1994): 8.
56. Ibid., 8.
57. Forrest, *History of Washington,* vol. 1, 425–26.
58. Connors, *Pennsylvania Historic Towns,* vol. 2, 27.
59. May 5, 1998, interview with Prof. V. Robert Agostino, author of *A Track through Time: A Centennial History of Carnegie Pennsylvania* (Pittsburgh: Wolfson Publishing, 1994).
60. Buck, *Planting of Civilization,* 516–17.
61. Connors, *Pennsylvania Historic Towns,* vol. 1, 17.
62. Buck, *Planting of Civilization,* 241.
63. Beveridge, "Fugitives," B1.
64. Ibid.

PITTSBURGH NETWORK

1. Leland D. Baldwin, *Pittsburgh: The Story of a City, 1750–1865* (Pittsburgh: University of Pittsburgh Press, 1937), 54.
2. Ibid., 108.
3. *Blacks in Pittsburgh: A Chronology* (Pittsburgh: Historical Society of Western Pennsylvania, n.d.), 1.
4. *Historical United States Census Data Browser.*
5. Wilson, *Standard History,* 810.
6. Ibid., 811–12.
7. Baldwin, *Pittsburgh,* 305.
8. Wilson, *Standard History,* 514.
9. *Pittsburgh Gazette* (February 10, 1832): 3.
10. Byrd, "Trackless Railroad," 18.
11. *Blacks in Pittsburgh,* 2.
12. Wilson, *Standard History,* 816.
13. Ibid., 817.
14. Ibid., 814.
15. Ibid., 817.
16. Jerry Byrd, "The Delany 'Solution,'" *Pittsburgh Press Roto Magazine* (October 17, 1982): 20.
17. Wilson, *Standard History,* 852.
18. Ibid., 817.
19. Kelly Flanagan, "Legendary History for Local Hotel," *South Hills Record* (January 15, 1998): 1, 12.
20. Byrd, "Trackless Railroad," 19.
21. Kalson, "Along the Freedom Path," 7.
22. *Blacks in Pittsburgh,* 1.
23. *Pittsburgh Gazette* (May 14, 1833): 3 and (June 14, 1833): 2.
24. Kalson, "Along the Freedom Path," 7.

25. Wilson, *Standard History,* 821.

26. Carnegie Library Homepage, *Bridging the Urban Landscape,* 1–3 (http://www. hrr.org/delany.htm).

27. Byrd, "Trackless Railroad," 18.

28. Letter from Martin Delany to Frederick Douglass, July 10, 1852. In C. Peter Ripley, ed., *The Black Abolitionist Papers,* vol. 4 (Chapel Hill, NC: University of North Carolina Press, 1991), 126–28.

29. *Blacks in Pittsburgh,* 1.

30. *Guidebook,* 12.

31. Letter from Lewis Woodson to Samuel E. Cornish, editor of *Colored American* (n.d.), *Black Abolitionist Papers,* vol. 3, 256–58.

32. Jerry Byrd, "Avery's Legacy," *Pittsburgh Press Roto Magazine* (October 17, 1982): 20.

33. Kalson, "Along the Freedom Trail," 7.

34. Wilson, *Standard History,* 517.

35. Byrd, "Avery's Legacy," 20.

36. Siebert, *Underground Railroad,* 431.

37. Byrd, "Trackless Railroad," 18.

38. Ibid.

39. Flanagan, "Legendary History for Local Hotel," 1; Baldwin, *Pittsburgh,* 305; and Kalson, "Along the Freedom Trail," 7.

40. Blockson, *Underground Railroad in Pennsylvania,* 156–57.

41. Byrd, "Trackless Railroad," 18.

42. Baldwin, *Pittsburgh,* 273; Kalson, "Along the Freedom Trail," 7.

43. Baldwin, *Pittsburgh,* 305.

44. Kalson, "Along the Freedom Trail," 7.

45. *Daily Morning Post* (July 29, 1850): 2.

46. Wilson, *Standard History,* 819–20.

47. *Daily Morning Post* (January 27, 1847): 4, (April 19, 1847): 4, (April 20, 1847): 4.

48. *Pittsburgh Daily Gazette* (April 17, 1847): 2.

49. *Daily Morning Post* (September 26, 1850): 2.

50. *Historical United States Census Data Browser* (for 1850 and 1860).

51. *Daily Morning Post* (September 30, 1850): 2.

52. *Daily Morning Post* (October 1, 1850): 2.

CRAWFORD–ERIE COUNTY NETWORK

1. Swetnam and Smith, *Guidebook,* 104.

2. Buck, *Planting of Civilization,* 235.

3. Ibid., 237.

4. Wallace, *Indian Paths,* 36, 43, 81, 170.

5. Ibid., 105.

6. Blockson, *Underground Railroad in Pennsylvania,* 122.

7. Siebert, *Underground Railroad,* 98, 432.

8. Ibid., 113.

9. Blockson, *Underground Railroad in Pennsylvania,* 122–23.
10. Swetnam and Smith, *Guidebook,* 106–7.
11. Siebert, *Underground Railroad,* 113.
12. Wallace, *Indian Paths,* 37.
13. Swetnam and Smith, *Guidebook,* 105.
14. Blockson, *Underground Railroad in Pennsylvania,* 122–24.
15. Siebert, *Underground Railroad,* 113.
16. Blockson, *Underground Railroad in Pennsylvania,* 123–24.
17. John R. Claridge, *Lost Erie: The Vanished Heritage of City and County* (Erie, PA: Erie County Historical Society, 1911), 5.
18. Swetnam and Smith, *Guidebook,* 115–16.
19. Wallace, *Indian Paths,* 37.
20. Ibid., 25–26.
21. Ibid., 171–73.
22. Ibid., 140.
23. Ibid., 85–87.
24. Ibid., 172–73.
25. Ibid., 25–26.
26. Buck, *Planting of Civilization,* 236–37.
27. Siebert, *Underground Railroad,* 113.
28. Ibid.
29. Blockson, *Underground Railroad in Pennsylvania,* 122–24.
30. Siebert, *Underground Railroad,* 113.
31. Swetnam and Smith, *Guidebook,* 124.
32. Blockson, *Underground Railroad in Pennsylvania,* 122.
33. Ibid.
34. Siebert, *Underground Railroad,* 113.
35. Blockson, *Underground Railroad in Pennsylvania,* 122.
36. John Elmer Reed, *History of Erie County, Pennsylvania* (Topeka, KS: Historical Publishing Co., 1925), 378.
37. Blockson, *Underground Railroad in Pennsylvania,* 122.
38. Siebert, *Underground Railroad,* 113.
39. Ibid.
40. Blockson, *Underground Railroad in Pennsylvania,* 122.
41. Reed, *History of Erie,* 378.
42. Blockson, *Underground Railroad in Pennsylvania,* 121.
43. Swetnam and Smith, *Guidebook,* 122.
44. Barbara N. Ekey, "Bound for Freedom through Sugar Grove," [Erie, PA] *Times-News* (March 1, 1992): 5K.
45. Reed, *History of Erie,* 378.
46. Ibid.
47. Blockson, *Underground Railroad in Pennsylvania,* 127.
48. Ekey, "Bound for Freedom," 5K

49. Ibid.

50. Ibid.

51. Blockson, *Underground Railroad in Pennsylvania,* 126.

52. Ekey, "Bound for Freedom," 5K.

53. Reed, *History of Erie,* 378.

54. Swetnam and Smith, *Guidebook,* 120.

55. Claridge, *Lost Erie,* 14.

56. Blockson, *Underground Railroad in Pennsylvania,* 121.

57. Reed, *History of Erie,* 378.

58. Siebert, *Underground Railroad,* 432.

CENTRAL ROUTE

1. Blockson, *Underground Railroad in Pennsylvania,* 142.

2. *Pennsylvania Atlas & Gazeteer,* 90.

3. Wallace, *Indian Paths,* 179.

4. *The Encyclopedia of Pennsylvania* (St. Clair Shores, MI: Somerset Publishers, 1983), 393.

5. Blockson, *Underground Railroad in Pennsylvania,* 142

6. Wallace, *Indian Paths,* 143.

7. *Encyclopedia of Pennsylvania,* 278.

8. Blockson, *Underground Railroad in Pennsylvania,* 143–44.

9. "Talk to Feature Local Stops on Underground Railroad," [Carlisle] *Sentinel* (September 12, 1999): www.cumberlink.com/local news/1999/09/local news.9.12.html.

10. Frederick A. Godcharles, *Pennsylvania Political, Governmental, Military and Civil Physical, Economic and Social Volume* (New York: The American Historical Society, 1933), 116.

11. Ibid., 155.

12. Wallace, *Indian Paths,* 177.

13. *Encyclopedia of Pennsylvania,* 273.

14. Blockson, *Underground Railroad in Pennsylvania,* 78–79.

15. George R. Crooks, *Life and Letters of the Rev. John McClintock, D.D.* (New York: Nelson & Phillips, 1876), 145–51.

16. "Talk to Feature Local Stops."

17. Ibid.

18. Ibid.

19. Blockson, *Underground Railroad in Pennsylvania,* 146.

20. Wallace, *Indian Paths,* 57–58.

21. Blockson, *Underground Railroad in Pennsylvania,* 145–46.

22. Ibid., 146.

23. Ibid.

24. Ibid.

25. "Historic Mansion Goes on the Market," [Carlisle] *Sentinel* (August 31, 1999): www.cumberlink.com/local news/1999/08/local news.8.31.html.

26. Blockson, *Underground Railroad in Pennsylvania*, 79.
27. Ibid., 146.
28. Ibid.
29. Siebert, *Underground Railroad*, foldout map.
30. Smedley, *History of the Underground Railroad*, 30.
31. Ibid., 36.
32. Blockson, *Underground Railroad in Pennsylvania*, 145.
33. Ibid., 144–45.
34. *Encyclopedia of Pennsylvania*, 339.
35. Smedley, *History of the Underground Railroad*, 36.
36. Fawn M. Brodie, *Thaddeus Stevens: Scourge of the South* (New York: W. W. Norton & Company, 1959), 64–65.
37. Smedley, *History of the Underground Railroad*, 36.
38. Blockson, *Underground Railroad in Pennsylvania*, 145–46.
39. Siebert, *Underground Railroad*, foldout map.
40. Blockson, *Underground Railroad in Pennsylvania*, 146.
41. Smedley, *History of the Underground Railroad*, 37.
42. Ibid., 37, 40, 45.
43. Robert Holt, "Underground Railroad Past Recalled," *Gettysburg Times* (November 19, 1998): www.gburgtimes.com/archives/archive98/november 11–19.html.
44. Ibid.
45. Smedley, *History of the Underground Railroad*, 37.
46. *Pennsylvania Encyclopedia*, 182–84.
47. *United States Historical Census Data Browser.*
48. Ibid.
49. Gerald G. Eppert, "'Two Steps Forward, a Step and a Half Back.' Harrisburg's African American Community in the Nineteenth Century," *African Americans in Pennsylvania: Shifting Historical Perspectives,* ed. Joe William Trotter, Jr., and Eric Ledell Smith (University Park, PA: Pennsylvania State University and the Pennsylvania Historical and Museum Commission), 223–27.
50. Ibid., 230–32.
51. Blockson, *Underground Railroad in Pennsylvania*, 75–77.
52. Godcharles, *Pennsylvania*, 110.
53. Wallace, *Indian Paths*, 122.
54. William H. Shank, *The Amazing Pennsylvania Canal* (York, PA: American Canal and Transportation Center, 1981), 18.
55. Godcharles, *Pennsylvania*, 146, 152, 155.
56. Still, *Underground Railroad*, 244.
57. Shank, *Amazing Pennsylvania Canal*, 18, 26, 30.
58. Harry A. Jacobs, *The Juniata Canal and Old Portage Railroad* (Hollidaysburg, PA: Blair County Historical Society, 1941), 19.
59. Blockson, *Underground Railroad in Pennsylvania*, 107.
60. McKnight, *A Pioneer History*, 281.

61. Blockson, *Underground Railroad in Pennsylvania,* 73, 105.
62. Wallace, *Indian Paths,* 78.
63. Siebert, *Underground Railroad,* 80.
64. Still, *Underground Railroad,* 43, 218.
65. Siebert, *Underground Railroad,* 79.
66. Still, *Underground Railroad,* 42–43.
67. Wallace, *Indian Paths,* 35, 161.
68. Blockson, *Underground Railroad in Pennsylvania,* 109.
69. "Governor Snyder Mansion," pamphlet (Selinsgrove, PA).
70. Charles M. Snyder, *Union County, Pennsylvania: A Bicentennial History* (Lewisburg, PA: Colonial Printing House, 1976), 243.
71. Nora Gray, *Historic Union County: Lewisburg, the Middle Years 1840–1880* (Mifflinburg, PA: *Mifflinburg Telegraph,* n.d.), 2–3.
72. *Pennsylvania Encyclopedia,* 414.
73. Blockson, *Underground Railroad in Pennsylvania,* 116.
74. Ibid., 116–17.
75. Ibid.
76. Ibid.
77. Wallace, *Indian Paths,* 152–53.
78. Wallace, *Indian Paths,* 159.
79. Blockson, *Underground Railroad in Pennsylvania,* 113.
80. Wallace, *Indian Paths,* 66, 67, 155.
81. Blockson, *Underground Railroad in Pennsylvania,* 114–16.
82. Wallace, *Indian Paths,* 160–61.
83. Blockson, *Underground Railroad in Pennsylvania,* 131.
84. Wallace, *Indian Paths,* 188–89.

SOUTHEASTERN CORRIDOR

1. Blockson, *Underground Railroad in Pennsylvania,* 83.
2. Siebert, *Underground Railroad,* foldout map.
3. Godcharles, *Pennsylvania,* 110.
4. Smedley, *History of the Underground Railroad,* 45–46, 48.
5. Blockson, *Underground Railroad in Pennsylvania,* 83.
6. Smedley, *History of the Underground Railroad,* 39.
7. Blockson, *Underground Railroad in Pennsylvania,* 147.
8. Smedley, *History of the Underground Railroad,* 46.
9. Ibid., 36–37.
10. Blockson, *Underground Railroad in Pennsylvania,* 83.
11. *Pennsylvania Encyclopedia,* 345.
12. Blockson, *Underground Railroad in Pennsylvania,* 146.
13. Wallace, *Indian Paths,* 105.
14. Ibid.
15. Blockson, *Underground Railroad in Pennsylvania,* 147.

16. Smedley, *History of the Underground Railroad,* 27.
17. *Pennsylvania Encyclopedia,* 291–92.
18. Godcharles, *Pennsylvania,* 110.
19. Smedley, *History of the Underground Railroad,* 27.
20. Blockson, *Underground Railroad in Pennsylvania,* 88.
21. Smedley, *History of the Underground Railroad,* 46.
22. Still, *Underground Railroad,* 736.
23. Speech by William Whipper delivered at the Colored Temperance Society of Philadelphia, January 8, 1834, *The Black Abolitionist Papers,* vol. 3, 119–29.
24. Letter from William Whipper to Frederick Douglas, October 1854, *The Black Abolitionist Papers,* vol. 14, 242.
25. Smedley, *History of the Underground Railroad,* 46, 49.
26. Ibid., 208.
27. Ibid., 63, 192.
28. Ibid., 49, 54, 57, 59.
29. Siebert, *Underground Railroad,* foldout map.
30. Smedley, *History of the Underground Railroad,* 85.
31. Ibid., 89.
32. Ibid., 31.
33. Blockson, *Underground Railroad in Pennsylvania,* 88, 96.
34. Smedley, *History of the Underground Railroad,* 31, 71, 227, 233.
35. Siebert, *Underground Railroad,* foldout map.
36. Smedley, *History of the Underground Railroad,* 80.
37. Ibid., 77
38. Blockson, *Underground Railroad in Pennsylvania,* 97.
39. Ibid., 88.
40. Smedley, *History of the Underground Railroad,* 182–86.
41. Ibid., 208.
42. Ibid., 31–32, 208.
43. Ibid., 90, 93, 100.
44. Ibid., 100–101.
45. Ibid., 33, 64, 134, 137, 164.
46. Ibid., 143.
47. Blockson, *Underground Railroad in Pennsylvania,* 61.
48. Smedley, *History of the Underground Railroad,* 33–34, 158.
49. Ibid., 32, 171, 174.
50. Ibid., 191–92, 194, 202, 204.
51. Blockson, *Underground Railroad in Pennsylvania,* 56.
52. Smedley, *History of the Underground Railroad,* 193.
53. Ibid., 211–13.
54. Blockson, *Underground Railroad in Pennsylvania,* 61.
55. Smedley, *History of the Underground Railroad,* 32, 208.
56. Still, *Underground Railroad,* 43.

57. Smedley, *History of the Underground Railroad,* 90–94, 132.

58. Ibid., 134–36.

59. Blockson, *Underground Railroad in Pennsylvania,* 60.

60. Ibid.

61. Smedley, *History of the Underground Railroad,* 32.

62. Ibid., 33–34.

63. Ibid., 100.

64. Still, *Underground Railroad,* 39–40.

65. Smedley, *History of the Underground Railroad,* 32.

66. Ibid., 273–74.

67. Ibid., 248–50, 253, 301, 308.

68. *Pennsylvania Encyclopedia,* 365.

69. Smedley, *History of the Underground Railroad,* 260–64, 266–67.

70. Blockson, *Underground Railroad in Pennsylvania,* 61.

71. Smedley, *History of the Underground Railroad,* 247–48, 282, 285–88, 301, 304.

72. Ibid., 288–89, 297.

73. Ibid., 33, 100.

74. Ibid., 100, 308, 337–38.

75. Blockson, *Underground Railroad in Pennsylvania,* 56.

76. Smedley, *History of the Underground Railroad,* 100, 338–39.

77. Ibid., 253, 323, 324.

78. Siebert, *Underground Railroad,* foldout map.

79. Blockson, *Underground Railroad in Pennsylvania,* 60, 64.

80. Siebert, *Underground Railroad,* foldout map.

81. Smedley, *History of the Underground Railroad,* 344, 346.

82. Blockson, *Underground Railroad in Pennsylvania,* 64.

83. Ibid., 60, 62.

84. Ibid., 63.

PHILADELPHIA NETWORK

1. Billy G. Smith, "Philadelphia: The Athens of America," *Life in Early Philadelphia: Documents from the Revolutionary and Early National Periods,* ed. by Billy G. Smith (University Park, PA: Pennsylvania State University Press, 1995), 3.

2. Ibid., 10.

3. Clement Biddle, *The Philadelphia Directory* (1791), as found in Smith, *Life in Early Philadelphia,* 15.

4. Ibid., 19, 21.

5. Robinson, *Historical Negro Biographies,* 5–6.

6. Gary Nash, "Slaves and Slave Owners in Colonial Philadelphia," *African Americans in Pennsylvania: Shifting Historical Perspectives,* ed. by Joe Williams Trotter, Jr., and Eric Ledell Smith (University Park, PA: Pennsylvania State University Press and the Pennsylvania Historical and Museum Commission, 1997), 41.

7. Ibid., 41, 44–50.

8. Ibid., 51–52.
9. Emma Jones Lapsansky, "'Since They Got These Separate Churches': Afro-Americans and Racism in Jacksonian Philadelphia," Trotter and Smith, *African Americans in Pennsylvania*, 94–96.
10. Nilgun Amadolus Okur, "Underground Railroad in Philadelphia, 1830–1860," *Journal of Black Studies* 25, no. 5 (May 1995): 554.
11. Washington, Letter to Robert Morris, April 12, 1786, vol. 28, 407–8.
12. G. S. Rowe and Billy G. Smith, "Prisoners for Trail Docket and the Vagrancy Docket," in Smith, *Life in Early Philadelphia*, 68–77, 80–86.
13. *Pennsylvania Gazette* (January 21, 1795): 3.
14. Okur, "Underground Railroad in Philadelphia, 1830–1860," 537.
15. Winch, *Philadelphia Black Elite*, 11.
16. Robinson, *Historical Negro Biographies*, 19–20.
17. Blockson, *Underground Railroad*, 211.
18. Blockson, *Underground Railroad in Pennsylvania*, 15–16.
19. Still, *Underground Railroad*, 611–12.
20. Blockson, *Underground Railroad*, 210.
21. Robinson, *Historical Negro Biographies*, 19.
22. Letter from James Forten to William Lloyd Garrison, May 6, 1832, *The Black Abolitionist Papers*, vol. 3, 86–87.
23. Ibid., 110.
24. Ibid., 127.
25. Okur, "Underground Railroad in Philadelphia, 1830–1860," 537.
26. Still, *Underground Railroad*, 323.
27. Ibid., 218.
28. Ibid., 316.
29. Frederick Douglass, *My Bondage and My Freedom* (New York: Arno Press and the New York Times, 1968; reprint, New York: Miller, Orton & Mulligan, 1855), 326.
30. Ibid.
31. Still, *Underground Railroad*, 316.
32. Ibid., 559.
33. Smedley, *History of the Underground Railroad*, 347.
34. Douglass, *My Bondage and My Freedom*, 326.
35. Still, *Underground Railroad*, 296.
36. Siebert, *Underground Railroad*, 121–22.
37. Still, *Underground Railroad*, 530.
38. Blockson, *Underground Railroad in Pennsylvania*, 12.
39. Smedley, *History of the Underground Railroad*, 347.
40. Still, *Underground Railroad*, 537.
41. Godcharles, *Pennsylvania*, 116.
42. Charles L. Blockson, "A Black Underground Resistance to Slavery, 1833–1860," *Pennsylvania Heritage* 4, no. 1 (December 1977): 30.
43. Ibid., 30–31.

44. Blockson, *Underground Railroad*, 207.

45. "Resolutions of a Committee of Philadelphia Blacks Presented at the Wesley AME Church in Philadelphia, October 14, 1850," *The Black Abolitionist Papers*, vol. 4, 68–70.

46. Blockson, *Underground Railroad in Pennsylvania*, 13–14.

47. Ibid., 15.

48. Still, *Underground Railroad*, 665.

49. Okur, "Underground Railroad in Philadelphia, 1830–1860," 551.

50. Blockson, *Underground Railroad*, 209.

51. Blockson, *Underground Railroad in Pennsylvania*, 17, 24, 26–27.

52. Blockson, *Underground Railroad*, 212–13.

53. Blockson, "A Black Underground," 33.

54. Still, *Underground Railroad*, 746.

NORTHEASTERN CORRIDOR

1. Blockson, *Underground Railroad in Pennsylvania*, 8.

 2. Ibid., 84.

 3. Smedley, *History of the Underground Railroad*, 215, 217.

 4. Wallace, *Indian Paths*, 107–8.

 5. Blockson, *Underground Railroad in Pennsylvania*, 85–86.

 6. Ibid., 84–85.

 7. Ibid., 86–87.

 8. Ibid., 49, 85–87.

 9. James A. Williams, "Slavery and Politics in Montgomery County, 1835–1855," *Bulletin of the Historical Society of Montgomery County* 27 (Fall 1988): 120–21, 129.

10. Smedley, *History of the Underground Railroad*, 30, 218, 221–22.

11. Blockson, *Underground Railroad in Pennsylvania*, 31.

12. Smedley, *History of the Underground Railroad*, 93, 192; Blockson, *Underground Railroad in Pennsylvania*, 48.

13. Blockson, *Underground Railroad in Pennsylvania*, 48.

14. Siebert, *Underground Railroad*, foldout map; also see Smedley, *History of the Underground Railroad*, 208, 222.

15. Godcharles, *Pennsylvania*, 116.

16. Wallace, *Indian Paths*, 102–3.

17. Blockson, *Underground Railroad in Pennsylvania*, 49.

18. Diane Stonebach, "Of Real Gingerbread Men, Tastes of South America," [Allentown] *Morning Call* (December 9, 1989): A73.

19. Hal Marcovitz, "Kostmayer Wants to Preserve Slaves' Railroad to Freedom," *Morning Call* (January 16, 1990): B01.

20. Smedley, *History of the Underground Railroad*, 208, 222.

21. Blockson, *Underground Railroad in Pennsylvania*, 35.

22. Marcovitz, "Kostmayer Wants to Preserve Slaves' Railroad to Freedom," B01.

23. Ibid.

24. "Milford Historians to Gather Tomorrow at Brick Tavern Inn," *Morning Call* (November 6, 1985): B09.
25. Scott Siebert, "Paintings Fulfill a Promise to Maintain a Family's Heritage," *Morning Call* (December 12, 1985): N03.
26. Blockson, *Underground Railroad in Pennsylvania*, 134.
27. Ibid.
28. Siebert, *Underground Railroad*, 122 and foldout map.
29. Wallace, *Indian Paths*, 157, 187–88.
30. Siebert, *Underground Railroad*, foldout map.
31. Blockson, *Underground Railroad in Pennsylvania*, 135.
32. Wallace, *Indian Paths*, 88–89.
33. Blockson, *Underground Railroad in Pennsylvania*, 133.
34. Christine Magnotta, "Dream Home Sours for Couple," *Pocono Record* (July 6, 1998): www.poconorecord.com/1998/local/tjd70360.html.
35. Blockson, *Underground Railroad in Pennsylvania*, 131.
36. Siebert, *Underground Railroad*, foldout map.
37. Blockson, *Underground Railroad in Pennsylvania*, 131.
38. Siebert, *Underground Railroad*, 122.
39. Wallace, *Indian Paths*, 124–25.
40. Blockson, *Underground Railroad in Pennsylvania*, 132–33.
41. Ibid., 131.
42. Siebert, *Underground Railroad*, 121 and foldout map.
43. Blockson, *Underground Railroad in Pennsylvania*, 131.
44. Wallace, *Indian Paths*, 72–74.
45. Blockson, *Underground Railroad in Pennsylvania*, 135.
46. Siebert, *Underground Railroad*, 121 and foldout map.
47. Ibid.
48. Blockson, *Underground Railroad in Pennsylvania*, 134.
49. Blockson, "A Black Underground," 32.
50. Blockson, *Underground Railroad in Pennsylvania*, 40, 47, 49.
51. Ibid., 35.
52. Ibid., 36.
53. Ibid., 48.
54. *Pennsylvania Gazette* (October 21, 1795): 2.
55. Blockson, *Underground Railroad in Pennsylvania*, 36.
56. Ibid., 48, 51.
57. Ibid., 48–49.
58. Ibid.
59. Marcovitz, "Kostmayer Wants to Preserve Slaves' Railroad to Freedom," B01.
60. Smedley, *History of the Underground Railroad*, 222, 326.
61. Blockson, *Underground Railroad in Pennsylvania*, 35.
62. Blockson, *Underground Railroad*, 216.
63. Blockson, *Underground Railroad in Pennsylvania*, 36.

THE ROLE OF ORGANIZED RELIGION

1. Samuel May, *Some Recollections of Our Antislavery Conflict* (Boston: Fields, Osgood & Co., 1869; reprint, Arno Press and the *New York Times,* 1968) 331.

2. Robinson, *Historical Negro Biographies,* 5–6.

3. Swetnam and Smith, *Guidebook,* 224.

4. John B. Harrison and Richard E. Sullivan, *A Short History of Western Civilization* (New York: Alfred A. Knopf, 1966), 442.

5. Mary Stoughton and A.M. Locke, *Anti-Slavery in America from the Introduction of African Slaves to the Prohibition of Slave Trade, 1619–1808* (Boston: Ginn & Company, Publishers, 1907), 146–47.

6. Ibid., 21, 416.

7. Ibid., 30.

8. Ibid., 25–26, 31.

9. Ibid., 31, 417.

10. Ibid., 417.

11. Coffin, *Reminiscences,* 223–30.

12. Ibid.

13. William W. Sweet, *The Story of Religion in America* (New York: Harper & Brothers Publishers, 1930), 175–79.

14. Buck, *Planting of Civilization,* 404–6.

15. Ibid., 407–8.

16. David Christy, *Pulpit Politics; or, Ecclesiastical Legislation on Slavery in Its Disturbing Influences on the American Union* (New York: Farran & McLean Publishers, 1862; reprint, Negro Universities Press, 1969), 343.

17. Ibid., 358–59.

18. Ibid., 349–51.

19. Ibid., 366, 369.

20. Harrison and Sullivan, *Short History,* 442–43.

21. Locke, *Anti-Slavery in America,* 41.

22. Ibid., 216, 224.

23. Ibid., 387–89.

24. Ibid., 400–1.

25. Buck, *Planting of Civilization,* 411.

26. Baldwin, *Pittsburgh,* 158.

27. Bausman, *History,* 1145.

28. Sweet, *Story of Religion,* 102, 119.

29. Buck, *Planting of Civilization,* 411–12.

30. Sweet, *Story of Religion,* 421–22.

31. Ibid., 428–32.

32. Sweet, *Story of Religion,* 347–49.

33. May, *Recollections,* 335–38.

34. Swetnam and Smith, *Guidebook,* 106–7.

35. Buck, *Planting of Civilization,* 413.

BIBLIOGRAPHY

Agostino, V. Robert. *A Track through Time: A Centennial History of Carnegie, Pennsylvania.* Pittsburgh: Wolfson Publishing, 1994.

American Slavery as It Is: Testimony of a Thousand Witnesses. New York: American Anti-Slavery Society, 1839; reprint, New York: Arno Press and the *New York Times,* 1968.

Baldwin, Leland. *Pittsburgh: The Story of a City, 1750–1856.* Pittsburgh: University of Pittsburgh Press, 1937.

Bausman, Rev. Joseph H. *History of Beaver County, Pennsylvania, and Its Centennial Celebration.* New York: Knickerbocker Press, 1904.

Bell, W. J., Jr. "Washington County, Pennsylvania, in the 18th Century Anti-slavery Movement." *Western Pennsylvania Historical Society Magazine* 25 (1942): 135–42.

Beveridge, Scott. "The Fugitives." *Washington Observer-Reporter* (February 23, 1997): 131, 133.

Biddle, Clement. *The Philadelphia Directory (1791).* In *Life in Early Philadelphia Documents from the Revolutionary and Early National Periods,* edited by Billy G. Smith. University Park, PA: Pennsylvania University Press, 1995.

Blackburn, E. Howard, and William H. Welfley. *History of Bedford and Somerset Counties, Pennsylvania, with Genealogical and Personal History.* New York: Lewis Publishing Co., 1906.

Blacks in Pittsburgh: A Chronology. Pittsburgh: Historical Society of Western Pennsylvania, n.d.

Blockson, Charles L. "A Black Underground Resistance to Slavery, 1833–1860." *Pennsylvania Heritage* 4, no. 1 (December 1977): 29–33.

———. *The Underground Railroad.* New York: Berkley Publishing Group, 1987.

———. *The Underground Railroad in Pennsylvania.* Jacksonville, NC: Flame International, 1981.

Brewster, R. W. "The Rise of the Antislavery Movement in Southwestern Pennsylvania." *Western Pennsylvania Historical Magazine* 22 (March 1939): 1–18.

Brown, Ira V. *Pennsylvania Reformers: From Penn to Pinchot.* University Park, PA: Pennsylvania Historical Association, 1966.

———. *The Negro in Pennsylvania History.* University Park, PA: Pennsylvania Historical Association, 1970.

Buck, Solon J., and Elizabeth Hawthorn Buck. *The Planting of Civilization in Western Pennsylvania.* Pittsburgh: University of Pittsburgh Press, 1967.

Burns, Edward M. "Slavery in Western Pennsylvania." *Western Pennsylvania Magazine* 7 (1925): 204–14.

Byrd, Jerry. "Avery's Legacy." *Pittsburgh Press Roto Magazine* (October 17, 1982): 20.

———. "The Delany Solution." *Pittsburgh Press Roto Magazine* (October 17, 1982): 20.

———. "A Trackless Railroad." *Pittsburgh Press Roto Magazine* (October 17, 1982): 18–19.

Calridge, John R. *Lost Erie: The Vanished Heritage of City and County.* Erie, PA: Erie County Historical Society, 1911.

Carnegie Library Homepage. *Bridging the Urban Landscape.* http://www.hrr.org/delany.htm.

Christy, David. *Pulpit Politics; or, Ecclesiastical Legislation on Slavery in Its Disturbing Influence on the American Union.* New York: Farran & McLean Publishers, 1862; reprint, Negro Universities Press, 1969.

Clark, William H. "Bedford County, from Indian Trail to Tourist Resorts." *Pennsylvania Heritage* (1986): 12–17.

Cockrum, Col. William M. *History of the Underground Railroad as It Was Conducted by the Anti-Slavery League.* New York: Negro Universities Press, 1969.

Coffin, Levi. *Reminiscences.* Cincinnati: The Robert Clarke Company, 1898; reprint, Arno Press and the *New York Times,* 1968.

Commager, Henry Steele, ed. *Documents of American History.* New York: Appleton-Century-Crofts, 1986.

Connors, Patrick. *Pennsylvania Historic Towns of Washington County.* 3 vols. Monongahela, PA: Historic Towns Publishing, 1996.

Craft, William, and Ellen Craft. *Running a Thousand Miles to Freedom; or, The Escape of William and Ellen Craft from Slavery.* London: William Tweedie, 1860; reprint, Arno Press and the *New York Times,* 1969.

Crooks, George R. *Life and Leggers of the Rev. John McClintock, D.D.* New York: Nelson & Phillips, 1876.

Douglass, Frederick. *My Bondage and My Freedom.* New York: Miller, Orton & Muligan, 1855; reprint, Arno Press and the *New York Times,* 1968.

————. *Narrative of the Life of Frederick Douglass, an American Slave, Written by Himself.* New York: Penguin Books USA, 1986.

Dunaway, Wayland F. *A History of Pennsylvania.* Englewood Cliffs, NJ: Prentice-Hall, 1948.

Eggert, Gerald G. "'Two Steps Forward, a Step and a Half Back': Harrisburg's African American Community in the Nineteenth Century." *African Americans in Pennsylvania: Shifting Historical Perspectives.* Ed. Joe Williams Trotter, Jr., and Eric Lidell Smith. University Park, PA: Pennsylvania State University Press and Pennsylvania Historical Museum Commission, 1997.

Ekey, Barbara N. "Bound for Freedom through Sugar Grove." [Erie, PA] *Times-News* (March 1, 1992): 4K–5K.

Elkins, Stanley M. *Slavery: A Problem in American Institutional and Intellectual Life.* New York: Grosset & Dunlap, 1963.

The Encyclopedia of Pennsylvania. St. Clair Shores, MI: Somerset Publishers, 1983.

Fairbanks, Rev. Calvin. *During Slavery Times.* New York: Patriotic Publishing Co., 1890; reprint, New York: Negro Universities Press, 1969.

Fitzpatrick, John C., ed. *The Writings of George Washington from the Original Manuscript Sources, 1745–1799.* Vols. 28 and 29. Washington, DC: United States Government Printing Office, 1931.

Flanagan, Kelly. "Legendary History for Local Hotel." *South Hills Record* (January 15, 1998): 1, 12.

Forrest, Earle R. *History of Washington County, Pennsylvania.* Chicago: S. J. Clarke Publishing Co., 1926.

Gara, Larry. *The Liberty Line: The Legend of the Underground Railroad.* Lexington, KY: University of Kentucky Press, 1967.

Godcharles, Frederick A. *Pennsylvania Political, Governmental, Military and Civil Physical, Economic and Social Volume.* New York: American Historical Society, 1933.

Gray, Nora. *Historic Union County: Leisburg, the Middle Years, 1840–1880.* Mifflinburg, PA: Mifflinburg Telegraph, n.d.

Hadden, James. *A History of Uniontown: The County Seat of Fayette County, Pennsylvania.* Akron, OH: New Werner Co., 1913.

Hanna, Rev. William. *History of Greene County, Pennsylvania, Containing an Outline of the State from 1862 until the Formation of Washington County in 1781.* Self-published, 1882.

Harpster, John W., ed. *Crossroads Description of Western Pennsylvania, 1720–1829.* Pittsburgh: University of Pittsburgh Press, 1938.

Harrison, John B., and Richard E. Sullivan. *A Short History of Western Civilization.* New York: Alfred A. Knopf, 1966.

Hendrick, Garrett, et al. "Resolution of the Germantown Mennonites." In *Documents of American History.* Ed. Henry Steele Commager. New York: Appelton-Century-Croft, 1958.

"Historic Mansion Goes on the Market." [Carlisle] *Sentinel* (August 31, 1999), www.cumberlink.com/local news/1999/08/local news.8.31.html.

Historical United States Census Data Browser, http://fisher.lib.virginia.edu/census/.

Holt, Robert. "Underground Railroad Past Recalled," *Gettysburg Times* (November 19, 1998), www.gburgtimes.com/archives/archive98/november 11-19.html.

Horton, James Oliver, and Lois Horton. *In Hope of Liberty, Culture, Community, and Protest among Northern Free Blacks, 1700–1860.* New York: Oxford University Press, 1997.

Howe, S. G. *Report to the Freedmen's Inquiry Commission, 1864: The Refugees from Slavery in Canada West.* Boston: Wright & Potter, Printers, 1864; reprint, Arno Press and the *New York Times,* 1969.

Hulbert, Archer Butler. *The Old National Road: The Historic Highway of America.* Columbus, OH: *Ohio Archaeological and Historical Publication* 9 (1901); reprint, 1954.

Jacobs, Harry A. *The Juniata Canal and Old Portage Railroad.* Hollidaysburg, PA: Blair County Historical Society, n.d.

Kalson, Sally. "Along the Freedom Path." *The Gazette* (February 6, 1994): 5–8.

Lapsansky, Emma Jones. "'Since They Got These Separate Churches:' Afro-Americans and Racism in Jacksonian Philadelphia." *African Americans in Pennsylvania: Shifting Historical Perspectives.* Ed. Joe Williams Trotter, Jr., and Eric Ledell Smith. University Park, PA: Pennsylvania University Press and Pennsylvania Historical and Museum Commission, 1997.

Locke, A. M., and Mary Stroughton. *Anti-Slavery in America from the Introduction of African Slaves to the Prohibition of Slave Trade (1619–1808).* Boston: Ginn & Company Publishers, 1907.

Lovejoy, J. C. *Memoir of Rev. Charles T. Torrey, Who Died in the Penitentiary of Maryland Where He Was Confined for Showing Mercy to the Poor.* Boston: John P. Jewett & Co., 1847; reprint, Negro Universities Press, 1969.

Magnotta, Christine. "Dream Home Sours for Couple." *Pocono Record* (July 6, 1998), www.poconorecord.com/1998/local/tjd70360.html.

Marcovitz, Hal. "Kostmayer Wants to Preserve Slaves' Railroad to Freedom." [Allentown] *Morning Call* (January 16, 1990).

May, Samuel. *Some Recollections of Our Antislavery Conflict.* Boston: Fields, Osgood & Co., 1869; reprint, Arno Press and the *New York Times,* 1968.

McDougall, Marion Gleason. *Fugitive Slaves (1619–1865).* Boston: Fay House Monographs, 1891; reprint, Bergman Publishers, 1967.

McKnight, W. J. *A Pioneer History of Jefferson County, Pennsylvania and My First Recollections of Brookville, Pennsylvania, 1840–43, When My Feet Were Bare and My Cheeks Were Brown.* Philadelphia: J. B. Lippincott Company, 1898.

"Milford Historians to Gather Tomorrow at Brick Tavern Inn." [Allentown] *Morning Call* (November 6, 1985).

Morison, Samuel Eliot. *The Oxford History of the American People.* New York: Oxford University Press, 1965.

My Pennsylvania: A Brief History of the Commonwealth's Sixty-seven Counties. Harrisburg, PA: Commonwealth of Pennsylvania, 1946.

Nash, Gary. "Slaves and Slave Owners in Colonial Philadelphia." *African Americans in Pennsylvania: Shifting Historical Perspectives.* Ed. Joe Williams Trotter, Jr., and Eric Ledell Smith. University Park: Pennsylvania State University Press and Pennsylvania Historical and Museum Commission, 1997.

Negro Population in the United States, 1790–1950. New York: Arno Press and the *New York Times,* 1968.

Okur, Nilgun Amadolus. "Underground Railroad in Philadelphia, 1830–1860." *Journal of Black Studies* 25, no. 5 (May 1995): 537–54.

Pennsylvania Atlas and Gazetteer. Freeport, ME: DeLorme Mapping Company, 1987.

Reed, John Elmer. *History of Erie County, Pennsylvania.* Topeka, KS: Historical Publishing Co., 1925.

Reitz, Ruth. "Slave Escape Network Passes through Brookville." [DuBois, PA] *Courier Express* (June 1, 1987): B8–B9.

Ripley, C. Peter, ed. *The Black Abolitionist Papers.* vol. 3–5. Chapel Hill, NC: University of North Carolina Press, 1991.

Robinson, Wilhelmena S. *Historical Negro Biographies.* New York: Publishers Company, 1967.

Searight, Thomas B. *The Old Pike: A History of the National Road with Incidents, Accidents, and Anecdotes Thereon.* Uniontown, PA: self-published, 1894.

Shank, William. *The Amazing Pennsylvania Canal.* York, PA: American Canal & Transportation Center, 1981.

Siebert, Scott. "Paintings Fulfill a Promise to Maintain a Family's Heritage." [Allentown] *Morning Call* (December 12, 1985).

Siebert, Wilbur. *The Underground Railroad: From Slavery to Freedom.* New York: The Macmillan Company, 1898; reprint, Russell & Russell, 1967.

"Slavery, Anti-Slavery, and the Underground Railroad." *Mercer County History* 4, no. 2 (fall 1974): 32–37.

Smedley, R. C. *History of the Underground Railroad in Chester and the Neighboring Counties of Pennsylvania.* Lancaster, PA: Office of the Journal, 1883; reprint, Arno Press and the *New York Times,* 1969.

Smith, Billy G. "Philadelphia: The Athens of America." *Life in Early Philadelphia: Documents from the Revolutionary and Early National Periods.* Ed. Billy G. Smith. University Park, PA: Pennsylvania State University Press, 1995.

Snyder, Charles M. *Union County, Pennsylvania, Bicentennial History.* Lewisburg, PA: Colonial Printing House, 1976.

The Statistical History of the United States from Colonial Times to the Present. Stamford, CT: Fairfield Publishers, 1965.

Stephenson, Clarence D. *Indiana County 175th Anniversary History.* 3 vols. Indiana, PA: A. G. Halldin Publishing Co., 1978.

Still, William. *The Underground Railroad. A Record of Facts, Authentic Narratives, Letters, & c.* Philadelphia: Porter & Coates, 1872; reprint, Arno Press and the *New York Times,* 1968.

Stonebach, Diane. "Of Real Gingerbread Men, Tastes of South America." [Allentown] *Morning Call* (December 9, 1989): H73.

Storey, Henry Wilson. *History of Cambria County Pennsylvania.* New York: Lewis Publishing Company, 1907.

Sweet, William. *The Story of Religion in America.* New York: Harper & Brothers Publishers, 1930.

Swetnam, George. *Pittsylvania Country.* New York: Duell Sloan & Pearce, 1951.

Swetnam, George, and Helen Smith. *A Guidebook to Historic Western Pennsylvania.* Pittsburgh: University of Pittsburgh Press, 1976.

"Talk to Feature Local Stops on Underground Railroad." [Carlisle] *Sentinel* (September 12, 1999), www.cumberlink.com/localnews/1999/09/local news.9.12.html.

Trotter, Joe Williams, Jr., and Eric Ledell Smith, eds. *African Americans in Pennsylvania: Shifting Historical Perspectives.* University Park, PA: Pennsylvania University Press and Pennsylvania Historical and Musuem Commission, 1997.

Wallace, Howard. *Historical Sketch of the Underground Railroad from Uniontown to Pittsburgh.* Self-published, c. 1888.

Wallace, Paul A. W. *Indian Paths of Pennsylvania.* Harrisburg, PA: Pennsylvania Historical and Museum Commission, 1971.

Ward, Samuel Ringgold. *Autobiography of a Fugitive Negro: His Anti-Slavery Labours in the United States, Canada & England.* London: John Snow, 1855; reprint, Arno Press and the *New York Times,* 1968.

Western Pennsylvania Historic Survey. *Guidebook to Historic Places in Western Pennsylvania.* Pittsburgh: University of Pittsburgh Press, 1938.

Williams, James A. "Slavery and Politics in Montgomery County, 1835–1855." *Bulletin of the Historical Society of Montgomery County* 27 (fall 1988): 119–31.

Wilson, Erasmus, ed. *Standard History of Pittsburg (sic), Pennsylvania.* Chicago: H. R. Cornell & Co., 1898.

Winch, Julie. *Philadelphia's Black Elite Activism, Accommodation, and the Struggle for Autonomy, 1787–1848.* Philadelphia: Temple University Press, 1988.

Youghiogheny River Lake. Pittsburgh: U.S. Army Corps of Engineers, 1995.

INDEX

Aaron, Samuel, 155, 156
Abbot, Abijah, 99
Abolitionist societies, creation of, 7–8
Act to Prohibit the Importation of
    Slaves (1808), 7
Adams County, 27
Addison, Alexander, 12, 70
Addison (town), 44
African Education Society, 82, 85
African Methodist Episcopal Church,
    9, 142, 149, 163, 166–67
Agents, 17
Albaugh, John, 32, 33, 169
Albion, 93, 94, 96
Aliquippa, 62
Allegheny County, 81
Allegheny Institute (Avery College), 86
Allegheny River route, 66
Allen, Richard, 9, 142, 143, 149, 166
Altoona, 36
American Anti-Slavery Society, 8
American Colonization Society, 8, 9
Anderson, John, 31
Antislavery laws, 6–7
Anti-Slavery Society (Philadelphia), 2, 8
Anti-Slavery Society (Pittsburgh), 82, 85
Armstrong, John, 30–31
Ashbury, Bill, 74, 78
Ashbury, Francis, 171
Atchison, George, 35, 36, 51
Atchison, William, 36
Avery, Charles, 82, 85, 86, *87*, 89
Avondale, 133, 136

Baden, 62
Baird, Absalom, 12, 70
Bald Eagle trail, 36
Baldwin, Henry, 82
Ball, John, 87, 88
Baptists, 173

Barber, A. A., 35
Barnes, 38
Barton, Levi, 92
Bear Lake, 99
Beaver County, 60–65, 69, 79
Beaver Dam, 99
Beaver Falls, 62–65
Bedford, 27, 29–36, 91
Bedford–Chambersburg Pike, 30
Beeson, Henry, 41, 169
Beesontown, 41–42
Bellefonte, 113–14
Belle Vernon, 58
Bendersville, 107–8
Benezet, Anthony, 168
Bensalem, 161
Berks County, 154–55
Bethel A.M.E. Church, 86, 110, 113,
    149, 154, 159, 166–67
Bethlehem, 157–60
Bethlehem Pike, 149
Biddle, Clement, 141–42
Bingham, Thomas, 84, 87
Birdsboro, 154
Black, George, 87, 88
Black, John, 82
Black, Joseph, 47, 170
Blackburn, E. Howard, 29–33, 36
Blackburn, James, 36
Black Lick, 50
Blair, David, 35, 171
Blair, William, 52
Blairsville, 49, 50
Bliss, George R., 116–17
Blockson, Charles, vii, 3, 4, 29–31, 35, 38,
    45, 47, 51, 52, 58, 62–66, 87–88, 92,
    93, 96, 97, 108, 109, 112–13, 114,
    117–18, 122, 153, 155–56, 158, 159,
    162, 163
Boiling Springs, 106, 107